CRAFTING SHORT SCREENPLAYS THAT CONNECT

CRAFTING SHORT SCREENPLAYS THAT CONNECT

Claudia Hunter Johnson

Focal
Press

Boston Oxford Auckland Johannesburg Melbourne New Delhi

Focal Press is an imprint of Butterworth–Heinemann.

R A member of the Reed Elsevier group.

Copyright © 2000 by Claudia H. Johnson

Butterworth–Heinemann supports the efforts of American Forests and the Global ReLeaf program in its campaign for the betterment of trees, forests, and our environment.

Library of Congress Cataloging-in-Publication Data
Johnson, Claudia (Claudia Hunter)
    Crafting short screenplays that connect / Claudia Johnson.
        p. cm.
    Includes bibliographical references and index.
    ISBN 0-240-80378-7 (pbk. : acid-free paper)
    1. Motion picture authorship.   2. Short films.   I. Title.
PN1996 .J62 2000
808.2'3—dc21   99-055863

British Library Cataloguing-in-Publication Data
A catalogue record for this book is available from the British Library.

The publisher offers special discounts on bulk orders of this book.
For information, please contact:
Manager of Special Sales
Butterworth-Heinemann
225 Wildwood Avenue
Woburn, MA 01801-2041
Tel: 781-904-2500
Fax: 781-904-2620
For information on all Butterworth-Heinemann publications
available, contact our World Wide Web home page at:
http://www.bh.com

10 9 8 7 6 5 4 3

Printed in the United States of America

So much of what I know about writing and teaching
I learned from three remarkable writers and teachers:

Janet Burroway
Sam Smiley
and the late Jerry Stern.

This book is for them.

"Most movies celebrate the ways we connect with each other."

—Jeremy Irons, at the 68th Annual Academy Awards

CONTENTS

PREFACE

This book is the distillation of a decade of teaching screenwriting and dramatic technique at Florida State University—and an epiphany I had halfway through.

During that decade, to my delight, I've seen the American short film (thirty minutes or less) rise in importance from a resume piece intended to launch a filmmaker's career to an art form in its own right. As interest and access increase, the short film is becoming the central short narrative form of our time, analogous to the short story in the 1940s, argues Ray Fielding, Dean of the Florida State University Film School.

"It's a new day for the short film," Fielding recently told me. "It's a phenomenon, a phoenix rising from the ashes. With the gradual perfection of wideband Internet transmission, and the already well-established market for long-play DVD discs, the short film is coming into its own. Not since the golden years of live television, when distinguished original dramatic plays were presented several times a week to national audiences, has the marketplace for short film and video drama looked so bright."

But during the past decade of teaching, I've found three things sorely missing: A nuts-and-bolt book about crafting short screenplays; access to short films and their screenplays so teachers and students can *see* the choices and changes—good, bad, or ugly—that were made in production; and any discussion in screenwriting books that there is more going on in good screenplays than conflict. To liquidate this lack over the years—often through trial and error—I designed a practical, hands-on approach to crafting short screenplays.

By craft I mean "the sum total of all means used to draw the audience into deep involvement, to hold that involvement, and ultimately to reward it with a moving and meaningful experience," as Robert McKee writes in *Story*.

In other words, to connect. This book is dedicated to the proposition that connecting—to oneself and to others—is the source of great screenplays, regardless of length.

And craft, I'm convinced, can be taught, though I agree with playwright William Gibson's wry observation, "The rest is art and up to God." Craft *must* be taught to those who want to write effective short films, which require "deft characterization, a compressed narrative style, and something to say that is focused and fresh in voice," as Michael Rabiger reminds us in *Directing the Film: Film Techniques and Aesthetics*. The shorter the film, in fact, the taller the order for craft. "A good five- to ten-minute film is actually more demanding to make than a passable thirty-minute one," Rabiger says.

Screenwriting is such a complex and difficult craft, I have found it most effective to break it into teachable, learnable pieces that students can tackle one at a time. This approach underlies the design of this book. You will write—and rewrite—five short screenplays of increasing length and complexity that focus on a different, essential aspect of dramatic technique and the craft of screenwriting. Each screenplay will build on the skills and techniques you learned in the previous one. Ideally, by the time you've written all five, you will have grappled with most of the issues, small and large, in screenwriting. I believe in learning by doing, and the book is designed to be interactive, from the exercises that prepare you to write to the margins that allow you to noodle ideas, details, dialogue, character, scenes or anything else that flashes to mind as you read the book.

My purpose has always been—and still is—to elicit the richest, most resonant work from my students—short screenplays that are, at once, unique and universal. The goal of this book is the same—to offer an experiential approach that will help you—or your students—craft short screenplays that connect. To that end, the book is divided into three sections:

Part One—Preparing to Write the Short Screenplay—explores essential preliminary issues: The importance of connecting to others; connecting to your unique material and vision; connecting to your own creative process; connecting to what screenplays *are* at their deepest level—patterns of significant human change—and to what they are on the surface level of screenplay format.

Part Two—Five (Not So) Easy Screenplays—guides you through crafting five short screenplays:

1. The Discovery: A three-page screenplay focused on a character making a discovery that makes a difference to the character.
2. The Decision: A five-page screenplay focused on a character making a decision that makes a difference to the character.
3. The Boxing Match (creating conflict): A five- to seven-page screenplay focused on one character wanting what another character does *not* want to give.
4. The Improbable Connection (creating connection): A seven-page screenplay focused on creating a plausible but not predictable pattern of human connection.
5. The Long Short Screenplay: A ten- to fifteen-page screenplay focused on telling the best story you can for the screen, using the techniques you've learned in the first four screenplays.

Part Three—Five Screenplays That Make It Look Easy—offers, for your illumination and, I hope, inspiration, the screenplays of five award-winning undergraduate and graduate F.S.U. thesis films from the Student Academy Award winner *Slow Dancin' Down the Aisles of the Quickcheck* to the Student Emmy Award winner *The Making of Killer Kite*.

I asked the five screenwriters to select the version of the screenplay that they wanted published. None is transcribed from the screen like so many published screenplays you'll find. As Bob Gray said when he sent me the screenplay for *Killer Kite*, "I resisted the temptation to rewrite the script and make it fit the edited film. This is the shooting script from which the film was made. It is, I think, a better educational exercise to see how a project can change from the final script to the completed edit."

I agree. And you will have the opportunity to see and study the changes that were made on that arduous journey from script to screen by comparing these five screenplays to their finished films, available on video from Focal Press.

In the brief introduction to each screenplay, I've let the writer describe how the screenplay changed in production. (Three writers—Thomas Jackson, Lani Sciandra, and Andy Zare—directed their films, *Slow Dancin' Down the Aisles of the Quickcheck*, *Cool Breeze and Buzz*, and *tongue*. Matt Stevens—who wrote the story for *The Making of Killer Kite*—directed the film, but Bob Gray wrote the screenplay. And Rachel Witenstein wrote *Lena's Spaghetti*, but Joe Greco directed.) Each introduction also describes where these talented writers are now and what they are doing.

Most are writing features, a testament to the often overlooked truth that the short film—while an art form in its own right—is excellent preparation for writing long screenplays. The dramatic principles explored in this book are found in all good screenplays, long and short. And even if you're writing long screenplays, crafting short scripts will help hone your skills (after writing five features, I took a whack at a short screenplay—*what a challenge!*—and came away with renewed respect and admiration for my students). Writing short screenplays that connect requires the craft and concentration of a medieval artist carving scenes in a walnut. And writing in a nutshell, in a nutshell, forces you to be more creative, resourceful. That is why I beg to differ with people who say that writing short scripts is as useful as lips on a chicken. It may well be the toughest screenwriting training you'll get.

And writing short screenplays is the best way to see your work on the screen and have others see it. "Getting seen is the precursor to getting noticed," Michael Rabiger says, "and for actuarial reasons alone short films are always more likely to be shown in festivals than long ones." Feature-length screenplays, alas, are like sperm: There's a one-in-a-million chance they'll get made.

This book is the first to explore connection as a crucial part of good screenplays and the screenwriting process. Including human connection in the stories they tell has helped my students write richer, more resonant short screenplays that have become award-winning films screened and celebrated at festivals all over the world. In the spirit of their own screenplays, they have competed and they have connected. I hope, with this book, you will, too.

ACKNOWLEDGMENTS

Eternal gratitude . . .

To Marie Lee at Focal Press, for loving the idea from the beginning, and to my editor, Terri Jadick, for your can-do editorial spirit that has made this process as painless as possible.

To Dean Ray Fielding, for your unflagging enthusiasm, and for so generously granting permission to include five of F.S.U.'s award-winning films on the companion videotape.

To my intrepid, resourceful, *amazing* assistants, Luke Crowe and Greg Marcks, for your warp-speed responses to my cries for help.

To my writing partner and former colleague, Matt Stevens, for letting me talk *ad nauseam* about these ideas while we wrote our own screenplays ("I'd like to say a word about connection . . .").

To my colleague, Valliere Richard Auzenne, for reading the proposal and test-driving many of these ideas in your class.

To my screenwriting students—especially those in my spring 1999 Screenwriting II class, for your input and patience as I wrote the book. I learned more from you than you know.

To Peter Stowell, for the time off to write it.

To my colleague Andy Ruben, for introducing me to Scriptware.

To Kathy Barber, for helping me keep up with all the awards these films have been winning; Meryl Warren, for helping me keep up with the writers; Linda Hensley, for candy and other kindnesses including loaning me her own copy of *Beauty and the Beast*; Marie Behm for the Atomic Fireballs; and Jennie Jarvis, for the photocopying.

To my former students Kate Gutman, Nancy Potter, and Kelly Rouse for sharing insights and information along the way.

To Rob McCaffrey, for sharing the process of developing the M.F.A. Thesis screenplay, *The Buse*.

To Mark Spragg, for our long conversations about screenwriting at Bread Loaf Writers' Conference.

To Linda Seger, for your time and teaching out in L.A.

To Jana Memel and Hillary Ripps at Chanticleer Films for your love of short films, and for sending me your own award-winning productions to screen.

To Farrar, Straus & Giroux, for permission to quote from Seamus Heaney's poem "Station Island."

To my *still*-lanky friend, Stuart Hample, for the quotation from Jay Allen Presson.

To my mother, for all the laughs and the lunches.

To my husband, Ormond Loomis, and our children, Anne and Ross Loomis—three of the best writers I know—for kicking around these ideas with me over dinner for the past decade. A special thanks, too, to Ormond, for teaching a low-tech writer about computers and taking care of the artwork.

Last but not least, to the five screenwriters featured here—Thomas Jackson, Lani Sciandra, Andy Zare, Rachel Witenstein, and Bob Gray—for letting me publish your screenplays. It's an honor to honor your work in this book.

INTRODUCTION: THE POWER AND IMPORTANCE OF HUMAN CONNECTION

For years I gently browbeat my students. "Dig deeper," I said. "The best stories are about the human heart."

I wasn't quite sure what I meant. I knew I didn't mean that old Hollywood saw—*throw in some love interest*! I meant something closer to Samson Raphaelson's remark about Shakespeare in *The Human Nature of Playwriting*, "[He] is not a realistic writer but he is overwhelmingly real because he reports the hearts of human beings."

I was teaching dramatic technique—first playwriting in the English Department at Florida State, then screenwriting when the Film School began—rounding up the usual suspects, conflict, crisis, and climax—but I had this nagging sensation that these overlooked something important in stories. I couldn't figure out what it was, so I hoped, if sufficiently coaxed, my students could.

WHAT WE TALK ABOUT WHEN WE TALK ABOUT DRAMA

Derived from the Greek *dran*—"to do"—drama means someone strives. Will meets obstacle, and this creates conflict. For two hundred years, perhaps more, we have talked about dramatic stories this way. George Bernard Shaw defined drama as "the conflict between man's will and his environment." Across the channel, Ferdinand Brunetiere said it was "the will of man in conflict." And so it has gone, like a roll call, each person casting a vote for drama's conventional wisdom.

"Since the early nineteenth century the 'conflict theory' of drama has dominated dramatic criticism and, to a considerable degree, the practice of

1

playwrights," Eric Bentley says in *Concepts in Dramatic Theory*. "It is a central assumption of most Twentieth-century dramatic theory."

In film, where the budgets (and insecurities) run wilder and the flops are more catastrophic, the rule of the game is more rigid.

"The basis of all drama is conflict," Syd Field says in almost every one of his books. "Without conflict there is no action; without action there is no character; without character there is no story. And without story there is no screenplay."

Most screenwriting books—about long or short screenplays—essentially say the same thing, though in *Screenwriting Tricks of the Trade*, William Froug is the most emphatic: "Without conflict, you might as well pack it in—you are in the wrong field of endeavor. Without conflict, your reader will fall asleep and you will never have to think about having an audience. The ball-game is over."

Conflict has shaped the way that we think about drama and the way that we think to shape it. In *Writing Great Screenplays for Film and TV*, Dona Cooper offers a new improved metaphor for the screenplay—a roller coaster. It's a rollicking image, more energetic and imaginative than most I have found in screenwriting books, but the author's graphic depiction—action that rises and rises and rises then falls—is merely a remake of a nineteenth-century model, Freitag's Pyramid (conflict, crisis, and resolution), which keeps cropping up in all kinds of books about writing, including former editions of Janet Burroway's *Writing Fiction*. But Janet—a friend and colleague—was increasingly uncomfortable, too, with this conflict-bound way of seeing the story.

Other writers, most of them women, were also uneasy.

But Ursula LeGuin came closest to articulating what I was feeling:

> People are cross-grained, aggressive, and full of trouble, the storytellers tell us; people fight themselves and one another, and their stories are full of their struggles. But to say that that is the story is to use one aspect of existence, conflict, to subsume all other aspects, many of which it does not include and does not comprehend.
>
> *Romeo and Juliet* is the story of the conflict between two families, and its plot involves the conflict of two individuals within those families. Is that all it involves? Isn't *Romeo and Juliet* about something else, and isn't it the something else that makes the otherwise trivial tale of a feud into a tragedy?[1]

Conflict was not incorrect, it was *incomplete*. It didn't get to the heart of the matter, to that level of story that engages most deeply. It was half the story, but I couldn't figure out what the other half was.

RUBY & ME

In January 1994, taking a shower, I saw it—the other half of the story. I don't know what it is about showers and baths that's conducive to insight, but the fact is well documented: Einstein reportedly claimed his greatest ideas occurred in the shower, and everyone knows about Archimedes. I'm a Pisces so I like to think it's the water, but it's more than likely the break from our work. "These insights tend to come suddenly and, characteristically, not when sitting at a desk working," Fritjof Capra writes in the *Tao of Physics*, "but when relaxing, in the bath, during a walk in the woods, on the beach."

I'd taken a break from researching a documentary film about the most famous murder in Florida, the trial of Ruby McCollum, an African-American woman in my small town of Live Oak convicted of shooting and killing the town's Great White Hope, Senator-elect Leroy Adams, her doctor and, allegedly, lover. When she fired the gun—if she, in fact, did it—her life also came to an end: Every major connection was severed; her husband died the next day of heart failure; she was separated from her children, other family, and friends for more than twenty years.

Immersed in Ruby's story, I wondered why it engaged me so deeply. She and I had nothing in common except for our gender and the small North Florida town where we lived. The surface events of her story were the stuff of soap opera—wealth, corruption, infidelity, murder—and this had no connection to my quiet life. There was something deeper at work.

Mulling over what it might be, I saw that it was connection itself. Underlying the conflict of Ruby's story, underlying the events of her life and mine—underlying any good story, fictitious or true—is a deeper pattern of change, a pattern of connection and disconnection. The conflict and surface events are like waves, but underneath is an emotional tide—the ebb and flow of human connection. It's just as essential to story as conflict but it has been essentially overlooked.

I'm no Einstein and I didn't run naked trailing bathwater into the street but I did shout "Eureka, I've found it!" I did. For the first time, I saw drama *whole*. Here was its deepest humanity, structure, and emotional rhythm, the "something else" LeGuin knew was missing.

Everything seemed to fall into place. I understood the emotional power of plays in a way that I hadn't before: What keeps *Romeo and Juliet* from being an "otherwise trivial tale of a feud" is the underlying pattern of connection and disconnection, not just between the two star-crossed lovers, but between them and those others who make up their web of connections—nurse, parents, Mercutio, Tybalt, Friar Lawrence, the Prince. What keeps *Death of a Salesman* from being a trivial tale of a failed businessman is Willy's tragic pattern of connection and disconnection with others, especially Biff.

I saw tragedy and comedy in a new light—comedy ends in connection, tragedy in disconnection. "The tragic side of tragedy," to borrow Aristotle's phrase, is more than the hero's fall from position and power. "Those who have had the misfortune to do or undergo fearful things," are, in the end, disconnected. We may pity the fallen because we fear falling but we fear it less, perhaps, than we fear disconnection. Even death, the ultimate disconnection, is less fearsome for some than life without connection.

"Ha! banishment," Romeo cries. "Be merciful, say 'death,'/For exile hath more terror in his look, /Much more, than death. Do not say 'banishment.'"

Connection is human sustenance, the substance of story. Its gain and loss provides the emotional power, as Aristotle implies in *The Poetics*:

> Let us determine, then, which kinds of happening are felt by the spectator to be fearful, and which pitiable. Now such acts are necessarily the work of persons who are near and dear (close blood kin) to one another, or enemies, or neither. But when an enemy attacks an enemy there is nothing pathetic about either the intention or the deed, except in the actual pain suffered by the victim; nor when the act is done by "neutrals"; but when the tragic acts come within the limits of close blood relationship, as when brother kills or intends to kill brother or do something else of that kind to him, or son to father or mother to son or son to mother— those are the situations one should look for.[2]

I understood, too, that connection and disconnection provided the emotional power of the films I had seen, even the best of the hard-boiled genres. *The Fugitive*—warmed-over TV show that it was—engages more deeply than most films in its genre because of the grudging but growing connection between the fugitive Kimble and Federal Marshall Gerard, the deeper emotional journey from Gerard's "I don't care," (a line Tommy Lee Jones rehearsed for days) to his closing line, "I care. Don't tell anyone." This unlikely connection is the heart of the story, its pattern of meaning. It fills the emotional void created by Kimble's wife's brutal murder. In story as in life, human nature abhors an emotional vacuum.

I went to see Janet. She said, "This is big." She pulled books from her shelves that touched on connection—Lewis Hyde's *The Gift* and Jean Baker Miller's *Toward A New Psychology of Women* and Carol Gilligan's *In A Different Voice*. She opened Hyde's book and showed me a passage from Pablo Neruda, a memory about a connection he made when he was a child, an exchange of small gifts—a pine cone and a faded toy sheep—with a boy about his own age, a stranger he did not see again:

> That exchange brought home to me for the first time a precious idea: that all humanity is somehow together.
> This is the great lesson I learned in my childhood, in the backyard of a lonely house. Maybe it was nothing but a

game two boys played who didn't know each other and wanted to pass to the other some good things of life. Yet maybe this small and mysterious exchange of gifts remained inside me also, deep and indestructible, giving my poetry light.[3]

This, I think, is the heart of it all: There are moments of change in our lives and stories that are not comprehended by conflict. These moments of change are connections, human exchanges, however fleeting or small—a faded sheep for a pine cone—or, as Stephen Jay Gould says in "Counters and Cable Cars," "people taking care of each other in small ways of enduring significance." Large or small, they are like gifts—they create ties between us.

Janet asked if she could mention my insight in her new edition of *Writing Fiction*:

> I'm indebted to dramatist Claudia Johnson for this further— and, it seems to me, crucial—insight about [LeGuin's] "something else": whereas the hierarchical or "vertical" nature of narrative, the power struggle, has long been acknowledged, there also appears in all narrative a "horizontal" pattern of connection and disconnection between characters which is the main source of its emotional effect. In discussing human behavior, psychologists speak in terms of "tower" and "network" patterns, the need to climb and the need for community, the need to win out over others and the need to belong to others; and these two drives also drive fiction.[4]

As a writer who has worked in four genres—plays, fiction, screenplays, and, most recently, memoir—I suspect these two drives drive most stories (I'll leave it to others to explore the exceptions). In *Metaphors of Interrelatedness: Toward a Systems Theory of Psychology*, Linda Olds acknowledges our "vertical strivings for power, achievement, knowledge, and accomplishment," but she adds:

> We no longer inhabit a universe capable of being represented vertically alone; the embeddedness of us all in an intricately interrelating dance of energy and spacetime, of connection and change, has become the inescapable heritage of our time. We must reach out for horizontal metaphors which speak the language of embrace and interconnection, rather than striving and rising above.[5]

The film *Red* does this with its powerful opening image of telephone cables carrying the young model's call at breathtaking speeds across land, under water, and across land again. One of the most compelling films that

I've seen, it is a story told with almost no conflict, a film, finally, about connection itself.

But most stories have both. Rooted in the same Latin prefix (*con-*, together), conflict (from the Latin *configere*—to clash or strike together) and connection (from the Latin *connectere*, to bind or tie together) are complementary forces. The physicist Niels Bohr introduced the concept of "complementarity," but as Capra points out in *The Tao of Physics*, it goes back 2,500 years: "The Chinese sages represented this complementarity of opposites by the archetypal poles of *yin* and *yang* and saw their dynamic interplay as the essence of all natural phenomena and all human situations." Connection and conflict are also dynamic and interrelated. They are woven together like strands of deoxyribonucleic acid, the double helix of drama.

A MODEL OF WHOLENESS

Like the newly pregnant woman who never noticed pregnant women before but now sees them wherever she goes, I noticed connection wherever I looked.

I saw its ebb and flow in the novels I read. Anne Tyler's *Ladder of Years* is a series of emotional movements of connecting and disconnecting and reconnecting as Delia drifts from her family, builds a new life, and returns to her own.

I saw connection and disconnection in films that I screened, even the wild-assed rides in *Pulp Fiction*—"Vincent Vega and Marsellus Wallace's Wife," "The Gold Watch," and "The Bonnie Situation." For all the vintage Tarantino violence and conflict, marvelous connections occur in each of the stories.

In *Apollo 13*, I noticed how painstakingly the story establishes Jim Lovell's web of connections—wife, children, colleagues—and how these become the real stake in the film, as important as survival itself, the reason survival matters to him at all.

Like Forster's once cryptic epigram, "Only connect," this made a new kind of sense. Eight months after my insight, on tour with my book, *Stifled Laughter*, I heard a lecture by Betty Friedan. It was an interesting update of Abraham Maslow who ranked connection (belonging) just below survival in his well-known hierarchy of needs. Friedan cited research that shows connection is no less a need. "Connectedness," as she calls it in *The Fountain of Age*, "has a direct effect on mortality." Epidemiological studies across the country show that men and women without significant human connection are twice as likely to die. Widowers, disconnected from their central and often their only significant connection, are "40 percent more likely to die in the first six months after their spouse's death than other men their age."

That women live longer than men is well known. The conventional wisdom says that men die younger because of too much striving and competition, but Friedan and others show it is also caused by too little connection. New studies on the male midlife crisis have linked men's psychological pain to the realization that they have (like dramatic theorists) neglected connection. This lack of "closeness, relatedness, and intimacy," Friedan says, contributes directly to men's shorter lives. To survive, men and women alike must have "purpose and intimacy," what Tolstoy called "work and love," goals to strive for and what Friedan bluntly calls "the life-and-death importance of connectedness."

I connect, therefore I am.

We cannot live by conflict alone; neither can a good screenplay. The best screenwriters understand this intuitively, but the rest of us will be better screenwriters if we think about both halves of the story—conflict and connection—when we think about the stories we're telling. In this way, we'll "facilate new ways of seeing" the story and work with "a model of wholeness," to borrow two phrases from Linda Olds. Most important, we'll open the aperture wider, to use a film metaphor, and give our stories more light.

NOTES

1. Ursula LeGuin, quoted in Janet Burroway's *Writing Fiction: A Guide to Narrative Craft*, Fourth Edition, HarperCollins, New York, 1996, p. 35.
2. Aristotle, *Poetics*, translated, with an introduction, by Gerald F. Else, Michigan University Press, fifth printing, 1978, pp. 40, 41.
3. Lewis Hyde, *The Gift*, Vintage Books, New York, 1979, pp. 281, 282.
4. Janet Burroway, *Writing Fiction: A Guide to Narrative Craft*, Fourth Edition, HarperCollins, New York, 1996, p. 35.
5. Linda E. Olds, *Metaphors of Interrelatedness: Toward a Systems Theory of Psychology*, State University of New York Press, 1992, p. xii.

PART I

PREPARING TO WRITE THE SHORT SCREENPLAY

CONNECTING TO PURPOSE

A screenwriter's purpose is to connect.

"Only connect," E. M. Forster tells us in *Howard's End*. He meant it as a rule to live by. I see it as a rule to *write* by. The best screenplays—long or short—are written by those who know how to connect—to themselves (their unique vision, material, process), to what drama *is*, and, most important, to others.

"You must never forget the umbilical cord is to real life, real people," Oliver Stone says in Linda Seger and Edward Jay Whetmore's *From Script to Screen*.

"I think of the medium as a people-to-people medium," Frank Capra says in Eric Sherman's *Directing the Film*, "not cameraman-to-people, not directors-to-people, not writers-to-people, but people-to-people."

"You know," Jean Renoir agrees, "if art doesn't take us as collaborators, art is dull. We must be in communion, the artist and the public. Without the collaboration of the public, to me, we have nothing."

Only connect. Write it down on a Post-it note or a three-by-five card and stick it on your computer, desk, forehead. This deceptively simple advice is the heart of the art of writing good screenplays.

It is also the impulse to write. "When talented people write well," Robert McKee says in *Story*, "it is generally for this reason: They're moved by a desire to touch the audience."

Thomas Jackson described this desire when I asked how he came up with *Slow Dancin' Down the Aisles of the Quickcheck*:

> I was driving back [from Bainbridge, Georgia, to Tallahassee] and I was thinking about a character, a grocery store manager who had a crush on his head cashier. You know, when I worked in this grocery store I had crushes on all the cashiers, you know, in some way or another, because

I was very shy and I didn't speak to them so I always had crushes on them. But I was thinking about this guy and I was thinking that, because I'm a songwriter, too, what if he played . . . I could just see this guy playing this woman a song, and it's not something that he normally does, and it's like he's pouring his heart out and it's just so unhim. And I'm describing this into a little tape recorder I keep with me all the time, and I got choked up. You can hear me get choked up on the tape because I'm getting emotional about this. And I say on the tape, I said, "Man, if I can just make people have that feeling, I'd feel like I did something." I thought, If I can get people to feel that way, I would feel like I did something.

You may have a different purpose in mind. If you're anything like the ambitious students I teach, you may well want to write the script for that short film that will open Hollywood's doors. And that can certainly happen—as I write, Thomas is at the Cannes Film Festival with *Slow Dancin'*—but it won't happen unless your screenplay connects. Connecting with others is what you must do to succeed as a screenwriter, and it will also be your greatest success.

Ask any dramatist—playwright or screenwriter. They'll describe the sheer wonder—and joy—of seeing an audience connecting to a story they've written. People lurching with laughter (in the right places) or staring rapt at the screen because they're so moved by the story they're seeing. And the worst times are those when an audience doesn't connect. Groans. Sighs of impatience or boredom. Bad laughs.

Years ago, during the intermission of one of my plays, I overheard two young men in the lobby discussing a dog. I like dog stories, so I sidled over to listen. The dog, I found out, was my play. That's what's so terrifying about writing plays or screenplays: Failure is so damn *public*.

Okay, you've been warned.

But even an evening of My Play As A Dog cannot cancel the incomparable pleasures I've had connecting to others, seeing an audience—to my everlasting joy and amazement—stand up and *cheer* for a short play I wrote. And, yes, that play opened doors—terrific reviews ("offers hope for humanity"), my first agent, and publication—but I promise you nothing—*nothing*—equaled the sense of achievement I felt when that play connected to others. And, when I keep that in mind, I'm a much better writer.

Maybe that's why Fritz Lang says:

I asked myself—why is the first work of a writer or a screen-writer, or of a playwright almost always a success? Because he still belongs to an audience. The more he goes away from the audience, the more he loses contact, and what I tried to do my whole life long was I tried not to lose contact with the audience.[1]

But even Fritz Lang—for all his magnificent films such as *Metropolis, M, The Big Heat*—wasn't always successful.

Why? Because connecting to others is one of the hardest things that we do. As Bruno Bettelheim observed in his book *Surviving*, human beings are like porcupines trying to stay warm on a cold winter night: We want to be close to one another for warmth, but we don't want to be too close for comfort. We're distinct—and we're not. We want to remain distinct, unique—and we don't.

Imagine a screening room full of strangers waiting to see the short film you've written—young, old, male, female, different ages, professions—a bag boy, a film buff, a periodontist who's had a bad day, an attorney who's just realized she hates practicing law. Put yourself in their place; this shouldn't be hard; you've been an audience member longer than you've been a writer. Like you and everyone else on this planet, they're preoccupied. Yet, somehow, the story you've written must engage—catch and hold—their attention. If it doesn't, they'll think, So what? Why are you telling me this? Wasting my time? What the hell does this have to do with my life? They'll daydream or rattle cellophane wrappers or get up and walk out.

"The first business of the playwright is to keep the audience from walking out," William Gibson says in *Shakespeare's Game*. This goes for screenwriters, too.

Luckily, audiences *want* to connect, though this desire may be unconscious, buried. "It is true that America is a high-tech, speed-driven, 'Gimme-the-fax/facts-and-get-on-with-it' society," Marylou Awiakta says in *Selu*. "Few can escape this dynamic. But it's also true that most of us, deep down, yearn for relationship, connection, and meaning."

Good stories satisfy this deep yearning. Once upon a time, we shared stories around a fire—sometimes we still do—but now we usually share them in movie theaters, and the flickering light on our faces comes from the images up on the screen. The stories we see may take place in a galaxy far away, on a sheep farm in New Zealand, or in a depressed Sheffield, England. The hero may be a rebel fighter or a piglet or an unemployed steelworker, but stories like *Star Wars* and *Babe* and *The Full Monty* not only entertain us, they make us more human. They show us in fresh and wonderful ways that we're not the only fool on the planet struggling with this Godawful difficult business of being alive. They "induce a moment of grace, a communion," Lewis Hyde says in *The Gift*, "a period during which we too know the hidden coherence of our being and feel the fullness of our lives."

As audience members, we spend a good deal of time and money in this culture to feel that sense of communion, to be fully engaged, to feel so tied to a story we're carried away.

"I want to be transported by the screenplay," Actor Peter Strauss says in *From Script To Screen*. "To go to the movie, to be in the dark and have magic happen."

I think it helps us as writers—I know it helps me—to think of a screenplay as a magic carpet ride, to ask these questions: How does my story lift an audience off the ground? Take them on a journey? Return them to their seats? And, perhaps most important, how does the ride make them *feel*?

"I look for passion, aliveness, hatred, rage, fear, pain, joy, bigness," Strauss continues. "I want to feel big, I want to be angry big, feel sad big."

Look at the language he's using. *I want to feel big. I want to be angry big, feel sad big*. He isn't content to see characters having emotions, *he wants to feel those emotions himself*.

The late great Paddy Chayefsky (*Marty, The Hospital*) put it bluntly, "Drama is concerned only with emotion." And, in interview after interview, even Tarantino insists that a story must work on an emotional level.

"A play"—or, in this case, a screenplay—"is the shortest distance from emotions to emotions," George Pierce Baker says in *Dramatic Technique*.

The stories we tell must create shared emotions, those golden threads that connect the audience to the characters up on the screen. Or on paper.

When Alan Arkin came to Tallahassee to direct a short film, I asked what he looked for in a screenplay. "I just want a good story," he said. "I want to be moved."

I just want a good story.

"You can't involve them with gimmicks, with sunsets, with hand-held cameras, zoom shots, or anything else," Frank Capra says in *Directing the Film*. "They couldn't care less about those things. But you can give them something to worry about, some person they can worry about, and care about, and you've got them, you've got them involved."

Involved. Engaged. Connected.

At the 59th Annual Academy Awards in 1987, accepting the Thalberg Award for his contributions to the industry, Steven Spielberg admitted he was more culpable than any other director for the popular practice of supplanting story with the camera and special effects. He pledged to inculcate in the next generation a greater interest in writing and to develop that interest himself.

It was this realization, this rededication to story, that led Spielberg back to that same stage to receive an Oscar for a film that connected to audiences worldwide with its wrenching disconnections and one of history's most improbable connections—Oscar Schindler caring for those on his list.

THE SCREENPLAY PARADOX

Joan Didion once said that the reason we write lies in the very vowel sounds of the phrase "Why I Write": *I, I, I.*

It has also been said that the reason audiences go to see what we've written can be summed up in the phrase: *Tell me about me.*

It's a miracle shared emotions happen at all.

Still, it's true: We go to *The Full Monty* to see a story about unemployed steelworkers who save relationships, self-respect, with a strip-show, but we also go because, on some level, we want to see our own life.

But we don't want to *see* our own life up there on the screen because we've seen it already, and that would be boring. We want to see our own life—and we don't.

Porcupines!

This seemingly contradictory statement is nonetheless true. A paradox. The Screenplay Paradox, I like to call it, though it's true for all stories.

So the screenwriter's job—our great sleight of hand—is to create a story that satisfies both.

NOT ABOUT ME

ABOUT ME

The burning question is *how?*

There's no formula, gimmick. If there were, Disney or Dream Works would own the rights to it. And the answer doesn't lie in cheap hooks, manipulation, second guessing, or pandering to what an audience likes.

Because nobody knows.

"Nobody knows anything," William Goldman says about Hollywood.

"By God," John Huston says in *Directing the Film*, "I don't know what my best friend or wife or son or daughter would like. I only know what I like, and I hope that there are enough like me to feel the way I do about it."

Why some stories connect and others do not is, ultimately, a mystery, but we move closer to the solution when we think about what stories that *do* connect have in common.

A few years ago, presenting the Academy Award for the best film in a foreign language, Jeremy Irons said, "Though our language may be different, our desires, our needs, are the same." If we substitute the word "lives" for "language," I think we move closer to understanding why some stories connect: *Though our lives may be different, our desires, our needs are the same.*

DIFFERENT LIVES
SAME DESIRES

I've never poured steel in my life, I've never been unemployed (knock on wood), and I've never danced on stage in a night club. I can't even understand some of the things the characters in *Full Monty* are *saying . . .*

> GAZ
> Dave, they're taking him away. All I need is
> seven hundred quid and they've got nowt on me.

> DAVE
> Gaz. No.

> GAZ
> Dave, he's me kid. Suppose they're nicking cars . . .

. . . but I connected like crazy. So did millions of others—bag boys, film buffs, periodontists, attorneys. Because under the surface particulars of the story, beneath its unique universe in Sheffield, England, lie the deeper, universal human patterns of striving, failing, and striving again as well as connecting, disconnecting, and reconnecting.

$$\frac{\text{NOT ABOUT ME}}{\text{ABOUT ME}} = \frac{\text{UNIQUE}}{\text{UNIVERSAL}}$$

We strive—some say compete—and we connect. We need to win and we need to belong. That's the human matrix—a vertical pattern of striving and a horizontal pattern of connecting. And these human patterns—recreated in unique ways—are the source of a story's shared emotions.

Art, Shakespeare tells us in *Hamlet*, holds a mirror up to nature. Human nature. And somehow, through the mysterious alchemy of art, we look at characters like Hamlet and Gaz and we see ourselves.

NOTE

1. Eric Sherman, *Directing the Film: Film Directors On Their Art*, Acrobat Books, Los Angeles, 1976, p. 310.

2

CONNECTING
TO SELF

There's a depressing rumor going around that there's nothing new under the sun. Every story's been told. When you go to the movies, it's easy to see how this rumor got started. Few films are fresh. Most are warmed-over versions of what we saw last year. We wander out of the theatre convinced that everything *has* been done. So how, my students ask, can their screenplays be unique?

The answer, I say, is *Le Menu*.

Le *what?*

Le Menu. A cross-section of their concerns. Self-analysis lite, so to speak, like those low-cal frozen dinners (I jokingly called it *Le Menu* one day in class. The name stuck).

I ask them to take out a pencil or pen and a clean sheet of paper and divide it into ten columns labeled *What I Love, What I Hate, What I Fear, What I Believe, What I Value, What I Want, What I Know About, People Who Made a Difference in My Life, Discoveries That Made a Difference in My Life, and Decisions That Made a Difference in My Life.*

When they're finished making the menu, the top row looks something like this:

Le Menu

What I Love	What I Hate	What I Fear	What I Believe	What I Value	What I Want	What I Know About	People Who Made a Difference in My Life	Discoveries That Made a Difference in My Life	Decisions That Made a Difference in My Life

Next, I ask them to fill in each column with their top five answers. Ten, if time allows. (If an answer is private, I ask them to flag it so I don't shoot my mouth off about it in class.) A few roll their eyes and I have to assure them it's not some pop-psychology gimmick. I'm not trying to find out who's crazy. "In a way, we're all crazy," one of my favorite writers, Joko Beck, says, and I'm content to leave it at that.

The exercise may *seem* a bit crazy—"touchy feely," as we said in the Sixties—but there is method in my madness. I've been giving this matter a great deal of thought since the literary manager of Actors Theatre of Louisville said to me a few years ago, "American dramatists lack passion and perception!" He was referring to playwrights, but the same could be said of screenwriters.

It isn't due to a lack of education or brilliance or vitamin K. It's due to our lack of awareness. We're all passionate and perceptive about certain things—we just have to figure out what they are.

"In order to create art works of any worth, each artist must have something to say, some values, some attitudes, some store of experience—a vision," my former playwriting teacher, Sam Smiley, said in *Playwriting: The Structure of Action*. Each artist must "identify those attitudes before they will ever energize a work of value."

That's what *Le Menu* is all about—identifying those attitudes, values, and experiences that will energize our work as screenwriters, creating a menu of what we know and care deeply about. It's one of the most important things we can do as screenwriters, because our unique material and vision is the source of unique screenplays.

So take a moment or an hour or a half-day to fill out the chart. Work in pencil, if possible; you will probably be erasing a lot; this is a harder task than it may seem at first. Noodle first on scrap paper if you prefer, then, when you're ready, fill in each column. You don't need to rank order your answers (but do if it makes you happy); just fill in the top five or ten.

And keep your answers small and specific. Hating phenomena like global warming is too general, or, as Mark Twain said about glacial epochs, "they are vague, vague." Hating nuclear war is too sweeping; these are *short* screenplays we're talking about. It's hard to tell *Dr. Strangelove* in fifteen minutes. Or seven. Or three.

But if hating nuclear war keeps turning up on your own menu, take a moment to figure out why. Shake it down. See what *specific* connections you have to this passionate feeling. Remember, there are no right or wrong answers. The point is to get down on paper what makes you tick. So dig deeper. Annihilation aside, why do you hate nuclear war? How does this hatred resonate with your own life?

This shaking-down process can be rich and revealing. Digging deeper usually is. Annihilation aside, I hate nuclear war because when I was a child in the Fifties and early Sixties, my South Texas elementary teachers made me and my elementary school colleagues crawl under our flimsy school desks and sit there hunched over, hugging our knees, as if that would do any good if Khrushchev (or later Castro) dropped the Big One.

This drill was supposed to make us feel safe, but it unleashed an unexpected emotional fallout among American schoolchildren—stark terror—not that we were going to die, but that we were going to die *apart from our parents*. Talk about *bomb scare*. I sat crouched under my desk plotting the fastest route home (through the cotton field next to my school). My future husband was in high school in a Connecticut prep school, a thousand plus miles from his parents in Florida, plotting how to steal a jeep and drive backroads all the way home so he could be with them before they all went *kablooey*. Ask any Boomer. It's a Christmas miracle if we're normal at all.

I think you see the point. It's hard to create a short screenplay from hating something as sweeping and vague as nuclear war, but you can begin to see possibilities in a terrified tomboy crouched under her South Texas school desk plotting short cuts through cotton fields or a high-school prep in Connecticut plotting to rip off a jeep.

The best short screenplays are deeply felt and highly specific.

Don't get me wrong. I'm not talking memoir. I'm not saying you have to write autobiographical screenplays. You may, of course; *Au Revoir, Les Enfants* is a beautiful film, but that's not the point. The point is to have a point of authentic connection to the screenplays you write. The best short screenplays I've seen over the years have sprung from a person or image or scene or belief, from *something* in the story that has deep resonance for the writer.

Thomas Jackson used to have crushes on all the cashiers; his main character, Earl, sprang from that root emotion. But the connection goes even deeper. In *Slow Dancin'*, Earl finally finds the courage to tell Maybelline that he loves her, and courage is a subject close to home for the writer:

> I like to explore courage in ordinary people, extraordinary courage in ordinary people. They're just ordinary people and what they're wanting to do is not like some grandiose thing but it's just like the moment of courage, taking that step, leaving home. I am these characters in the sense that, you know, I'm still in Bainbridge. I'm afraid to take that step out, and so that's why it's interesting to me because these are characters that are afraid, just like I am, but they actually take that little leap of faith that it takes to make the move.

I've learned the hard way that the *best* idea in the world can be hell to write if it doesn't resonate with you on some level. *Le Menu* is a very good place to look for ideas that do. It's your secret weapon, a menu of the passions and perceptions that make you—and your screenplays—unique. So finish the menu (though you're never really finished because your answers will change and evolve as you do), and for heaven's sake, don't throw it away. When I teach, I always keep a copy of my students' menus on file.

Inevitably, some of them tell me they don't have an idea. Or they'll try to write an idea that doesn't have real resonance for them. More times than not, the idea doesn't work out. The student comes to me in a panic.

One student, Lani Sciandra, worked on such an idea for her thesis script, but it blew up in her face halfway through the semester. She came to my office, dazed and confused. Ready to throw in the towel. I asked her what she wanted to write about. She didn't know. So we did menu stuff (the idea for the menu was beginning to take shape in my mind). I asked her what kinds of things gnawed on her bones, as Faulkner once put it.

She said, "Like what?"

"Oh, like shame, envy, hate, love."

She talked about her relationship with her father. It was troubled. He was rarely around.

"Well," I said, "what about that?"

Lani left my office to think about this. A few weeks later she returned with a screenplay titled *Cool Breeze and Buzz*—a deceptively simple story of a young girl, Paula (a.k.a. Cool Breeze), who is living on a river with her Aunt Barbara when her father, Buzz, drives back into her life in a red Cadillac he won playing poker and invites her to go live in Las Vegas with him.

Lani was living on the Wakulla River south of Tallahassee at the time, and the story sprang from that "magical kingdom—hermetically sealed from forces unnatural to itself," she told me.

> An image echoed in my mind—from the river—gliding downstream with the current—a discovery—a secret revealed—drawing from the part of me that had the most resonance—it had to do with identity and responsibility— my mother, who raised me, was the obvious choice—but as I played off the title it transformed into something less immediate, transparent—a fantasy of the absent father, the true figure in the shadow—I liked the idea of contrasting elements—the image of a man like Buzz in his red Cadillac crashing in on this pristine microcosm—and the dynamics this creates when posed with the question, "to go or not to go"—where do you really belong?—what is home?

Cool Breeze and Buzz may be a simple story on the surface, but like the river that inspired it, there are deeper currents that have a profound connection to Lani. As a result, the story is so deeply felt and so rich in detail, emotional honesty, and humanity that it has won more awards than any other undergraduate film produced at the Florida State Film School—first prize at film festivals across the United States and numerous recognitions abroad. And, for the same reason, *Slow Dancin'*, *tongue*, *Lena's Spaghetti*, and *The Making of Killer Kite* have won numerous awards, too.

Ultimately, an authentic connection to the screenplays you write will be more important than any gimmick, sunset, hand-held camera, or zoom shot in the film that you or someone else makes. Michael Rabiger puts it this way:

> Setting out to develop a style or an artistic identity, as students often feel they must do in fine art schools, leads to superficialities and attention-demanding gimmickry. Far more important is to develop your deepest interests and to make the best cinema you can out of the imprint left by your formative experience. Working sincerely and intelligently is what can truly connect your work to an audience.[1]

It's the Screenplay Paradox: The best way to connect with others is through the honest expression of our unique experience of being human.

DEPART THE *DONNÉE*

Your menu will be a goldmine for *germinal ideas*, as Sam Smiley calls them—undeveloped inspirations for stories—but feel free to depart the *donnée*—French for "given"—as Henry James said. Make the leap into making the rest of it up.

For Lani, the world of the river was familiar. "I started with what I knew in order to explore what I didn't, and the seed was planted so to speak."

So did Rachel Witenstein in *Lena's Spaghetti*, the story of two lonely people—a young girl, Hannah, and a mailman, Herbie—who connect as pen pals:

> Like Hannah, I was the "misfit new kid." I was also a late-bloomer. As an adolescent, I used my journal as a time-travel machine; I frequently sought the advice of my "older self," who I knew would one day read what I was writing. I would write out all my questions and thoughts, then concentrate really hard and try to hear my adult voice answering back. I guess this story was a way for me to explore the implications of taking this "older self" into the real world, into a real relationship. The concept of using your imagination to overcome obstacles such as insecurity or loneliness was familiar territory. With Herbie, I tried to create a character who would benefit from the imagination of this girl. Even though she wasn't particularly honest with him, he was better off in the end because of their relationship.

Matt Stevens knew a lot about campy cult horror films and, as an M.F.A. student, the horrors of filmmaking. With these two areas of knowledge as his springboard, he created the wacky unique mockumentary, *The Making of Killer Kite.*

As Grace Paley so wisely put it, "Write about what you know that you don't know."

Find something you're passionate or perceptive about or something that gnaws on your bones and then ask, What if? See where the creative river takes you.

That's what another student, Andy Zare, did after I threw a hissy fit in my screenwriting class because all the ideas were so familiar. Boring. Sleep city. Yawners.

I said, "Okay, next time I want you to bring me the most outrageous idea you can think of." And I walked out of class, leaving my students there, a bit stunned.

Andy went home and brainstormed.

> I was always fascinated by superheroes. *Superfriends* was my favorite cartoon when I was a kid. Superman wasn't my favorite because he could do anything. I was more intrigued by the less-than-mainstream heroes that had odd abilities like Aquaman and the Wonder Twins. It's good that we had Aquaman to fight all that crime that goes on under water. The Wonder Twins were my favorites because they were so absurd. One could turn into an animal and the other would turn into some form of water. This of course was quite useful.

But the original spark came from Andy's old high school friend, Joe Wagner, the name he gave his main character.

> Joe heads a comedy sketch group in L.A. called "Laughing-stock." He had this comedy routine about a superhero called "The Tongue" who fought crime with his super sense of taste. His nemesis would force him to brush his teeth so as to dull his taste buds. I took this idea and turned him from a superhero into an "Ordinary Joe." I was basically more interested in the downside of his ability and what type of problems it would create.

So Andy explored what those problems might be.

> I figured that the thing that Joe Wagner would dread more than anything else would be to kiss anyone. So it's really just a simple love story. It's your typical "Boy meets girl; girl wants to kiss boy; boy has super-sensitive tongue and doesn't want to kiss girl" story. There were a lot of areas to explore with Joe's tongue, but I wanted to focus it around his fear of kissing.

Andy came to the next class and pitched *tongue*—one of the freshest ideas I'd heard and one of our most successful undergraduate films. Unlike any film you've ever tasted, just as Andy said it would be. And it started with a passion for superheroes and a person he knew.

Whatever your own experiences, relationships, passions, and perceptions, these will be the greatest source of uniqueness in the screenplays you write.

"We bring our life experience into the theatre," Sam Shepard said. The same is true of the movie theatre.

Unfortunately, we don't always trust this. We give into the Tarantino Temptation. Surrounded by success—and hungry for it ourselves (hey, we're just human)—we begin to believe it's easier to imitate someone like Tarantino than develop our own vision and voice. But as Anne Lamott says in *Bird By Bird*:

> The truth of your experience can *only* come through in your own voice. If it is wrapped in someone else's voice, we readers [or viewers] will feel suspicious, as if you are dressed up in someone else's clothes. . . . Sometimes wearing someone else's style is very comforting, warm and pretty and bright, and it can loosen you up, tune you into the joys of language and rhythm and concern. But what you say will be an abstraction because it will not have sprung from direct experience.[2]

Imitating others can be instructive. And it can feel like a shortcut to success—but in the long run it will short-circuit your own talent and creativity. Because your own vision, based on your direct experience, is the *source* of your creativity and the stories you tell, as Ray Bradbury reminds us in his inspiring essay, "How to Keep and Feed a Muse":

> Be certain of this: When honest love speaks, when true admiration begins, when excitement rises, when hate curls like smoke, you need never doubt that creativity will stay with you for a lifetime. The core of your creativity should be the same as the core of your story and of the main character in your story. What does your character want, what is his dream, what shape has it, and how expressed? Given expression, this is the dynamo of his life, and your life, then, as Creator. At the exact moment when truth erupts, the subconscious changes from wastebasket file to angel writing in a book of gold.
>
> Look at yourself, then.[3]

If you're in this for the long haul, you'll write many screenplays, short and long. It takes five to ten years to learn your craft, if you're lucky. So don't waste time seeking overnight success (which, by the way, takes fifteen years).

Seek yourself, your experience, your unique vision. In the end, that's the most valuable thing you have to offer.

"All you can give us is what life is about from your point of view," Anne Lamott tells us.

Everything else has been done.

NOTES

1. Michael Rabiger, *Directing: Film Techniques and Aesthetics*, second edition, Focal Press, Boston, 1997, p. 213.
2. Anne Lamott, *Bird By Bird: Some Instructions on Writing and Life*, Pantheon Books, New York, 1994, p. 199, 200.
3. Ray Bradbury, *Zen in the Art of Writing: Releasing the Creative Genius Within You*, Bantam Books, New York, 1992, p. 47.

---3---

CONNECTING TO PROCESS

There's another half to the self-knowledge story: You need to know your own writing process. I'm not talking about the specific steps in the process of screenwriting; I'll talk about that in Part II. I'm talking about understanding how you *work* as a writer—your own creative process—and how to create optimum conditions for that to occur.

No one can tell you your process. Every writer's is different. Individual. Idiosyncratic. That's the point. But you need to understand yours. You may not have been writing long enough to know what it is. That's okay, just start paying attention. And start asking yourself the following questions:

When do you work best? What are your own creative rhythms? Do you write best at night? In the morning? High noon? If you don't know, try different times until you figure out what works best for you, then *do everything in your power* to work on your screenplays during that time.

"Yeah, right," I hear some of you snicker. "C'mon, I'm in *film school*."

I know. So am I. I work long hours, too. And I see my students stagger into my classroom after an all-nighter in the editing suite with that stunned look on their faces that cartoon characters get when other characters bash them on the head (I've learned not to take it personally when they nod off in class). Still, I tell them what I'm telling you: *Clear time and space for your writing*. Not just any time and space—the time and space that works best for them. More often than not, they snicker, too.

And I understand. For the past twenty years, I've had to write around raising children, which meant grabbing a couple of hours before they woke up. *Early* mornings. O'dark thirty, as we say in our family. Or when they were at school. I assumed I worked best in the morning, but recently, while writing this book, I've discovered if I start writing later, I go into a deep and productive creative trance in the late afternoon. So even if you know your creative process, it will probably change with your circumstances, evolving as you evolve as a writer.

Where do you do your best writing? I'm speaking geographically now, as Mihaly Csikszentmihalyi does in *Creativity*:

> At the macro level, the question may be whether you feel you would be happiest if living at the seashore, surrounded by mountains or plains, or in the bustle of a big city. Do you like the change of seasons? Do you hate snow? Some people are physically affected by long sunless periods.[1]

If you're a student or otherwise tied to one place, this discussion might strike you as silly, but it's sillier not to think about it, according to Csikszentmihalyi:

> There can be many reasons why you might feel trapped in the place that you live, without a choice to move. But it's a great waste of time to spend your entire life in uncongenial surroundings. One of the first steps in implementing creativity at the personal level is to review your options of life contexts and then start thinking about strategies for making the best choice come true.[2]

In the long run, this kind of thinking is absolutely essential. A writer's *first concern*, Tennessee Williams once said, must be "to discover that magic place of all places where the work goes better than it has gone before, the way that a gasoline motor picks up when you switch it from regular to high octane. For one of the mysterious things about writing is the extreme susceptibility it shows to the influence of places."

Some of our faculty at the Film School swear they work better in Tallahassee than they do in L.A. The novelist Sheila Ortiz-Taylor works best at writers' retreats. I write best at our farm in rural north Florida, on the porch overlooking the meadow. And Sam Smiley just sent me a postcard from Ireland, where he's writing a screenplay. "Somehow creativity really flows when you're away from home."

You may be too young or inexperienced as a writer to know this right now, but, again, start paying attention. And, granted, even if you know the place you work best, you might not be able to pick up and go at the moment, but it will help your writing career a great deal if you figure out where that "magic place of all places" is for you and make plans to get there. At least now and then. The sooner you do so, the sooner you'll get where you need to be.

On the micro level, ask yourself what kind of *space* works best for you? As a young writer in Paris, Hemingway loved to work in cafes. Later, in Key West, he worked in a study detached from his house. David Mamet recommends writing in restaurants, and I solved some major structural problems in a book proposal because of the white noise of voices in the food court at our Student Union.

"Again," says Csikszentmihalyia, "it is not what the environment is like that matters, but the extent to which you are in harmony with it."

Once you're found your space, fill it—to the extent that you want it filled—with objects that have significance for you. Anne Lamott keeps a one-inch picture frame on her desk. "It reminds me that all I have to do is write down as much as I can see through a one-inch picture frame. This is all I have to bite off for the time being."

Along with a dozen or so family pictures, I keep four small model planes on my desk, partly to remind me of my father—an aviator—and partly to remind myself to take off now and then in my writing. Take chances. Lighten up. *Soar.* My daughter gave me a Venetian glass fountain pen that I keep on my desk to remind me, when I hit rough patches in writing, that a writer was what I've always wanted to be. A friend sent me a small sign that says WRITE THAT BOOK when I started this one, and it sits at the end of my desk right next to my printer where I tape quotations that inspire or move me or remind me that my writing doesn't have to be perfect.

Again, this may sound silly. It's not.

> The kind of objects you fill your space with also either help or hinder the allocation of creative energies. Cherished objects remind us of our goals, make us feel more confident, and focus our attention. Trophies, diplomas, favorite books, and family pictures on the office desk are all reminders of who you are, what you have accomplished. . . . Pictures and maps of places you would like to visit and books about things you might like to learn more about are signposts of what you might do in the future.[3]

How do you work best? In long stretches or short bursts? The screenwriter Mark Spragg prefers total immersion. "I work seven days a week, all day long, 'til I drop, so the subconscious is so saturated, it's what I dream about. When I meditate, it comes up, I've already done so much thinking about it."

Writing tools may seem like a trivial consideration, but you need to know what works best for you: Pencil and paper? Pen? A computer? A typewriter like Barton Fink? (William Faulkner outlined his books on his study *wall*, but I don't recommend this for renters.) I need pen and paper when I start a project—or a piece of one, like this chapter. I need to noodle in longhand before I turn on the computer. I love the scratch of a good fine-point pen across paper; it gets the creative juices going for me while I brainstorm. And noodling (a similar technique is called clustering) is nonlinear, so it keeps me loose, keeps the ideas flowing, keeps the raging perfectionist in me at bay.

Know thyself and thy hangups.

I noodled this chapter before I started writing (see page 29):

It may look like chaos to you—isn't that where order comes from?—but this noodling helped me see connections, which I noted with arrows. As the chapter began to take shape in my mind, I assembled the various prewritten pieces on the computer, and I was ready to write a rough draft.

When I'm writing a screenplay, I'll noodle a much longer time—*piles* of pages—until the characters and story are clear in my mind; then I work out the structure on my drafting table. I need to know my scenes—at least their dramatic purpose—and the order I'll tell them before I turn on the computer and start drafting the screenplay. Even then, as I reach a new scene, I'll stop and noodle the dialogue and action before I start typing. Some writers work more organically, writing the screenplay to *find out* where the story is going. Barry Levinson dictated the screenplay for *Avalon* into a tape recorder.

Do you work better in silence or with music playing? I never *thought* about writing with music until I began writing scripts with Matt Stevens, and he always did. Vivaldi's *Four Seasons* seems to work best, and it's playing now as I write this chapter.

"Music played an important role in composing the atmosphere of the written page," Lani Sciandra said about writing *Cool Breeze and Buzz*.

> I was listening to a lot of electronic music at the time and used a mixed tape of songs I thought captured the feeling of what (I suspected) was going on—sometimes rewinding a track for hours until I got through a scene—St. George Pierre (the composer) was a great influence in shaping the mood from the beginning—I felt his score provided another dynamic to the expectations of a story told against a rural backdrop.

Are there *rituals* that help you write better?

"Small rituals, self-devised, are good for the soul," Julia Cameron says in *The Artist's Way*:

> Burning incense while reading affirmations or writing them, lighting a candle, dancing to drum music, holding a smooth rock and listening to Gregorian chants—all of these tactile, physical techniques reinforce spiritual growth.[4]

If you're not from California, you might want to try something else. A Midwesterner, Hemingway began each writing day by sharpening pencils. Southerners, Matt and I make fresh iced tea. When we start writing, one of us paces while the other one types. Hemingway wrote standing up (though not, I suspect, in cafes in Paris); when I write alone, I sit down, usually in the half-lotus position (sitting this way helps my back). Toni Morrison—or is it Maya Angelou?—plays cards until her Muse starts to talk. In a way, that's what all writers are doing—seducing the Muse, getting her to start talking. So figure out what works for you and your Muse and do more of that. If nothing works—hey, you're creative—create something that does.

You'll work best when you're taking care of yourself, no small cheese for film students, I know. But remember to eat, and eat well. Get as much sleep as you can; writer's block is often the result of exhaustion. Hit your writing each day, but take breaks, especially when you feel blocked. That way your unconscious as well as your conscious mind can work on it. Ray Bradbury calls the unconscious "the Muse." In *A Writer's Time*, Kenneth Atchity calls it "the out islands." I've nicknamed my unconscious "the elves," and I find my writing goes best when I remember to leave it alone and let the elves work on it for a while.

Go for walks, runs, or long drives. Nothing gets the Muse talking faster than motion. Just be sure, when she does, that you can take notes. Thomas Jackson always carries a small tape recorder in his car. I carry a folded four-by-six card and a pen when I go for long walks. When I drive, I keep a clipboard and a pen on the seat right beside me. I strongly recommend pulling over before you start writing. If you don't, pay attention.

For that matter, pay attention *all* of the time. That's the best thing you can do for yourself as a writer. "Be a person upon whom nothing is lost," as Henry James said.

And forgive yourself if your writing's not perfect. Perfectionism is a form of self-hatred, "a circus man strapped to the flaming wheel, turning," to borrow a phrase from the poet Bea Hampton. I know because I'm a recovering perfectionist ("And you want your recovery to be perfect," as one friend drolly said).

"Perfectionism is not a quest for the best. It is a pursuit of the worst in ourselves, the part that tells us that nothing we do will ever be good enough," Julia Cameron reminds us:

> Perfectionism has nothing to do with getting it right. It has nothing to do with fixing things. It has nothing to do with standards. Perfectionism is a refusal to let yourself move ahead. It is a loop—an obsessive, debilitating closed system that causes you to get stuck in the details of what you are writing or painting or making and to lose sight of the whole. Instead of creating freely and allowing errors to reveal themselves later as insights, we often get mired in getting the details right. We correct our originality into a uniformity that lacks passion and spontaneity. 'Do not fear mistakes,' Miles Davis told us. 'There are none.'"

"When all else fails, lower your standards," my father loved to say. Especially on your "shitty first draft," as Anne Lamott calls it, and she's right. As Hemingway said, "The first draft of anything is shit."

Writing is hard—a "shit grind," Janet Burroway says—and Thomas Jackson agrees. "Writing to me is like pulling teeth. I don't know how it works, you just do it every day and eventually something materializes out of all these characters."

So hang in there and keep writing, a little each day. Something will materialize. And you'll have good days and bad. After twenty-plus years of writing, I've decided that both are essential: I need two rotten days writing before I can get to a good one.

I hate that.

And keep in mind, too, that trying to write and hitting internal and external obstacles *is* the dramatic paradigm, as you'll see in the next chapter, so pay attention to your own struggle. You'll be a better dramatist for it.

Most of all, trust the process. Make some mistakes, takes some chances. Lighten up, take off, *soar*. As I'll say more than once in this book, the last word in screenplay is *play*. In this bottom-line business (grosses and grades), it's much too easy to lose sight of that.

NOTES

1. Mihaly Csikszentmihalyi, *Creativity: Flow and the Psychology of Discovery and Invention*, HarperPerennial, New York, 1996, p. 354.
2. *Ibid.*, pp. 354, 355.
3. *Ibid.*, p. 356.
4. Julia Cameron, *The Artist's Way: A Spiritual Path to Creativity*, G.P. Putnam's Sons, New York, 1992, p. 189.
5. *Ibid.*, pp. 119, 120.

4

CONNECTING TO SCREENPLAYS

A screenplay is a film unfolding on paper. A story told for the screen. A story told to be *seen*. And, like all drama, told *in* scenes.

"The scene is unique to drama—though used sporadically in all storytelling—in being its very bonework," William Gibson says in *Shakespeare's Game*.

A screenplay is a story told in scenes for the screen.

But what is a story?

Definitions abound, but most are similar to the one I just found in the *American Heritage Dictionary* that sits on my desk: *The narrating or relating of an event or series of events, either true or fiction.*

I'm a bit of a word freak, so I took a moment to look up "event": *An occurrence, incident, or experience, especially one of significance.*

Then I looked up "significance": *The state or quality of importance, consequence. From signify, to have meaning or importance.*

A story is the relating of events that have meaning, importance, consequence. That *matter*. That make a *difference*, however subtle, in the character's life. If a screenplay can't answer the question, "How is this day (week, month, year) different from any other?" it will raise the dread question "So what?" That age-old challenge, "What difference does it make?" is not idle talk. It's what we want to know when we watch the events of a movie unfold.

Making a difference, in fact, is the first definition of change, at least in my dictionary: *To cause to be different; alter.* And change is the heart of it all.

After more than twenty years of writing and ten years of teaching, I've found the most useful, least rule-bound definition of story is *a pattern of human change.*

A screenplay is a pattern of human change told in scenes for the screen.

That pattern of human change has other names—spine, through-line, action—but essentially they mean the same thing. As Sam Smiley says in *Playwriting: The Structure of Action*, "Simply defined, action is human change."

33

As a writer and teacher, I prefer thinking of the screenplay as a pattern of human change because it's dynamic. It's a *process* that an audience can see *beginning* (an event occurs that has meaning, importance, consequence), *developing* (the consequences of this event—and others—are played out), and *ending* (the outcome of the events is finally known at the climax). William Gibson says:

> A play is an energy system, and the business of the precip-
> itating event is to introduce a disequilibrium, that is, to
> release energy. Characterization, language, mood and
> tempo, meaning, all the other attributes which will give the
> play its identity, wait upon that release; it animates them,
> they cannot begin to exist without it. And once begun, the
> "play" is that of contradictory energies working to arrive at
> a new equilibrium, if it kills everybody.[1]

Gibson posits that a play—and, I would add, any screenplay—is made up of moves. The precipitating event is the first move, but hardly the last. "It is as in chess, also an energy system, one move provokes another." The example Gibson chooses is *Hamlet*:

> Horatio, once he has seen the ghost, must act; the move is
> his. It requires a decision, and he can decide his eyes are
> failing and go off to the oculist, or the Denmark fog is too
> much and go south for the winter, but these decisions will
> take him and us into a different game, not too inviting. In
> truth, he has no choice, the one decision that moves this
> game forward is
>
> > Let us impart what we have seen tonight
> > Unto young Hamlet; for, upon my life,
> > This spirit, dumb to us, will speak to him.[2]

Jump-started by the precipitating move, the energy system, game, story, pattern of human change is set in motion and will continue until the last move is made, until the energy system comes to an end, until the outcome is known. Until the climax. Until checkmate.

The best screenplays—long or short, serious or comic— create an energy system—a credible, compelling pattern of human change. That's what good screenplays do. That's what we pay our money to see. And we connect because our own lives—good, bad, or ugly—are also patterns of change.

In *The Full Monty*, Gaz—an unemployed steelworker on the brink of losing his son—becomes a one-night-stand stripper to make enough money to regain his son and, in the process, regains self-respect.

In *As Good As It Gets*, Melvin—an obsessive-compulsive writer who doesn't love anything in this world—falls in love with a dog and a waitress.

I could go on all day about features, but the subject here is short screenplays. And when you're writing short screenplays, thinking about story as a pattern of human change is even more useful. Why? Because this definition includes even small, subtle change, *as long as it matters deeply to the character*.

I've had students come into my office and slump in my yellow papasan chair and tell me that so-and-so said their short screenplay isn't a story. Then I ask, "Well, is there a pattern of change and does it make a difference to your character?" If the answer to both questions is yes, I assure students that they have a story. It may need rewriting (all screenplays do); nevertheless, they have a story, and with a lot of work and a little luck, they can figure out how to tell it in a way that connects.

What you're looking for when you write a short screenplay is that small subtle shift, that tiny turn of the screw in a character's inner or outer life. Preferably both. But small is the point. A simple but meaningful pattern of human change. As Patrick Duncan (*Courage Under Fire, Nick of Time*) said in *Creative Screenwriting*, "Let the story be simple and let the characters be complicated." (I'd jot that on a three-by-five card and stick it next to the one that says "Only connect".) And Duncan is referring to *features*. It's far more true for short screenplays.

The worst short scripts I've read suffer from what I call *narrative cram*. Too many big events occurring in too little time. ("Two pounds of shit in a one-pound sack," as we say in the South.) A feature plot packed into one or two dozen pages. There's so much going on that nothing seems to matter. Important moments can't *breathe*. The result is suffocating.

In short screenplays, smaller is better.

Small stories that make a big difference.

In *tongue,* Joe meets a young woman, Anna, who helps him overcome his fears of connection—and kissing.

In *Slow Dancin' Down the Aisles of the Quickcheck*, thanks to external events, Earl is finally able to say—or sing—how he feels to Maybelline.

How do screenwriters make these changes—some might say "miracles"—happen? By creating a pattern of change in their characters' outer life that changes their inner landscape forever. Hamlet was right. Art *does* hold a mirror up to nature, because our lives work the same way—*external events force inner change.*

SURFACE AND DEEP ACTION

When I'm writing a screenplay (or a novel or play or memoir, for that matter), I find it useful to break the story I'm telling into the external and internal patterns of change. I call these the story's *surface action* and the *deep action*. Just as the best screenplays interweave striving and connecting, they interweave the surface and the deep action. The best drama, in fact, is a dance between the external and the internal: Horatio sees the ghost of

Hamlet's father (*external*), struggles to decide the best action to take (*internal*), and tells Hamlet (*external*). And so it goes until death do him depart.

So it's enormously helpful, when you're preparing to write a screenplay, to clarify what these dual actions are. Do so in terms of the main character and an *-ing* verb. This reminds you that both actions are dynamic. And it reminds you that both, though interrelated, are, in fact, different. The surface action is the *external pattern of change*, the events we see happen up on the screen. *Gaz is trying to retain joint custody of his son.* To do this, he has to raise the money he owes his ex-wife. But he refused to work at her factory. So he tries to put together an all-male strip-tease act.

The deep action—also known as the *character arc*—is the *internal pattern of change* that is occurring in the character in response to external events. *Gaz is regaining his self-respect.*

Boiling your surface and your deep action down to one sentence is harder than it looks—my students are always amazed how tricky this is—so it may take a good deal of thinking and noodling to nail them. Once you do, write them down. You may find that they change as you write (material often has a mind of its own). Fine. Rewrite them. But keep them in plain sight because they're your compass, pointing you in the right direction as you write your screenplay.

MAKING CHANGE

So a screenwriter's job, in a nutshell, is making change. (And, alas, sometimes that's all you'll make for a while.) Articulating the surface and deep action is just the beginning. Now you have to *make* those patterns of human change happen in a compelling credible way.

But how? How do you build a pattern of change? Think of it as a pathway your character is moving along. What is that path made of?

Stepping stones.

In screenwriting, these stepping stones are specific *moments of change*. Events that make a difference, a.k.a. *dramatic events*. And once you can write a credible, compelling moment of change, you're well on your way to writing good screenplays. So it's of vital importance that you grasp—really grasp—what a moment of change *is*.

As you might expect, I looked up the word "moment," and to my joy and amazement I read: *A brief, indefinite, interval of time . . . A particular period of importance, significance . . . Outstanding significance or value; importance.*

Why did I feel such joy and amazement? Because the word "moment" is screenwriting summed up in one word. It's an interval of time (a scene), but also an interval of time that's important, significant (moment of change), and it comes from the Latin *momentum* which comes from the Latin *movere*—to *move*. And that's what good screenplays do.

We create stories told in scenes, patterns of human change out of moments of change, moments that matter, moments of moment, if you will, and these moments move our screenplays forward.

Moments of moment create momentum.

Yes, I'd jot that down, too.

But what *kinds* of moments create change in our lives and in the stories we tell? To figure this out for yourself, take a shot at:

THE MOOD EXERCISE

So here goes.

In the space provided below, describe a brief scene (in prose, present tense) in which a character's mood changes. Whatever mood he or she is in when this small scene begins, make sure it has changed by the time the scene's over. (This works best if done in a class or a group, but if you're doing it by yourself, write several brief scenes before you move on in the book. Multiple scenes is what matters.)

If you're not in the mood to make something up, describe a brief scene from your life. Mine might look something like this:

> I'm writing away on this book when the telephone rings. My son, Ross, sixteen, says, "Mom, I'm in trouble." My heart goes *squish squish.* But he's safe. He just ran out of gas, so he pushed the car off the road and walked on to school. "Could you bring me five gallons?" I agree, deciding to be Zen about it. I drive to school humming, then I lurch forward and shriek, "Oh, my *God!*" Up ahead I see his car *nose down in a ditch!* When he pushed it off the road, he pushed it over the edge, a minor detail he failed to mention.

My mood changed a number of times in that scene, but you only have to make your character's mood change once, as students did in these examples submitted anonymously in a screenwriting workshop I taught in Tampa:

> Megan's car turns the corner in front of the school. Mozart is playing on the radio. She smiles, searching for Eddie. She hums the concerto and taps her fingers eagerly awaiting Eddie. Fourteen year old Eddie spots the car, gives his friends a shove, and high-fives a goodbye. He opens the door and gets in.
> "What's new?" Megan says. "How are you, sweetie?"
> "Nothing's new. Don't talk to me."
> Megan shuts off the radio and looks at a pigeon flying by.

Or:

> A young man goes to an electronics store. He purchases a big-screen TV. Young man goes home. In his living room, with a huge ribbon on top, is a big-screen TV.

Or:

> She reaches into her mailbox at the college. Mostly junk. But there were two envelopes. She recognizes the handwriting, the return address. She thought he would send maybe a Christmas card, a note inside. She doesn't dare open it now and get caught reading it. She doesn't trust herself not to cry when she reads his advice about being a scholar. She runs upstairs to her office, tears the letter open, and realizes he's sent the wrong letter. It begins, "Oh, my darling, I love you and I love you and I love you." It was a mistake. And then she sees her name. It was to her.

You get the picture. Short and sweet. A character starts in one kind of mood and ends in another. Don't spend more than five minutes on this. Keep it simple. And don't agonize. It doesn't have to be art ("Let Art do his *own* work," as my friend, Stu Hample, says). So turn off the perfectionist machinery and write a quick scene:

Okay, you've finished your scene. If you haven't, wrap it up. The point isn't perfection. It's making change.

There. Good. Thank you.

If you're in a class or a writing group, collect the scenes and read them aloud. Have each writer identify the *precise* moment of change. What *specific event* happened that altered that character's mood? List these events on the board.

Did the character learn something? Hear some bad news? (I learn that Ross ditched his car.) Good news? (A woman realizes that the love letter she received is really to her.) A surprise? (A young man finds a big-screen TV in his living room.)

When you've finished listing the moments of change and why they changed the character's mood, look at the verbs that you used—in this case, *learning, finds out, finds, realizes*. Circle them and ask what these words have in common. "Is there one word that includes all of them?" I asked my workshop students in Tampa.

"They're all discoveries," said one of my students.

"Bingo!" I said. Because a realization or epiphany is a discovery, too.

When I do this exercise with groups of students, its almost always a discovery that alters the character's mood. Now and then it's a decision (I decided to be Zen about taking Ross five gallons of gas). Both are correct. Because, as Sam Smiley once taught me, discoveries and decisions are the two major categories of change in our lives and the stories we tell.

Sam also included deed and accident on his list. I tend to think of an accident as a discovery, but deed—or doing—while not a precise *moment* of change—is an essential part of any pattern of change. Remember, "drama" comes from the Greek *dran—to do*. Doing flows out of decisions, and decisions flows out of discoveries.

Again, it's a dance: Horatio sees the ghost of Hamlet's father (*discovery*), struggles to decide the best action to take (*decision*), and tells Hamlet (*doing*, but also a *discovery* for Hamlet). And so the game, the energy system, the pattern of change, continues to flow until Hamlet can no longer discover, decide, do—or be.

THE PEARL IN THE OYSTER

Each moment of change—discovery or decision—occurs in a scene— the bonework of drama—be it in a play or a screenplay. Which is where we came in.

A screenplay is a story told in scenes for the screen.

I like to think of a scene as an oyster and the moment of change as the pearl—the scene's reason for being. And the pearls—strung together in scenes—are the screenplay's pattern of human change.

It's important to note that some scenes *do not* contain a moment of change. Sometimes a scene is for atmosphere, mood. Or it establishes a situation. Sometimes a character is simply being or doing, absorbing the events that have happened, like Ulee tending his bees in *Ulee's Gold*.

Ulee's writer/director, Victor Nunez, said to me years ago that it's good just to be with your characters for a while in your screenplay. Hang out. It's lovely, important advice. Granted, you don't have much time to do this in short screenplays, but you do need to give your characters and events time to breath.

But keep in mind that scenes like Ulee tending his bees work because moments of change have already occurred. We sense what he's going through. We're connected to his emotions while he tends his bees. If we weren't—if no moments of change had occurred in the film to stir his emotions (and ours)—then watching him tend his bees—however exquisitely acted, lit, shot—would be far less compelling.

Remember, your purpose is to connect, and you connect through your character's emotions. It's the discoveries and decisions in your story—and the deeper currents of striving and connection—that create emotion in your characters. And this emotion *flows* from scene to scene, from one moment of change to another, holding your story together.

EMOTIONAL FLOW

Just as emotion is the invisible thread that connects an audience to characters up on the screen, *emotional flow* is the invisible thread that connects the individual scenes.

Each scene in a screenplay is separate, distinct. By definition, a new scene occurs when the camera changes time or place (not placement within a scene):

EXT. LIGHTHOUSE – NIGHT

INT. LIGHTHOUSE – NIGHT

EXT. BEACH – DAY

And so forth. The story *leaps* from one scene to another, blessedly leaving the boring stuff out. We see the pieces of the story that matter, that make a difference, that create—or process—emotion in the characters. And we're able to stay connected to the story—in spite of the leaps—because we follow the emotional flow.

It's analogous to *the persistence of vision:*

> If, while one is looking at an object, it suddenly disappears, the image of it will remain on the retina of the eye for a brief space of time (approximately one tenth of a second) and during that time one will continue to "see" the object although it is no longer before the eye.[3]

I like to call it *the persistence of emotion:*

> If, while one is looking at an emotion (the boy reacting to his mother being killed by the bus in *Central Station,* for example) it suddenly disappears because the story leaps to a new scene, the emotion remains on our mind (heart? both?) and we continue to "feel" this emotion during the leap although it is no longer before our eyes.

We—and the character—carry this emotion forward. It *flows* to the next scene when we see him—hunched over, heartbroken. If he were laughing and singing, we'd say, *Huh?* The emotional flow wouldn't work. His happy emotions wouldn't feel *earned* (unless we learned he was in deep denial). When we watch a film, we're connecting the emotional dots and connecting to the characters as we do. The story—leaps and all—moves forward in what seems to be a seamless emotional flow. And we move forward with it.

The opening of *tongue* leaps from Joe Wagner's bathroom to a flashback of a kiss in a gazebo and a fistfight on a playground back to Joe's bathroom in the present to his bedroom to his job at with a florist—all in a matter of minutes—but we're able to follow—and care—because of Joe's emotional flow.

As I said, not all scenes contain a moment of change. *tongue's* opening scene simply establishes Joe's situation, his supersensitive tongue. But all moments of change *are* contained in scenes. Pearls in oysters. And sometimes the richest most resonant scenes have more than one pearl. Which brings me to Charlie Chaplin. . . .

EVERYTHING YOU NEED TO KNOW YOU CAN LEARN FROM *CITY LIGHTS*

Okay, that's a bald overstatement. You can't learn *everything* you need to know about writing screenplays from *City Lights*, but you can get pretty close if you pay close attention to one scene in the film.

You've probably seen it—Charlie Chaplin meets the blind flower vendor—but I recommend that you screen it again.[4] Several times, if you can. The scene is only two and a half minutes long. Here's the scene, summarized:

> The Little Tramp (Chaplin) sees a policeman and avoids him by ducking into a parked car and stepping out the other side onto a sidewalk where a young woman (Virginia Cherrill) is selling flowers. She hears the car door slam, assumes he's rich (or affluent enough to own an automobile), and asks him to purchase a flower. It's a silent film and there's no dialogue card for these lines, but you can read her lips, "Flower sir? Buy a flower?" A moustache-twitching moment of deliberating. He's torn. Poor.
> "Would you buy a flower, sir?"
> He decides that he will.
> She holds up two flowers. He points to the one in her right hand. She offers the other. A little impatient, he touches her right hand. When the flower accidentally falls on the sidewalk, he picks it up. She stoops to get it but when she can't find it, she says in a second dialogue card, "Did you pick it up, sir?" He gives her an "oh, come on" look, holds out the flower, but she doesn't see it. He moves the flower in front of her face and realizes she's blind.

Deeply moved, he tips his hat and gently puts the flower in her hand. She pins it to his lapel and waits for her money. He digs in his pocket for what may be his last coin, looks longingly at it, and puts it into her hand. She curtsies and backs up toward her change box on the cement wall. The Little Tramp takes her hand and helps her sit down.

As she starts to make change, the rich man returns to his car, slams the door, and drives away. She calls to him and a second dialogue card appears, "Wait for your change, sir."

In a lovely form = content shot, the camera pans back and forth from the car to the flower vendor as the Little Tramp puts it together: She thinks *he's* rich. Deciding he'd like to keep it that way, he tiptoes around the corner out of sight.

But offscreen he decides that he wants to see her again, so he sneaks back around the corner and sits by the fountain and watches her adoringly as she walks to the fountain and rinses her water bucket. Unaware that he's there, she chucks the dirty water right in his face. He tiptoes past her out of the frame.

What can you learn from this scene? Five easy lessons:

First, dialogue is *not* essential to creating a pattern of human change in a screenplay. Film is visual. Volumes of speech are conveyed by the actors. As my friend and former colleague, Charlie Boyd, said, "*Thoughts* register on film."

Don't get me wrong, I'm a great fan of talk. If it's highly entertaining and/or illuminates or moves the pattern of human change forward. *Pulp Fiction*—one of the talkiest films in the world—does this better than most. So I don't buy that old saw that talk in screenplays is bad. *Bad* talk is bad. Dialogue that doesn't move the story forward (more on this later), that's too familiar, too cliched, or too on-the-nose can be deadly.

Second, this scene from *City Lights* shows us that significant human change can occur in a very short time.

In this case, two and a half minutes. As he humors the flower vendor by buying a flower, the Little Tramp is profoundly changed.

So third, this scene is a wonderful illustration of external events forcing internal change. There's a clear surface action—buying a flower—and deep action—falling in love. And, I would argue, gaining compassion.

Falling in love/gaining compassion is the Little Tramp's character arc. I find it useful to draw the character arc, and, using my sophisticated screenplay notation, it looks something like this:

In two and a half minutes, because of external events, the Little Tramp's internal landscape is altered forever (or, at least, for the rest of this film).

Amazing.

Fourth, this excerpt shows that a rich and resonant scene often has more than one moment of change. It's an oyster with numerous pearls. Let's look at the scene one more time, this time looking for discoveries and decisions that the Little Tramp makes:

> The Little Tramp (Chaplin) sees a policeman (*discovery*) and avoids him by ducking into a parked car (*decision*) and stepping out the other side onto a sidewalk where a young woman (Virginia Cherrill) is selling flowers. She hears the car door slam, assumes he's rich (or affluent enough to own an automobile—*a false discovery*), and asks him to purchase a flower (a *discovery* for him). It's a silent film and there's no dialogue card for these lines, but you can read her lips, "Flower sir? Buy a flower?" A moustache-twitching moment of deliberating. He's torn. Poor.
>
> "Would you buy a flower, sir?"
>
> He decides that he will (*decision*).
>
> She holds up two flowers. He points to the one in her right hand (*decision*). She offers the other. A little impatient, he touches her right hand. When the flower accidentally falls on the sidewalk, he picks it up. She stoops to get it but when she can't find it, she says in a second dialogue card, "Did you pick it up, sir?" He gives her an "oh, come on" look, holds out the flower, but she doesn't see it. He moves the flower in front of her face and realizes she's blind (*discovery*).
>
> Deeply moved, he tips his hat and gently puts the flower in her hand. She pins it to his lapel and waits for her money. He digs in his pocket for what may be his last coin, looks longingly at it, and puts it into her hand (*decision*). She curtsies and backs up toward her change box on the cement wall. The Little Tramp takes her hand and helps her sit down.
>
> As she starts to make change, the rich man returns to his car, slams the door, and drives away. She calls to him and a second dialogue card appears, "Wait for your change, sir."
>
> In a lovely form = content shot, the camera pans back and forth from the car to the flower vendor as the Little Tramp puts it together: She thinks *he's* rich (*discovery*). Deciding he'd like to keep it that way (*decision*), he tiptoes around the corner out of sight.
>
> But, offscreen, he decides (*decision*) that he wants to see her again, so he sneaks back around the corner and sits by the fountain and watches her adoringly as she walks to the fountain and rinses her water bucket. Unaware that he's

there, she chucks the dirty water right in his face (a *discovery* for him). He tiptoes past her out of the frame (*decision*).

Thirteen moments of change in two and a half minutes. Six discoveries, seven decisions. You might find more. Each moment of change shifts the direction of the scene's energy and emotional flow. That means the scene has tiny reversals. These give it richness and texture. "Every scene is made up of the texture of the minor reverses a character encounters trying to get his or her way," Brady and Lee write in *The Understructure of Writing for Film and Television*.

If you diagrammed this *City Lights* scene, those reverses would look something like this:

In *Making Shapely Fiction*, Jerry Stern calls this "zigzagging." "Microplotting." "Creating fluctuations of feeling to maintain a high degree of attention." But more important than keeping your audience's attention, Stern says, is psychological truth.

> Zigzagging reflects psychological reality, the way hopes and fears alternate, how in our desperation we leap at solutions that we quickly reject, how human situations can change drastically from one moment to the next. And for readers [or audiences] zigzagging makes each scene electric with suspense.[5]

I like to call zigzagging a scene's EKG. But a scene without change (unless, as previously noted, it provides important mood, atmosphere, or time with the character) looks more like this:

And what have you got? A dead scene.

Fifth, the *City Lights* scene illustrates emotional flow. The Little Tramp comes into the scene concerned about the police who were angry at him in scene one after he was discovered under the tarp at the statue's unveiling (if you haven't seen the whole film, you'll have to take my word for this). So now, when he sees the policeman, he ducks into the car. After meeting the flower vendor and falling in love, he leaves the scene with new emotion, and that will flow to the next scene he's in, the invisible thread connecting the scenes.

Of course there's much more to learn from this scene; I learn something new each time I watch it. Like the brilliant use of surprise: Just as the scene's getting sappy, the Little Tramp gets a bucket of water smack in the face. What a great comic instinct. As Billy Crystal once said, describing what good comedy does, "Take 'em one way, then take 'em another."

And that's the screenwriter's job. Taking the story one way, then taking it another. Making change. Knowing your story's moments of change, why they make a difference to your character, and writing them so well they matter to us. Crafting a credible, compelling pattern of human change out of discoveries and decision and the action and emotions that flow in between. Narrating them in screenplay form.

Which brings us to format, something that throws a whole lot of people the first time they see it.

"To this day I remember staring at the page in shock," William Goldman writes in *Adventures in the Screen Trade*. "I didn't know what it was exactly I was looking at, but I knew I could never write in that form, in that language."

What he was looking at wasn't a screenplay, it was a shooting script, full of numbered slug lines and medium shots and close ups and medium long shots. He didn't know that, so he invented his own screenplay form, an extreme and highly creative reaction, to say the least, but then, this is William Goldman we're talking about.

Screenplay format is really quite simple. It's the *easy* part of screenwriting, once you understand it. And though I don't recommend reinventing the wheel, there's still plenty of room for invention.

DEMYSTIFYING FORMAT

Screenplay format breaks down into five easy pieces:

1. The *scene heading* or *slug line*
2. The narrative description of the *action*
3. The *name of the character speaking*
4. The *parenthetical directions* and *dialogue*
5. *Transitions*

More and more, my students are using screenplay software (me, too). Talk about *easy*. In most people's opinion, it's worth every penny, but it can be pricey (I've listed different software names and phone numbers in the Appendix so you can check on the price and computer compatibility). It is possible to create professional-looking screenplay format yourself. To that end, the TAB settings are:

1"	Left margin
2.6"	Dialogue
3.3"	Parenthetical
3.9"	Character name (ALL CAPS)
5.9"	Transitions
7.5"	Right margin (turn off justification)

In either case, use 12-point Courier type, justify your left margin but not your right, leave one-inch margins all around, limit the number of lines per page to 54, number your pages (with a period after the number) in the upper right corner of each page—except for the title page and the first page of dialogue—but don't number individual scenes.

Your title page should be simple—the title in caps, centered, one-third down the page, with "by (your name)" a few spaces beneath it, also centered, or "by" double-spaced and centered beneath it and "your name" double-spaced and centered below that. You can put contact information in the bottom left-hand or right-hand corner.

It's most useful to see how each part appears on the page, so here's the opening scene of *tongue* (you'll find the entire screenplay in Part Three):

FADE IN:

INT. SMALL BATHROOM – NIGHT

The screen is covered by an unidentified pink object.

> JOE (V.O.)
> Many people like to say they're different. But I
> really am.

CAMERA PULLS BACK TO REVEAL THE OBJECT: A
HUMAN TONGUE.

Crowded up next to his bathroom mirror is JOE
WAGNER, twenty-something. He is skinny, frail, and
sporting a bad haircut. He pokes and prods his tongue in
intense examination.

> JOE (V.O.)
> My name is Joe Wagner, and I have been cursed.
> Cursed with a most unusual ability: my tongue. It
> tells me things I don't want to know. I don't know
> why or how, but I can't stop it . . . or live with it.

The five easy pieces of the format make perfect sense when you remember that *a screenplay is story told to be seen in scenes for the screen.*

1. The *scene heading* or *slug line*—all CAPS, flush left with the left margin—tells where and when a scene happens:

INT. SMALL BATHROOM – NIGHT

This is the *master scene* heading, and the action and dialogue can flow uninterrupted. Occasionally you may want to use *mini slugs*—POV, BACK TO

SCENE, INSERT, INTERCUT—which appear in CAPS flush left. *Mini slugs*—especially a character's name or an object used as a mini-slug—have spawned a lively new style of screenwriting known as *writing down the page* or *detailing*, which Matt Stevens and I used in our feature, *Behind the Eight Ball*:

```
EXT. BOOKER JUNIOR HIGH LAWN - DAY

Conrad's car shoots across the lawn.

MRS. MCFADDEN

steps in front of Conrad's approaching car. And puts her
hand out like a traffic cop.

CONRAD

tries to slow down.

                      CONRAD
         Get outta the way! Get outta the way!

MRS. MCFADDEN

lifts her chin. No way she's getting out of the way!

She leaps up on Conrad's windshield and hangs on like a
suction-cup Garfield!

CONRAD'S POV - Mrs. McFadden's face pressed against
the glass.

                   MRS. MCFADDEN
         Conrad Howell! I knew you'd get in trouble.

The momentum of his car throws her off the windshield
and onto the ground.

She picks herself up and straightens her lapels.

                   MRS. MCFADDEN
                    (indignant)
         Hmph!
```

Writing down the page can give a scene great energy, so it's especially useful in action sequences, but it can also eat up a great deal of space, so it's rarely used in short screenplays, particularly if the writer has a page limit.

My students do find it useful at times in short screenplays to use MONTAGE or SERIES OF SHOTS to show the rapid passage of time. A montage is a series of MOS (no dialogue) shots, but more and more, MONTAGE and SERIES OF SHOTS are used interchangeably. Some writers number or letter the scenes; some don't. In our feature *Obscenity*, Matt Stevens and I chose to number our scenes:

A SERIES OF SHOTS:

1. Sara and Joe confer with Bailey about rental figures.

2. Sara and the OWNER of another video story go over adult figures. Joe makes notes on his clipboard.

3. ANOTHER OWNER tears off a computer printout and shows it to Sara and Joe.

4. In the conference room, Linda, Joe, and Sara pore over the data. The table is littered with reference books, legal documents, and Chinese food containers. Sara posts figures on a chart on the board.

My colleague, Andy Ruben, letters his scenes and slugs his montages with more information:

INT. LAB – MONTAGE – NIGHT/MORNING

Again, no two screenplays are exactly the same. Just make choices that make your screenplay readable and professional.

2. The *action*—also flush left, single-spaced, with a double space between it and the slug—describes what we see in Joe Wagner's bathroom:

The screen is covered by an unidentified pink object.

The action also describes what is happening *as it happens*, so it's *always* written in present tense. If your description runs longer than four or five lines, break it into smaller sections. Characters' names appears in ALL CAPS the first time we see them.

> Crowded up next to his bathroom mirror is JOE
> WAGNER, twenty-something. He is skinny, frail, and
> sporting a bad haircut. He pokes and prods his tongue in
> intense examination.

Too many screenwriting students think describing the action isn't important, but to a master like Hitchcock, it was one form of filling the frame, to him the heart of filmmaking.

> The one thing that the student has got to do is to learn that
> there is a rectangle up there—a white rectangle in a
> theatre—and it has to be filled . . . I only consider the screen
> up there, and the whole film to me should be on paper from
> beginning to end.[6]

What you're doing in a vivid, economical way is filling the screen, describing what's in it (*mise en scene*) and what's going on.

Mark Spragg described to me how much care he takes with describing the action, consciously filling the frame as he writes. In a scene in his screenplay *Blue Wind*, his main character, Frank, reencounters his step-daughter, Jolee, in a bar. It's been fifteen years since he's seen her.

> I wanted to show big-time contrast, shabby *versus* pearl-
> button cowboy sitting next to him. Contrast. She wears short
> sleeves. Show her strong arms. She owns her own land-
> scaping biz. Minimalism, but within it, I use words like
> 'cacophony.' I use metaphors. I say a scene has the color
> spectrum of a Rembrandt. I make it beautiful. And I never
> pissed off a director by doing this.

When he talks about composing a 16 mm frame, Andy Ruben tells students, "It's a square. Make it *pretty*."

Good screenwriters tell their stories this way. Visually. They fill the frame. They make it beautiful, pretty. They *use* it to help tell their story.

3. The *name of the character speaking* tells who's talking:

JOE (V.O.)

Occasionally, you will need a (V.O.) to the right of the character's name to indicate that the speech is a *voice-over*, i.e., not spoken within the scene. (O.S.) indicates that the character is speaking *off-screen*, ie., spoken within the scene but not within the frame.

4. The *parenthetical* indicates tone or inflection, but should be used sparingly. Don't give actors line readings. If the line is well-written, the tone should be clear, but there are exceptions:

> BOB
> (hostile)
> Of course I love you.

And the *dialogue* is the speech that Bob says. Or Joe in *tongue*:

> JOE
> Many people like to say they're different. But I really am.

It's important to note that dialogue forms a *column* that is roughly 3.5 inches wide. It does not go all the way to the right-hand margin of the page.

If you have to break dialogue at the end of a page, always end after the last complete sentence, then center (more) beneath the dialogue block. When resuming the speech at the top of the next page, reslug the character's name and add (CONT'D) beside it. When you're breaking a character's speech to describe action, you don't need (CONT'D). Just reslug the name and continue the speech.

5. *Transitions* appear sparingly in screenplays to help move the story from one scene to the next. FADE IN: and FADE OUT (usually followed by a period at the end of the screenplay) appear flush left on the page. CUT TO: and DISSOLVE TO: appear on the right-hand side of the page (Tab 5.9). You do not need a CUT TO: between every scene; the cut is implied with each new slug line. DISSOLVE TO: means one image is slowly replacing another, usually to show the passage of time. Both are a bit out of fashion, at least for the moment.

Once you understand the basics, the five easy pieces of screenplay format—*the slug line, the action, the name of character speaking, the parenthetical and dialogue,* and the *transition*—and why they're used in a screenplay, you're ready to use screenplay format.

As you do, remember your goal—*to make the film unfold on paper.*

"The whole film to me should be on paper from beginning to end," Hitchcock said.

So the reader can *see* it unfolding. You want to create a seamless read—"a vivid and continuous dream," as John Gardner once said—for the reader. The *last* thing you want to do is interrupt your own film-on-paper with bad grammar or spelling or boring descriptions or confusing actions. Keep it simple, visual, vivid, and clear. Your goal is to make the film *happen* in your reader's head.

That's connection.

And don't forget how *flexible* screenplay format can be. It's constantly evolving. You have more freedom than you may realize. The more screenplays you read, the more you'll understand what I mean. Read long and short screenplays, preferably in manuscript form, to see how other screenwriters use format. Screenplays in manuscript are available from Script City (1-800-672-2522 or on the Web at www.scriptcity.net), among other places, but these, too, can be pricey. Books sometimes are cheaper, but only a few like *Pulp Fiction* are actually printed in manuscript form. *Scenario: The Magazine of Screenwriting Art* (212-463-0600) publishes four issues a year with four screenplays in each—in the version the screenwriter wishes—and offers deeply discounted student subscriptions. If you're enrolled at a film school, of course, you can check screenplays out of your film library. The point is to read all you can.

Ultimately, the best way to learn to write screenplays is to write them yourself. The conventional wisdom for features says you have to write five before you sell one. I think, with short screenplays, once you've written (and rewritten) the five screenplays here, you'll be well on your way to understanding the craft.

That's what this book is really about.

NOTES

1. William Gibson, *Shakespeare's Game*, New York, Atheneum, 1978, p. 7.
2. *Ibid.*, p. 9.
3. Ernest Lindgren, *The Art of the Film*, New York, Collier Books, 1970, p. 26.
4. *City Lights* is available from CBS/FOX. Their public relations office phone number is 310-369-5369.
5. Jerome Stern, *Making Shapely Fiction*, New York, Norton, 1991, p. 255.
6. Eric Sherman, *Directing the Film*, Acrobat Books, Los Angeles, 1976, p. 331, 332.

PART II
FIVE (NOT SO) EASY SCREENPLAYS

THE DISCOVERY

As you learned in the Mood Exercise, the most frequent moment of change in our lives and our characters' lives is the *discovery*. Learning. Finding out. Realizing.

The best stories are *patterns of discoveries* that make a difference, however subtle, to the characters, like the discovery Hannah makes in *Lena's Spaghetti*:

INT. HANNAH'S BEDROOM – LATER

Hannah jumps on the bed. She flops onto her stomach, picks up the comics, looks them over with a straight face. She turns the page and sees the personal ads. She brightens as she reads.

INSERT – PERSONAL AD

    Like to write? Single male seeks unique female for pen-pal. Please write: Herbert Mack. 8013 Duck Lane. Savannah, Georgia 41256.

MUSIC SWELLS.

Though small and simple, this discovery has great significance for the story, launching Hannah's correspondence with Herbie, a correspondence that alters each of their lives. Likewise the discovery that Paula makes early in *Cool Breeze and Buzz*:

EXT. TRAILER – DAY

ANGLE ON PAULA

skipping along the river's edge reading the comic book. She reaches a clearing and the trailer comes into sight.

HER POV

of the trailer. The red Cadillac is parked in front.

She approaches the Caddy and proceeds to investigate.

CLOSE ON

A) her finger running along the side of the car through a thick layer of dust

B) her hand wiggling the hood ornament

C) the license plate on the front that reads "JACKPOT"

Then suddenly, we hear a MALE VOICE:

> MALE VOICE (O.S.)
> Beauty, ain' she?

HER POV

of a man, BUZZ MCKINNEY, 42, standing in the door at the top of the steps smoking a cigar.

> BUZZ
> (beat)
> Hey, Coolbreeze.

She drops the bag and freezes.

> PAULA
> (staring up at him)
> Hey.

He stands in slacks and a tight short-sleeved v-neck. Upon his belly, a huge brass buckle with a race horse and a large ring on either pinky.

Aunt Barbara appears from behind him.

> AUNT BARB
> Paula, honey, yer daddy's come
> to see you.

The rest of the story flows from this moment, as it does from the discovery that Joe makes early in *tongue*:

INT. LEO'S FLORIST – LATER

Joe is kneeling down taking inventory of the plants in
the aisles. ANNA ZHELIA, a petite girl with a natural
smile, a sparkle in her eyes, and a bounce in her step,
enters the shop. Her energy is contagious. She is
beautiful, but not dangerously beautiful. She approaches
Joe.

ANNA

Excuse me, I'm Anna Zhelia. Are you Leo?

Joe is startled. And when he looks up at Anna, he
becomes frozen by her simple beauty and composure.

JOE

No, he's in back . . . Can I help?

ANNA

I need to speak to him about the job.

JOE
(suddenly puzzled)

The job?

And the story is moving.

Moments of moment create momentum.

In each case, we *witness* a watershed moment in each character's life, a
discovery that forces the energy system of their life and emotion to flow a
different direction (in *tongue* and *Cool Breeze and Buzz*; in fact, there
are double discoveries—Anna and the job; the Caddy and Buzz—that make
the scenes especially rich). The *precise* moment of change is clearly rendered
on paper and thus ends up on screen. We *see* the discovery *happen*—that's
what we pay our money to see—and we *feel* its emotional impact. We
connect.

It's an excellent exercise to have everyone in your class or writing group
cue up a favorite movie scene where a significant discovery occurs, as my
colleague, Dr. Valliere Richard Auzenne, asks her students to do each semester. Screen them. Compare them. Analyze them. Chart their EKG structure.
Then, when you're fully acquainted with how discoveries are crafted in the
films you admire, you're ready to craft one yourself.

"If you can write a good discovery, you can write a good screenplay,"
Sam Smiley says. I agree. So learning to craft a convincing, significant
discovery is one of the most important aspects of dramatization that you
will master.

THE FIRST SCREENPLAY—THE DISCOVERY

To that end, write a three-page screenplay about a character making a discovery that makes a difference to the character. And follow these guidelines:

1. The discovery—the *precise* moment of change—must be clearly rendered on paper and therefore on screen. There's a tendency, especially with beginning screenwriters, to have their discoveries happen off screen. Not in this screenplay. The discovery has to *happen* on screen.

2. The audience must *understand* the difference the discovery makes to your character. They must be able to *see* the shift—however subtle—in your character's life.

3. *Do not go over three pages.* Normal margins and twelve-point Courier type. I know, my students howl, too—*three pages!* But when they're done, they often admit, like Michael Piekutowski (a.k.a. "Pick"), "It makes you focus on what's important. Then you write as much as you can in as few words as possible." Or Kim Baird, "I liked the restrictions. They made you think about what you wanted to say. There was no time for rambling."

"There's no time for lassitude in the screenplay," Mark Spragg told me, and he was talking about *features.*

"What is drama, after all," as Hitchcock once said, "but life with the dull bits cut out?" One of his writers, Jay Presson Allen, described how Hitch did it:

> There was a scene in *Marnie* where a girl is forced into marriage. And I began in the theatre; I only knew to do absolutely linear things. So I wrote the wedding, and the reception, and leaving the reception, and going to the boat, and the boat leaving. You know, I kept plodding, plodding, plodding. And Hitch—I can't imitate it, I'm sorry I can't because it's so lovely—he said: "Why don't we cut some of that out, Jay. Why don't we shoot the church and hear the bells ring and see them begin to leave the church. Then why don't we cut to a large vase of flowers and there is a note pinned to the flowers that says "Congratulations." And the water in the vase is sloshing, sloshing, sloshing. . . ." You know, I think of that all the time. When I get so wordy and so verbose I suddenly stop and say: think of that vase of water.[1]

In short, cut to the vase. The art of screenwriting is often subtraction. Believe me, I know. After writing features for years, I decided to adapt one of my one-act plays for a short screenplay. The limit was twenty-five pages;

my play was thirty, so I thought, *Piece of cake*. Then I started typing the scenes and I realized the screenplay would be sixty pages or more. All that yakkety-yak that worked so well on stage had to go. I had to hit my scenes later, cut dialogue that wasn't working hard for the story, boil down my descriptions, select only the most important details, and let the rest go. I cut entire scenes—*everything* that wasn't absolutely essential to telling the story.

Painful? Yes, at first, I admit it, but the finished twenty-five page screenplay was so much better for it, I was delighted. I'm a far better *feature* writer for having done this and a better teacher because I have new sympathy—and *respect*—for my students who have written such rich and resonant short screenplays.

So stick to three pages. Feel free to write a loose and baggy first draft if you want—far be it from me to tell writers their process—but cut it and shape it until it fits in three pages.

4. Remember that you're writing a *screenplay*, not just a scene. Your goal is to write a small story about a discovery and the difference it makes to your character. Like Jay Presson Allen, take advantage of the freedom of the form—the story leap, the power of the image. If your story is built on one conversation, open it up, move it around (this *is* moving pictures we're talking about) the way Nora Ephron does in *When Harry Met Sally*:

```
EXT. CAR – DAY

The car tooling along a beautiful stretch of highway.

                    SALLY (V.O.)
          You're wrong.

                    HARRY (V.O.)
          I'm not wrong.

                    SALLY (V.O.)
          You're wrong.

                    HARRY (V.O.)
          He wants her to leave. That's why he puts her on
          the plane.

                    SALLY (V.O.)
          I don't think she wants to stay.

                    HARRY (V.O.)
          Of course she wants to stay. Wouldn't you rather
          be with Humphrey Bogart than that other guy?
```

EXT. CAR EXITING (INDUSTRIAL) – MAGIC HOUR

EXT. DINER – NIGHT

Sally's car rounds the corner near some refinery tanks, heads into a diner parking lot.

> SALLY (V.O.)
> I don't want to spend the rest of my life in Casablanca married to a man who runs a bar. That probably sounds very snobbish to you, but I don't.

The car pulls in front of a diner straight out of the fifties, Harry driving.

> HARRY (V.O.)
> You'd rather have a passionless marriage—

> SALLY (V.O.)
> —and be First Lady of Czechoslovakia—

> HARRY (V.O.)
> —than live with the man ...

INT. CAR – NIGHT

> HARRY
> ...you've had the greatest sex of your life with, just because he owns a bar and that's all he does.

> SALLY
> Yes, and so would any woman in her right mind. Women are very practical.

She takes out a can of hairspray, sprays her hair.

> SALLY
> Even Ingrid Bergman, which is why she gets on that plane at the end of the movie.

EXT. DINER PARKING LOT – NIGHT

> HARRY
> (getting out of car)
> Oh, I understand ...

. . . he says, realizing she's saying all this because she's never had great sex. A discovery.[2]

One argument, five locations, and two characters making a number of discoveries about each other that seem insignificant, even silly, until Harry comes to his realization that Sally's never had great sex, and she discovers that's what he thinks, and this spawns a new argument that raises the central dramatic question of the screenplay—can a man and woman be good friends? Sally says yes, Harry says no because "the sex thing" is always "out there." They spend the rest of the film working out the answer to this central question.

5. Last, don't let this screenplay's brief length lull you into thinking you're writing a skit. You're writing a significant moment in your character's life. It may be funny or sad or any tone in between, but it isn't a skit. Skits are shallow. Significant discoveries are not.

CHOOSING AN IDEA

The best way to stay out of shallow water with your screenplay is to work with material that you connect to, that has resonance for you as a person. And the best place to find this material is right on your menu. After all, one of the columns is *Discoveries That Made a Difference in My Life*. You might find an idea for a discovery that makes a difference by looking at your own life. If you do, of course, feel free to depart the *donnée* and fictionalize the idea for the screenplay you write.

Look at the other columns on your menu—your loves, hates, fears, beliefs. You may have a strong passion or opinion that spawns an idea. This can be a wonderful place to begin. One of my students, Fatima Mojadiddy, believed passionately that the homeless should work, and she wanted to write a short screenplay about this. I agreed, on one condition: She had to talk to homeless people at the Shelter in Tallahassee. And there, to her surprise, she discovered that many of the homeless *do* work, an important discovery for Fatima as a human being and screenwriter, and, as it turned out, a discovery that makes a difference to the main character in her screenplay.

You may decide to set your menu aside and create an idea from something entirely different—a bit of dialogue you overheard or an image that struck you just as the image of the river struck Lani Sciandra. Maybe even a sound. Once, walking by a dumpster, I heard a cell phone ringing inside. That scene has stuck with me, and one of these day's I'm going to start a screenplay that way—a character hearing a cell phone ring in a dumpster and making a discovery that makes a difference when she answers the phone.

Whatever idea you choose, be sure that you feel some connection. And be sure that the idea's small and specific so you can create a pattern of human change that we can see happen on screen in three minutes.

DEVELOPING CHARACTER

Why the discovery makes a difference depends entirely on the character you create. In *Lena's Spaghetti*, Hannah has just moved to a new town. She's lonely, disconnected. When she discovers a personal ad from Herbie, she answers.

In *tongue*, Joe has deliberately taken a job in a florist shop so he can keep his distance from people. The discovery that a lovely young woman, Anna, has joined the staff is *not* good news—at least in the beginning.

And in *Cool Breeze and Buzz*, Paula's discovery that her father is back has tremendous significance for her because she hasn't seen him in years.

You have to know—and show—your character so that your audience understands why the discovery matters. Some writers write a character bio, but I find it most helpful to start by answering the following questions:

Character Checklist

1. Name?
2. Physical appearance?
3. Backstory? (the character's story before the screenplay begins)
4. Present circumstances? (occupation, income, geographic location, dwelling, key relationships)
5. Values, beliefs, worldview, attitudes, opinions?
6. Loves?
7. Hates?
8. Fears?
9. Wants?
10. Imperfections and contradictions?

Answer these questions for your character. All this information, of course, cannot end up in your screenplay. Knowing isn't showing. To show, you have to find what Thornton Wilder called "shortcuts to the imagination." Ways of embedding important information—preferably visually—in your screenplay. Ways to give important glimpses into your character and your character's world.

A good place to start is carefully crafting your *Character I.D.*—the brief but *vivid* description of your character when you introduce him for the first time in your script, the way Lani describes Buzz McKinney:

```
He stands in slacks and a tight short-sleeved V-neck.
Upon his belly, a huge brass buckle with a race horse
and a large ring on either pinky.
```

The huge brass buckle with a race horse is a glimpse—just a glimpse—into his life as a gambler. A shortcut to our imagination.

When you craft an I.D., you want your character to walk off the page into the head of the reader and stay there the whole screenplay. It drives me crazy when I can't *see* characters the first time I meet them. I know, I know, many screenwriters don't bother, but the very best do. Look how brilliantly William Goldman describes Butch Cassidy the first time we meet him:

> A man, idly walking around the building. He is Butch Cassidy and hard to pin down. Thirty-five and bright, he has brown hair, but most people, if asked to describe him, would remember him blond. He speaks well and quickly, and has been all his life a leader of men, but if you asked him, he would be damned if he could tell you why.[3]

Or how vividly George Lucas, Gloria Katz, and Willard Huyck describe Toad when he first appears in *American Graffiti*:

> Terry Fields ("The Toad") maneuvers the scooter next to Steve's Chevy but misjudges and ricochets off the trash can before stopping. Terry grins sheepishly. He's seventeen, short but plenty loud, both vocally and sartorially in his pink and black shirt, levis, and white bucks. He looks slightly ridiculous but always thinks he's projecting an air of supercool.[4]

It's one of my great pleasures in screenwriting classes to explicate these two passages, showing how they briefly but brilliantly give us a glimpse of three crucial aspects of character (3-D I.D.s, I like to call them): (1) what the character *looks* like, (2) how the world perceives him, and (3) how he perceives himself.

Talk about exquisitely *crafted*. Perfectly packed little snowballs. Okay, they're a bit on the long side—I'd shoot for two or three sentences, max, especially in short screenplays—but notice that they don't stop the story. Each I.D. is *floated on action*—casing a bank and ricocheting off a trash can— and even as we're introduced to Butch and the Toad, the story keeps flowing.

So take all you know about your character from the Checklist and boil it down into a beautifully crafted 3-D I.D. Avoid like the plague cliches like "avoid like the plague" or sleep-city descriptions like "an attractive female" or "a typical Dad" or the overloaded APB description—six feet tall, brown hair, blue eyes, big feet—actually, big feet has nice possibilities. Select *high* details—specific, illuminating details—that give us a glimpse of the outer and inner person, and write the finished I.D. in the space provided below or on a separate sheet of paper.

DEVELOPING STORY AND STRUCTURE

Now that you know your character, you need to develop your pattern of change. When and where does the story begin? What discovery does your character make? Where? When? And what difference does it make?

When your character makes the discovery—early, middle, or late—in your screenplay is up to you—but the audience *must understand* the difference it makes to your character. *Why* it makes a difference. If the discovery happens early, the rest of your short screenplay might be dramatizing the difference it makes. If the discovery happens late in the screenplay, you'll have to set up your character and situation carefully so we understand the significance of the discovery when it occurs. If you've set your character and situation up well enough, you may not even need dialogue when the discovery happens. In film, such a moment is often more powerful without words.

In *Grosse Pointe Blank*, Martin Blank is speechless when he discovers his home is now an UltiMart. But as he stands there stunned, staring, as this awful information sinks in, we *know* what he's thinking—and feeling. We supply his thoughts and emotions. This is the height of connection between character and audience and the height of success for a screenwriter. The moment is so beautifully crafted, character and viewer become one.

One way to dramatize the difference a discovery makes is to show the shift—however subtle—in your character's life. Martin Blank is heading home, but when he discovers it's an UltiMart, the physical and emotional flow of the story shifts. "You can't go home again," he says to his shrink, "but I guess you can shop there." He calls his secretary, tells her to find his mother, and when he finds her in a mental ward, he finds that she doesn't know who he is. "You're a handsome devil. What's your name?"

The best stories are patterns of discoveries.

Once you've created a pattern of change out of one or more discoveries, decide how your screenplay will end. You don't have to—or want to—tie up all the loose ends. That leads your story into hunky-dory land, and few of us believe it exists. Just find a simple way to bring the magic carpet and your audience back to the ground.

Once you've developed your story, you're ready to create a *Scene-by-Scene*—a list of scenes in the order they occur. I strongly recommend that you work on index cards first—one scene per card—so you can move the scenes around on your desk or table or floor until you find the most effective order and emotional flow. Sticky notes work well, too. The point is to stay flexible, to see all the possibilities your material offers, before you lock yourself and your story into a structure. Andy Zare found cards extremely useful when he worked on *tongue*:

> I used the index card method of organizing my scenes. I'd brainstorm and come up with ideas which would become index cards. And I'd try to see how it would work into the story. Some cards I knew were keepers, such as Joe's dates with Anna. Others were ideas for Joe's nightmares. Those

scenes were more fun than they were crucial to the story. Basically, I wanted to keep the nightmares that best illustrated his fear.

If you get inspired about a scene and the index card isn't big enough for the notes or dialogue that you want to write, write them out on a separate sheet of paper (*never* argue with your Muse) and file it, making a note on the index card to look it up later.

Once the order of your scenes is working, type up your Scene-by-Scene. There are no rules about the right way to do this, but I find it useful to give each scene a slug line, double space, then give a brief description of what happens and why, ie., your dramatic purpose in the scene. An example from *tongue* might look like this:

INT. SMALL BATHROOM – NIGHT

Joe examines his tongue. Establishes that he has a problem with his tongue, but we don't know what it is.

EXT. LAKE – DAY – FLASHBACK

A younger Joe kisses Sara and discovers she's just kissed his best friend, Mike. Establishes the nature of the problem.

EXT. SCHOOL PLAYGROUND – DAY – FLASHBACK

Mike beats the tar out of Joe and tells him to keep his tongue out of other people's business. Establishes why Joe now avoids contact with people and is terrified of kissing.

EXT. LEO'S FLORIST SHOP – MORNING

Joe arrives at work, and his boss, Leo, tells him he has good news. Establishes that Joe's only comfortable working with plants and that Leo has a surprise.

INT. FLORIST – LATER THAT MORNING

Joe meets Anna; he's struck by her simple beauty and composure—and the news that Leo's hired her. Establishes attraction and throws story in new direction.

You may find it helpful to make a note about the emotion you hope to elicit from the audience in the scene, but don't bog down in too much detail. The simpler your Scene-by-Scene is, the better. That way you—and others—can read your screenplay in a skeletal form, letting the movie run in your—their—head, and confirm that your story and structure are, in fact, working.

DRAFTING THE SCREENPLAY

With your outline as a guide, write with energy and enthusiasm. "Turn the dogs loose and see where they go," as Mark Spragg likes to say. Stir in the I.D. you've already crafted. Make your characters come alive on the page. And make time to work on your screenplay each day, even if you have to get up earlier or stay up later to do it. The cumulative effect of writing each day is amazing.

If your rough draft is too long, grit your teeth and start cutting. A happy problem—subtraction is easier than addition. Try cutting your narrative description (but not necessarily your main character I.D.) in half, making it *more* vivid, visual, and economic. Cut dialogue that isn't essential, that doesn't work hard for you or your story. This is almost *always* a vast improvement as you will see when you read the five student screenplays in Part III and compare them with their films. Again, a visual reaction from a character is often stronger than words, as Lani Sciandra discovered as she was shooting *Cool Breeze and Buzz*:

> I trusted the notion that less is more—how can we say this without saying it?—redirecting the burden of meaning from writer to viewer—in the script, Paula shouts after the man who dusts her on the dirt road in the red Cadillac— this is an example of me trying too hard to punctuate the point—in the film, it's a silent reaction shot which I felt enhanced the mystery—I realize now how much more I could've let go but I suppose that's how the lesson goes.

When your characters *do* need to speak, let the *text* (what is said) be simple, and let the *subtext* (the river of emotion that flows underneath what is said) be complex.

When your screenplay is finished—at least in this incarnation—give it a title if you haven't done so already. I *never* accept an untitled work. The title is crucial. It's the first thing your audience sees, your first chance to connect with them and focus their mind on your story.

If you don't have a title, sit down and noodle everything that the story's about. Odd bits and details from the world of your screenplay. Slang for nudity—*The Full Monty*. A wonderful title! I love to do title workshops in class. As I jot miscellaneous words on the board, students start seeing connections. We did this for Chris Tomko's brilliant but untitled short screenplay about two young losers who kidnap a Sharpei dog so they can make enough money to get out of town. And, lo, someone shouted, "Sharpei Diem! Seize the Dog!" It set up the tone and the subject without *telegraphing* (giving the story away). The title stuck—and I love it—bad Latin though it may be.

If you try this alone or in class and you're *still* stuck in what the late great Jerry Stern called "Title Hell"—a place I've been many times—give your screenplay a working title and hand it in. Someone who reads it just might come up with a better one for you.

REWRITING THE SCREENPLAY

Repeat after me: Screenwriting is rewriting.

I'm not the first person to say it and I won't be the last. Because truer words that we don't want to hear were never spoken.

"Here is what I always say about screenwriting," Nora Ephron says in the Introduction to *When Harry Met Sally*:

> When you write a script, it's like delivering a great big beautiful plain pizza, the one with only cheese and tomatoes. And then you give it to the director, and the director says, 'I love this pizza. I am willing to commit to this pizza. But I really think this pizza should have mushrooms on it' . . . then someone else comes along and says, 'I love this pizza, too, but it really needs green peppers' . . . then someone else says, 'Anchovies.' There's always a fight over the anchovies. And when you get done, what you have is a pizza with everything. Sometimes it's wonderful. And sometimes you look at it and you think, I knew we shouldn't have put the green peppers onto it. Why didn't I say so at the time? Why didn't I lie down in traffic to prevent anyone's putting green peppers onto the pizza?"[5]

But even *before* a director or producer starts throwing green peppers on your script, you'll be rewriting—to make it better. If you're serious. If you want to be a successful screenwriter. The version published here of *Slow Dancin' Down the Aisles of the Quickcheck* is Thomas Jackson's *fifteenth* draft. "I didn't even have a *story* in my first draft," he told me.

Not long ago, I read the sixth draft of an M.F.A. Thesis screenplay-in-progress, *The Buse*, and I told the co-writer, Rob McCaffrey, what worked for me and what didn't, what was clear and what wasn't, where I thought the emotional flow wasn't working, where a character's emotion wasn't quite earned, what emotional beats he might add to make it work better. A week later, Rob said the screenplay was "beginning to go in the right direction." And it was an excellent script when I read it.

Screenwriting is rewriting.

This truth is so important, so fully acknowledged in the profession, that it's spawned a peculiar ritual at the Sundance Screenwriters Lab. "It has become a Lab tradition for the Fellows to burn their scripts to symbolize their acceptance that the writer's work is never done and that the script can always be better," said a 1998 fellow, William Wheeler.

Screenwriting is rewriting. Write it down. Pin it up. Make it your screenwriting mantra. And keep in mind that it isn't bad news.

"Revision," Kurt Vonnegut reminds us, "can make a fool look like a genius."

And as you rewrite, these guidelines might help you along in the process:

1. Be sure you're giving your readers the best script you can, however many drafts this may take. Recently a student gave me a short screenplay with a long note attached telling me she had "literally ripped her hair out" writing and rewriting the script. She wanted to know if there was a way to avoid all that angst and hard labor in the future. Alas, no, I told her, at least none that I've found. Screenwriting *is* rewriting. Over and over. But I was happy to tell her that her script was terrific. Not perfect, of course, but close. And you should work as hard on your own. As Jerry Stern used to say, "Don't give your writing to a reader until there's nothing more you can do."

2. Get feedback, responses, from the right kind of readers—people who care about you and your work and your future. If the guy who runs your dry cleaners offers to read it, think twice, unless he fits the criteria mentioned above. (I've had my worked trashed by one shopkeeper who turned out to be a frustrated writer waiting to take out his frustrations on the first writer stupid enough to offer her work. Now, when I've finished a draft of a screenplay, I only give it to readers I trust). If you're in a class or a workshop, you may not be able to choose who sees your work, but there will be those you should listen to more than others. And you will become that same kind of good critic for others.

I try and keep the critiques in my screenwriting classes constructive and carefully focused on one common goal—helping the writer strengthen the screenplay. Students tell the writer what is working for them in the script and what isn't. What is clear or unclear; this may be the most helpful feedback of all. What's strong and what could be stronger. How? Is the character's emotional flow working? Why or why not? They must be specific or it just isn't helpful.

You want to know if the precise moment of discovery is clearly rendered. How could it be clearer? Have you clearly shown the difference it makes? Does your audience get it? If not, what could you add or subtract to make sure they do? Are there breaks in the emotional flow? Emotions that seem unmotivated, out of the blue? If a character's emotion doesn't feel earned, we don't buy it. Your job then is to figure out what to add or shade in your script so the emotion *is* earned. And, when you add, of course, you'll have to find something else to subtract.

Take notes as people respond; you'll be amazed how many wonderful suggestions you'll forget. Before the critique is over, your head will feel like an overstocked fishpond.

Most of all, listen closely to everything that is said. More than once I've snickered (to myself) at someone's suggestion only to discover later it's the key to my screenplay. So be open. Check your ego at the door. Constructive criticism is a gift. Your purpose here is creating a screenplay that works. And connects. To do this, you need other people.

3. Look for consensus. If more than one person thinks a moment isn't working, it's probably wise to take a close look. If only one person thinks it doesn't work, and you disagree, diplomatically disregard it. Ultimately you'll have to run the responses—consensus or not—through your own creative Cuisinart and decide what's best to do.

4. Set the script aside as long as you dare so you can see it fresh when you return to rewrite. "Revise" means *to look or see again*, and you need distance to do this.

5. Make the changes necessary to make your script stronger—from your character I.D. to your curtain line. Sometimes this involves outlining the entire script over again and completely rewriting (*a page one rewrite*); sometimes this involves what Jerry Stern called *embeddings*—small additions you can embed in your existing script that make your story clearer—and stronger.

6. Take heart. Yes, you may have to cut something you love yet doesn't quite work to make room for something that does. But that, as William Wheeler discovered at Sundance, is the nature of the beast. "As I watched my pages curl, smoke and disappear into the flames," Wheeler said, "I realized the feeling of loss and rebirth was one I would always have, one way or another, for the rest of my writing life."

NOTES

1. I am indebted to Stu Hample for sending this quotation from *On Writing*, a collection of interviews held at Writers' Guild of America, East, edited by Arlene Hellerman.
2. Nora Ephron, *When Harry Met Sally*, Knopf, New York, 1992, pp. 7, 8.
3. William Goldman, *Butch Cassidy and the Sundance Kid*, Bantam Books, New York, 1969, p. 1.
4. George Lucas, Gloria Katz, Willard Huyck, *American Graffiti*, Grove Press, New York, 1973, pp. 5, 6.
5. Ephron, p. xiii, p. xiv.

---6---

THE DECISION

Discoveries are often beyond our control, but decisions are not. They come straight from our unique Central Control—experience, values, worldview.

"The quickest and best way to know someone is to see that person make a significant decision," Sam Smiley says.

I agree. Our decisions define us. They also define the lives that we lead. It's no wonder, then, that major decisions are powerful moments in screenplays. True watershed moments. In long and short scripts, a character's most important decisions are often the *turning points* of the story—those moments of change that throw the story in a whole new direction.

Rainman is a perfect example: The first turning point at the end of Act I is Charlie Babbitt's decision to kidnap his autistic brother, Raymond, from the institution where he's lived all his life. The climax of the story is the much-changed Charlie Babbitt's decision to let Raymond return to the same institution. This second decision is a *measure* of how much Charlie Babbitt has changed in the process. So is Hannah's decision to end the correspondence with Herbie in *Lena's Spaghetti*. And Earl's decision to profess his love in *Slow Dancin' Down the Aisles of the Quickcheck*. Their growth—character arc—is revealed by the decisions they make.

Decisions are made by characters, and characters are made by decisions.

Who we are dictates the decisions we make and the action we take.

Who = Do

Again, it's a dance—discovery, deliberation, decision, and doing. So a crucial part of designing that dance is learning to craft a decision.

THE SECOND SCREENPLAY—THE DECISION

Write a three- to five-page screenplay about a character making a decision that makes a difference to the character. The guidelines are similar to those for your last screenplay:

70

1. The decision—the *precise* moment of change—must be clearly rendered on paper and therefore on screen. You can say "he decides" or be a little more subtle, as long as the decision is *clear*. Look at Andy Dufresne's decision to play Mozart's *Marriage of Figaro* over the prison loudspeaker in *The Shawshank Redemption* after he discovers boxes of records and one phonograph donated by the Library District:

INT. GUARD STATION/OUTER OFFICE — DAY (1955)

Andy shoots a look at the bathroom . . . and smiles. Go for broke. He lunges to his feet and barricades the front door, then the bathroom. He returns to the desk and positions the P.A. microphone. He works up his courage, then flicks all the toggles to "on." A SQUEAL OF FEEDBACK echoes briefly . . .

INT./EXT. VARIOUS P.A. SPEAKERS — DAY (1955)

. . . and the Mozart is suddenly broadcast all over the prison.

After finding the record—*discovery*—he shoots a look at the bathroom (where the guard is)—*deliberation*—and smiles. Go for broke—*decision*. He lunges to his feet and broadcasts the music—the *doing* that follows. The decision is clearly rendered, and the dance of discovery, decision, and doing is beautifully—and *clearly*—choreographed.

2. The audience must understand why your character makes this decision. And you must show—or at least indicate—the difference it makes, the shift, however subtle, in your character's life and emotional flow.

3. *Do not go over five pages.* There's no art without limitation. A real artist welcomes limitations and then finds ways to transcend them.

4. Remember that you're writing a screenplay. Design a small but significant story told in more than one scene about a character who makes a significant decision. You may need a discovery or two to precipitate the decision—that's up to you—but your purpose is making us *see and understand* the decision and the difference it makes.

5. And remember—no skits. Dig deeper.

CHOOSING AN IDEA

As you begin to look for ideas for a significant decision a character might make, it's useful to remember that there are two main kinds of decisions in drama—*expedient* and *ethical*, as Sam Smiley points out:

Expedient decisions have to do with choice of means, and ethical decisions concern specific ends. Deciding something expediently, such as whether to use a knife or a pistol for a murder, has little relation to good and evil, or rightness and wrongness of conduct. Ethical decision or moral choice, such as deciding whether to murder or not to murder, reveals the quantity of evil in a person and the quality of good in him.[1]

You may want to create a story about a character making an ethical decision or an expedient decision or, if you can manage it in five pages, both, like the women in Aristophanes' great comedy *Lysistrata*.

"The key to the action," Smiley says, "is the ethical decision of the women to join the title character in attempting to end the war; the comedy in the play arises from their decision about how to force men to stop fighting."

This doesn't mean your character has to contemplate murder; taking candy from a baby—or not—is an ethical decision, too. And ethical decisions are the most revealing. As Smiley says, summarizing the thought of philosophers from Aristotle to Sartre, "A man is the summary of his ethical decisions." The same, of course, goes for women.

Look at your menu, at the decisions you've made that made a difference, and see if there's an idea there. Check out your own values and beliefs and think about the decisions they've helped you make—or regret. Consider the people you've known and the difference they've made to you; there might be terrific material there. And feel free to add to any of the columns at any time (one of my students, Amanda Farinos, keeps her menu on her computer screen and adds to it all the time).

If an idea doesn't materialize from your menu, step outside your own life and go sit in a busy mall, a bus stop, airport, and people watch. Make up stories for perfect strangers. What decisions have they made that brought them here now or made them who they are? Or create a surface or a deep action for them: *So and so is coming to decide . . . what?* And what difference does it make? If all else fails, come up with the most outrageous idea you can think of, like Andy Zare when he came up with *tongue*.

Less is usually more in screenwriting, except when you're coming up with ideas. Brainstorm like crazy. Creative composting, I call it. Go wild. Free associate. Noodle. Write it all down. And don't censor yourself. Be *playful* (the last word in screenplay *is* play). When you're done, choose the idea you love the most and save the rest for future screenplays (I keep a file for story ideas, character details, and bits of dialogue that I like). Just make sure you connect to your idea in some significant way. And keep it small and specific.

DEVELOPING CHARACTER

The decisions our characters make—like our own—are hotlines to who they are and what they value and believe.

"People seem not to see that their opinion of the world is also a confession of character," Emerson writes in his essay "Worship," and he said a mouthful, as we say in the South.

So zeroing in on these items on your Character Checklist is an ideal place to start developing your main character. What does she believe? What are her values? Worldview? Opinions? Once you know, you'll be closer to knowing the decisions she'll make.

It's a terrific exercise to write a monologue for your character. Let her tell you *in her own voice* what she values, believes. Let her rip—emote—about her beliefs. Make them specific. You'll find your character's voice—it's never too soon to do that—and you'll discover who she really is. The speech may or may not end up in your script. That doesn't matter. You're developing character now.

You may discover that you *do* want a piece of it in your script; after all, values and beliefs are a wonderful shortcut to character for your audience, illuminating your character's decisions and actions. Look at the way Crash Davis's beliefs in *Bull Durham* dictate what he does after Annie Savoy says she's choosing him or Ebby to "hook up with" this season:

> CRASH
> Why do *you* get to choose? Why don't I get to choose?

> ANNIE
> Actually none of us on this planet ever really chooses each other. It's all quantum physics and molecular attraction. There are laws we don't understand that bring us together and break us apart.

> EBBY
> Is somebody gonna go to bed with somebody or what?

> ANNIE
> You're a regular nuclear meltdown honey—slow down.

> Crash rises to leave, and heads for the door.

> CRASH
> After 12 years in the minor leagues, I don't tryout. Besides—I don't believe in quantum physics when it comes to matters of the heart . . . or loins.

> ANNIE
> (challenging him)
> What *do* you believe in?

Crash at the door.

> CRASH
> I believe in the soul, the cock, the pussy, the
> small of a woman's back, the hanging curve ball,
> high fiber, good scotch, long foreplay, show tunes,
> and that the novels of Thomas Pynchon are
> self-indulgent, overrated crap.
> (beat)
> I believe that Lee Harvey Oswald acted alone, I
> believe that there oughtta be a constitutional
> amendment outlawing astro-turf and the
> designated hitter, I believe in the "sweet spot,"
> voting every election, soft core pornography,
> chocolate chip cookies, opening your presents on
> Christmas morning rather than Christmas eve,
> and I believe in long, slow, deep, soft, wet kisses
> that last for 7 days.[2]

You'll notice a number of changes in this speech when Costner says it on screen, but, again, the gist is the same. And these beliefs motivate—and illuminate—his decisions and actions. He doesn't believe in quantum physics when it comes to matters of the heart. And he's an experienced catcher who doesn't try out. So he walks.

In *Sex, Lies & Videotape*, Graham tells Ann his beliefs about keys and responsibility:

> GRAHAM
> Well, see, I have this one key. And this one key is
> all the responsibility I have. Everything I own is
> in my car. If I get an apartment, that's two keys.
> If I get a job, maybe I have to open and close
> once in awhile, that's more keys. Or I buy some
> stuff and I'm worried about getting ripped off, so
> I get some locks. Pretty soon I've got a dozen
> keys, all indicative of responsibility.

> ANN
> You don't like responsibility?

> GRAHAM
> I don't like being responsible for other people.[3]

This wonderfully specific speech helps us understand why Graham can't commit—or connect—to others, especially women, why he makes such peculiar decisions. Incapable of having sexual relationships with women, he videotapes them talking about sex, then finds in these the gratification he needs. In the hands of a lesser screenwriter, this might be cheap and gratuitous, but there's real humanity here because Soderbergh lets Graham let us in on who he is as a person—his beliefs, values, *fears*. And his decisions and actions flow out of that.

DEVELOPING STORY AND STRUCTURE

Spinning story out of character is one excellent strategy for this screenplay (any screenplay). Take your character, his beliefs, values, worldview, and place him in a situation where he has to make a decision that will make a difference to him and his story. Crash Davis's decision to refuse Annie's offer alters the flow of the scene—and the story. It takes the rest of the screenplay for events to bring the two of them back together again.

Another strategy is to spin story out of event (though you begin to see that character and event are inseparable. As Henry James said, "What is character but the determination of incident? what is incident but the illustration of character?"). Several years ago, working with script consultant Linda Seger out in L.A., roaring down the Santa Monica freeway in her red sports car, I asked what she considered the greatest weakness in screenwriting.

"Development," she said, without hesitating. "Developing story. American screenwriters don't play the *consequences* of the events that they write. Events occur in a script but they don't make a real difference. Nothing flows out of them. Nothing *develops*."

That phrase "play the consequences" has helped me immensely as a writer and teacher. It goes right to the *generative* nature of event—*Moments of change generate more moments of change.* When Crash Davis discovers he's a prospect for Annie's sexual spring training, he decides to walk out. So does Anna in *tongue*, when Joe decides to tell her why he hasn't kissed her.

JOE

Anna, there's a reason why I can't kiss you . . .

(beat)

It's my tongue.

ANNA

(in disbelief)

Your tongue?

> JOE
> (rambling)
> I have this super sense of taste. It's awful. I'm
> afraid to kiss anyone. I'd know their whole past.

> ANNA
> What are you saying?

> JOE
> If I kiss you, I'd know too much about you.

But a beat or so later Anna calls his bluff:

> ANNA
> Okay, kiss me and tell me something about me.

> JOE
> I can't.

Anna gets up and starts to leave. Joe gets up a split
second later.

> JOE
> Wait.

> ANNA
> Joe Wagner, you're a liar and a coward, and I
> never want to see you or your tongue again.

Anna leaves. Joe starts to pursue her, then stops. He
watches her until she is out of sight.

Joe's decision to tell Anna the truth has consequences. So do most
decisions. Explore them fully and you'll find your story.

Once you've developed your story, jot the events you plan to include on
index cards or sticky notes and arrange and rearrange them until you come
up with a structure that works. Your character's decision might occur late in
your screenplay, the consequence of a discovery or a series of discoveries she
makes (just make sure we understand the difference it makes). Or the decision might occur early (make sure we understand it), and the consequences
unfold for the rest of the screenplay. That's up to you. It's your character,
story. As long as it works in five pages.

Again, you're designing a dance, a pattern of change, an energy system
that your audience can see beginning (*the setup*), developing (*playing the
consequences*), and coming to an end (*climax and resolution*).

Your setup has to be fast. Start your story, your pattern of change, on page one. You can do this with an *inciting event*—the precipitating move or *catalyst* of your story/energy system; dramatists call it the *disturbance*—or you can drop us smack in the middle of things (*in medias res*) the way Tarantino does in *Pulp Fiction*. We fade in—*bang!*—on an argument. The energy system is already flowing.

Don't burn valuable time or pages giving us information about your character's situation. If you want us to know that your character works at a bike shop, don't stop the story to give us that information. *Embed* it. Visually. Let your story flow *through* the bike shop—your character could make a discovery or decision there or process one she's already made—and we'll understand where she works.

Put your scenes in the service of story, not information.

Make sure, in the middle, that we see your story develop. And make sure we see your story come to an end.

When you're through designing your screenplay on cards, type up your Scene-by-Scene, take a break or a deep breath, and start writing.

DRAFTING THE SCREENPLAY

This time, raise the stakes on yourself as you draft your screenplay. Work harder for *significant details* in your Character I.D. and narrative description. "A detail is *concrete* if it appeals to one of the five senses," Janet Burroway writes; "it is *significant* if it also conveys an idea or a judgment or both." Look at the description of Shawshank Prison in *The Shawshank Redemption*:

> A malignant stone growth on the Maine landscape. The
> moon hangs low and baleful in a dead sky. The headlight
> of a PASSING TRAIN cuts through the night.

A little purple, perhaps, but "malignant stone growth" is a fresh, vivid description of a prison that conveys a judgment about how evil it is.

Make your dialogue sound more *natural* this time. When your scenes are written, take a look at your characters' speeches. Are they all the same length? This is deadly. Read your script aloud and you'll see how monotonous it is—downright mind-numbing—to hear this. No sweat. Redo it. Remember that we interrupt one another—and ourselves—when we talk. Long sentences rarely flow like fountains out of our mouths. We talk in fragments. Sometimes. Especially when our emotions are rising. Eisenstein created *montage*—editing—accelerating the pace of the cuts to reflect a scene's rising emotion, a technique Hitchcock perfected in *Psycho*. The same principle applies—within reason—to the way that we talk. When we're upset, our sentences, well, begin to—Break down. Just don't overdo it. Or. It. Could. Look. Pretentious.

Good dialogue is like music—it has rhythm and pace. Crescendos and rests. A pause. Or a silence. Or a *beat*—a snap pause or an indication that a character is changing the subject mid-speech. And, like music, good dialogue has its own notation. When a character is interrupted, it's a *cut line*. You indicate this with two hyphens—at the end of the sentence:

> BOB
>
> Look, Sue, I'm—

> SUE
> (bitter laugh)
>
> Sorry?

Or a character might interrupt herself:

> ANNIE
>
> I hook up with one guy a season—I mean it takes me a couple of weeks to pick the guy—kinda my own spring training...

Or her voice might trail off, as Annie's just did at the end of the speech. You indicate this with ellipses . . . three dots, no spaces between them in a screenplay.

This lesson in dialogue notation usually precipitates a snowstorm of ellipses in student screenplays . . . Use them sparingly . . . or you'll drive people . . . crazy.

Also don't overdo *punching words* (putting them in italics) for emphasis:

> CRASH
>
> Why do *you* get to choose?

Essentially, you're giving actors line readings, so go easy. Let the actors play, too. And note that capitalized words in dialogue indicate shouting. Edward Albee does this AD NAUSEAM! Do it occasionally—for dramatic effect—or you can simply say in a parenthetical (shouting). Any technique that you overuse calls attention to itself and pops the reader out of the vivid and continuous dream that every screenplay should be. Unless you're trying to make your dialogue sound stylized, work to make it sound natural. Nothing more, nothing less.

REWRITING THE SCREENPLAY

Again, get the best feedback you can and look for consensus. Does your pattern of change begin on page one? Does it develop? Is necessary information embedded in scenes? Is your character's moment of decision clearly rendered? Do we understand it? Can we *see* the difference it makes? Take careful notes when your screenplay's critiqued, then put the notes and your screenplay away for a couple of days if you can. You'll be amazed how much work your unconscious—I call mine "the elves"—will do for you while you're away.

When you return, you'll be ready to reshape your screenplay. Cut what is weak to make room for what isn't. Think of it as pruning a plant; after careful cutting, a plant is healthier, stronger. When you cut away what isn't important, you make room for what is.

NOTES

1. Sam Smiley, *Playwriting: The Structure of Action*, Prentice-Hall, Englewood Cliffs, New Jersey, 1971, p. 88.
2. Ron Shelton, *Bull Durham*, screenplay manuscript dated 5-1-87, pp. 23, 24.
3. Steven Soderberg, *Sex, Lies and Videotape*, screenplay manuscript dated February 21, 1988, p. 17.

THE BOXING MATCH

Since the day you thought about writing screenplays, you've no doubt been told that they must have conflict. As I've said, this is only half true—connection is also important. And this advice about conflict is not very helpful if you're trying to learn the craft of screenwriting. It gets you obsessing about the wrong thing. You begin to think that conflict is some secret ingredient in a screenwriter's potion—the dramatist's eye of newt—and you wonder where the heck you can find some to throw in your script. But you don't *find* conflict, you *create* it.

Like so many others, Linda Cowgill insists in *Writing Short Films*, "Action in drama and fiction depends upon conflict, which is the starting point of all drama."

With all due respect, this is backwards.

Conflict is not the starting point of drama, drama is the starting point of conflict.

Drama done well is complex, but the root of all drama is simple. Again, the word comes from the Greek *dran, to do*. To perform, execute, bring about, effect, cause, take action. We do because we want something badly. You'll hear different words for it—want, will, desire, intention—but it's all the same thing. Want, if you will, or will, if you want, is the heart of great drama from *Oedipus Rex* to *Pulp Fiction* to *Shakespeare in Love*.

Oedipus wants to end the plague in his country.

Marsellus Wallace wants to get his briefcase back.

Shakespeare wants to finish his play.

Colin, the director in *The Making of Killer Kite*, wants to finish his film and he goes to great (and illegal) lengths to do so. Earl wants Maybelline. Hannah wants connection. Buzz wants reconnection. Joe Wagner doesn't want any connection at all. Anna does. Whatever the story, desire motivates doing.

"An action is an activity designed to bring about an 'end,'" Colin Hardie says, explicating Aristotle's *Poetics*, "We have a desire or wish for a certain state of affairs. From this we argue back by a chain of means, until we arrive at something we see to be in our power here and now."[1]

We desire, deliberate, decide, do. And, where conflict's concerned, doing always runs into trouble. Will hits obstacle. That's the dramatic paradigm. Why is this so satisfying? Why have we gathered for centuries to see it played out over and over? Because it's half of *our* story. Unless we're fully realized *bodhisattvas*, we also want badly. Sometimes we don't get what we want. Sometimes we do, and, being human, we want something else. We strive, fail, suffer, strategize, and strive again. So we find it fascinating—and a whole lot more entertaining—to see others do the same thing. It's a major umbilical point between us and the characters we're watching up on the screen. They want. We want. A connection is created between us.

And *conflict* is *created* when will meets obstacle. Again, it's useful to remember the root of the word—*confligere*—to clash or strike together. There is no conflict *until* human will clashes with or strikes an obstacle. We want something badly, but life has other ideas. It thwarts us, comes out of left field, hurls obstacles in our path. Or we hurl them in our own path, like Earl's self-doubt in *Slow Dancin' Down the Aisles of the Quickcheck*. There are all kinds of obstacles—external and internal—and great drama, like *Hamlet*, like *life*, offers a rich mixture of both.

Say you're late for class. You rush to campus. You try to park. You've paid a whopping fee for a parking permit which is, you discover, little more than a hunting license. All the parking spaces are taken. First obstacle. Your will is thwarted. Conflict is created. You could park illegally, but you're not that kind of person. Or maybe you are, but you're broke and you already have a half-dozen parking tickets to pay before you can graduate. But you *won't* graduate if you're late for this class. . . .

Suddenly—*aha!*—you see a car pulling out and you race toward it only to realize a van is heading for the same space from the other direction. *Oh, no way!* you think, and you floor it. So does the van. But your car is faster, and you get there first. A little amazed at yourself (or a little ashamed, as I was one day), you turn off the engine, glance in the rear view mirror, and see the other driver pull up behind you with a look on her face that says, *I want to eat your intestines.* . . .

The conflict increases in energy, intensity—and interest—when another person comes on the scene. Why? There are two wills at war. Two agendas. One person wants. The other opposes. Dramatists call this a *boxing match*—one character wants what another character does not want to give—and the best dramatists use it over and over to create compelling conflict. In *Pulp Fiction*, according to my calculations, Tarantino (with his co-story-writer, Roger Roberts Avery) creates *thirty-eight* boxing matches. The screenplay *opens* in the middle of a boxing match between a young man and young woman. The opening line presents the first obstacle to the young woman's desire to rob liquor stores:

YOUNG MAN
No, forget it, it's too risky. I'm through doin' that shit.

But her will is strong; she won't take no for an answer. So the boxing match continues as she tries to persuade him to do it anyway, but he won't.

> YOUNG MAN
> ... It ain't the giggle it usta be. Too many
> foreigners own liquor stores. Vietnamese,
> Koreans, they can't fuckin' speak English. You
> tell 'em: "Empty out the register," and they don't
> know what it fuckin' means.

She wants/he opposes, and we understand why. Conflict is created. So is audience interest, because the outcome of the boxing match is unknown.

It's important to note that boxing matches are *not* arguments. An argument is "a discussion in which disagreement is expressed about some point," but a boxing match is a pattern of change. Change does not necessarily happen in arguments; in fact, as Harriet Lerner argues in her book, *Dance of Anger*, we often have the same argument over and over to *avoid* changing. Characters often argue in a boxing match, but change is also occurring. In *Pulp Fiction*, the young woman *discovers* that the young man has another idea—robbing the restaurant they're in—and she *decides* they should do it.

> YOUNG WOMAN
> I'm ready, let's go, right here, right now.[2]

And they do, though Tarantino decides to postpone showing the robbery until the end of the film—thirty-seven boxing matches later—when the robbery has the greatest dramatic and ironic impact.

Whatever the situation or character or will or obstacle, the point is the same: *Conflict isn't the root of drama, it's a by-product of drama.* Once you understand this, you can create all the conflict you want.

THE THIRD SCREENPLAY—THE BOXING MATCH

Write a five-page screenplay about a character (A) who wants something badly that a second character (B) does *not* want to give. And follow these guidelines:

1. Character A's want must be clear.
2. We have to understand *why* your character wants it. This gets at stake—what's lost if the character doesn't get what he wants.
3. We must understand why Character B does not want to give it. In *tongue*, for example, Anna wants Joe to kiss her. He won't. Thanks to Andy Zare's ingenious setup, we understand why.

4. Let Character A fail at least once, regroup, and try again. This is a screenplay, not just a scene, but even in the best scenes characters try to get what they want with energy and resourcefulness. Let your character try more than one strategy. Let us *see* the dance of deliberation, decision, and doing.

5. The outcome must be clear. Does Character A succeed or fail? There's no right or wrong answer; do what's best for your story, but make sure the outcome is clear.

6. Do not go over five pages.

7. But no skits. Dig deeper and find out what your boxing match is *really* about. One of my students, Ben Edwards, was writing a boxing match about a young soldier in Vietnam trying to get a comic book from another soldier who doesn't want to give it to him. Ben wasn't happy with his rough draft; he said it felt shallow, more like a skit. Then, right in the middle of class, he realized what it was really about. "It isn't about a comic book, it's about how scared this kid is and how he needs diversion, entertainment to keep his mind off his fear."

At Bread Loaf Writers Conference, Terry Tempest Williams told our workshop, "If your writing isn't interesting, you aren't dropping through to what your story is really about." She was talking about nonfiction, but her advice applies with equal force to screenwriting. When Ben realized that his boxing match between two soldiers over a comic book wasn't about the comic book, it was about fear, he found the universal dimension we all can connect to. This deeper level gave the screenplay greater resonance for Ben and—once he rewrote it—for his audience.

CHOOSING AN IDEA

There's a whopping temptation with boxing matches to grab those big TV subjects—rape, murder, drugs. We think, of course! He wants *her* but she doesn't want to give herself to him. Or: She's desperate for a fix but her best friend won't pony up the horse. Or: He wants to take his enemy's life but his enemy has other ideas—survival, for instance.

Ideas like this are known as The First Things That Swim By. They swim by first because TV has cut such deep grooves in our consciousness that our imagination shoots down these grooves faster than the dumped water down sluices in *Chinatown*, but as one writer said—I think it was Grace Paley—don't take the first thing that swims by. Keep brainstorming. Piddle around with your passions and perceptions until you come up with a fresher idea, something we haven't already seen in syndication. You may decide to come back to that first idea. That's fine. If you do, there may be a good reason.

When one of my students, David Cypkin, pitched an idea about a boy growing up among drunks and drug dealers at a Miami beachfront hotel, a story that climaxed with a knife fight between a cocaine dealer and a client who still owed him money, my kneejerk reaction was, "Nah, too TV." Then the student explained that he *grew up* at this hotel in Miami, hanging out in the bar with this cocaine dealer who seemed like a nice enough guy until he sliced up a sad, obese client. It was a journey from innocence to experience for him. This deep connection—though no guarantee that the material would make a good screenplay—gave David authentic insight and a shot at making the material more than warmed-over TV.

Having said that, let me quickly add that one of the better boxing matches I've seen recently is Pick's (Michael Piekutowski) gangster genre piece, *Up To Here*, that opens with two hit men, Marty and Rollins, burying a body they've just murdered. What lifts this story above familiar TV subject matter is the *specificity* of the boxing match that ensues when Marty wants the car keys so he can drive the "aged Cadillac" but Rollins refuses to give them to him. By the time the boxing match ends, *nobody's* driving because Rollins and the Cadillac have sunk in the swamp. The screenplay ends with Marty trudging down the road alone.

There simply aren't any rules. The ideas that produce the best boxing matches do, on some level, have resonance for the writer, but like Pick's screenplay, the connection is often *not* autobiographical. Rob Caragiulo's *momma . . . ?* is about Junior, "an eighteen-year-old, mildly inbred son," who wants his exhausted mother to massage his head. He finally gets what he wants, but as the boxing match heats up, his relationship with his mother subtly changes.

In another outstanding boxing match screenplay, *The White Face* by Eric Buscher, Bill Tift, "a lanky man about thirty, wearing messed-up jeans and a long-sleeve shirt untucked with a coffee stain on the pocket," wanders into a bar for a shot of Jack Daniels, unaware that it's a mime bar. Failing to get a real drink, Bill's finally thrown out by the mime bouncer, but he's ever so slightly changed in the process. Neither idea came from these writers' lives, but Rob and Eric did admit to mild obsessions with the mentally impaired and mimes, respectively, and they tapped that obsession to write their screenplays. You might want to add a column to your Menu—What I'm Obsessed About—and look to your own obsessions for good ideas.

Above all, notice that in each of the boxing matches mentioned above, Character A's want is small but significant and *highly* specific. A car key. A head massage. A shot of Jack Daniels. Students sometimes try to write a boxing match about a character wanting someone else's love or respect, but it's tricky to photograph that. That doesn't mean you won't try such a scene in the future; for my money, the greatest boxing match ever written is the final scene between Biff and Willy Loman in *Death of a Salesman*. Biff wants Willy to see—finally *see*—who both of them really are, but Willy refuses. In the hands of Arthur Miller, the scene is breathtaking, heartbreaking, as your scenes and screenplays may be someday, but for the purposes of this screenplay, keep your character's want concrete.

And the best dramatists often do the same thing. Think of Marsellus Wallace's briefcase or Desdemona's handkerchief in *Othello*. As the playwright Jeffrey Sweet says:

> The great plays are filled with brilliant negotiations over objects. You can often dramatize what is going on between your characters through the way they negotiate over an object. This technique is particularly useful because it allows the audience to figure a good deal out for themselves, obviating the writer from having to go through tedious explanations
> ... How much more effective it is to allow the viewer, by analyzing the negotiation ... to arrive at his or her own conclusions as to the nature of the relationship between the characters.[3]

An object lesson for us all. And one that Arthur Miller follows himself in the boxing match between Willy and Biff.

What Biff wants isn't an object, but the scene takes off when Biff whips out the piece of rubber tubing Willy keeps by the gas furnace in the basement because he's contemplating suicide. And the epiphany that Biff recounts in the scene, the discovery that precipitated this great boxing match scene, revolves around an object—the fountain pen that he stole before a job interview:

> I ran down eleven flights with a pen in my hand today. And suddenly I stopped, you hear me? And in the middle of that office building, do you hear this? I stopped in the middle of that building and I saw—the sky. I saw the things that I love in this world. The work and the food and the time to sit and smoke. And I looked at the pen and said to myself, what the hell am I grabbing this for? Why am I trying to become what I don't want to be? What am I doing in an office, making a contemptuous, begging fool of myself, when all I want is out there, waiting for me the minute I say I know who I am![4]

The pen, *per se*, is unimportant, but it precipitates Biff's realization about what he really wants, and that precipitates the boxing match final scene that changes his relationship with Willy forever. So, as you choose an idea for your boxing match, make Character A's want specific, concrete. Then let your boxing match reveal its significance, meaning.

DEVELOPING CHARACTER

Your character's want is twice blessed: It defines character *and* story. A character's actions flow from the character's want and the character's want flows from who the character *is*.

Suppose you meet someone for the first time. You've never met him before, but you *need* to know who he is. Not resume stuff, who he is *as a person*. Maybe you need to know badly—he's going to give you a ride or marry your daughter. If you only had time for one question, what would it be? It's funny, but that old chestnut that fathers used to ask their daughter's suitors, "What are your intentions?" isn't far off the mark. If you ask this person, "What do you want?" and he answers sincerely, you're well on your way to knowing this person. (And, as the scene with Biff shows, knowing what you want is also an avenue to self knowledge.)

In *Zen In the Art of Writing*, Ray Bradbury says:

> We know how fresh and original is each man [and each woman], even the slowest and dullest. If we come at him right, talk him along, and give him his head, and at last say, What do you want? (Or if the man is very old, What *did* you want?) every man will speak his dream. And when a man talks from his heart, in his moment of truth, he speaks poetry.[5]

Like Biff when he says what he really wants—"the work and the food and the time to sit and smoke."

Let your character speak her want, in her own voice. Write an "I Want" speech for her. Let her say flat out what she wants, like Wayne in *Wayne's World* when he sees the guitar of his dreams:

                    WAYNE
    It will be mine. Oh, yes, it *will* be mine.

Or Elliot in the opening moments of *Hannah and Her Sisters*, as he watches his sister-in-law:

                  ELLIOT (V.O.)
    God, she's beautiful. She's got the prettiest eyes.
    She looks so sexy in that sweater. I just want to
    be alone with her and hold her and kiss her and
    tell her how much I love her. Stop it, you idiot,
    she's your wife's sister!

Sometimes a character says what he wants and *doesn't* want, like Lloyd Dobler in *Say Anything* when Diane Court's father says, "Yeah, Lloyd, what are your plans for the future?"

> LLOYD
> Spend as much time as possible with Diane before
> she leaves.

>> MR. COURT
> Seriously, Lloyd.

> LLOYD
> I'm totally and completely serious, sir.

>> MR. COURT
> Oh, really?

> LLOYD
> You mean like career?
>> (Mr. Court nods)
> Um, I don't know. I've—
>> (clears throat)
> I thought about this quite a bit, sir. I would have
> to say, considering what's waiting out there for
> me, I don't want to sell anything, buy anything,
> or process anything as a career. I don't want to
> sell anything bought or processed or buy anything
> sold or processed or process anything sold, bought
> or processed, or repair anything sold, bought, or
> processed, you know, as a career. I don't want to
> do that. So my father's in the army. He wants me
> to join, but I can't work for that corporation. Um,
> so what I've been doing lately is kick boxing.

He continues to talk about career longevity, the uncertain future of the sport and himself in the sport, then he finishes his monologue by returning to the original want:

> LLOYD
> I don't know. I can't figure it all out tonight, sir.
> I'm just gonna hang out with your daughter.

Again, the speech you write may not end up in your screenplay, but you'll learn a great deal about your character as you write it. If you want to learn more, ask your character *why* she wants what she wants—or doesn't want what she wants—and let her answer (you can develop Character B by asking *him* why he won't give it). Ask Character A what's at stake? What will she lose if she doesn't get what she wants?

We can see stake clearly in "The Bonnie Situation" in *Pulp Fiction*. Jimmie's friend, Jules, has just arrived with a backseat full of brains, but his marriage is at stake if his wife, Bonnie, finds out.

> JIMMIE
> —I ain't through! Now don't you understand that if Bonnie comes home and finds a dead body in her house, I'm gonna get divorced. No marriage counselor, no trial separation—fuckin' divorced. And I don't wanna get fuckin' divorced. The last time me an' Bonnie talked about this shit was gonna be the last time me an' Bonnie talked about this shit. Now I wanna help ya out, Julie, I really do. But I ain't' gonna lose my wife doin' it.

Tarantino is following time-honored dramatic advice—get your character up a tree and throw rocks at him. Jimmie is torn. He wants two things—to stay married and to help his friend, Jules. This creates a *dilemma*.

And we connect because it feels true. We're all torn. We want cheesecake but we want to lose weight. We want to take that job out of town but we don't want to leave our significant other. Our lives are one damn difficult choice after another. And, as Jimmie discovers, deciding is hard. But he makes a decision born of *both* wants. He'll let Jules and Vincent clean up the mess, but they only have ninety minutes before Bonnie comes home. It's one of the oldest dramatic tricks in the book—the time bomb—a sure-fired source of suspense. Will Jules and Vincent get the car cleaned in time? It wouldn't matter to us if we hadn't heard Jimmie's passionate speech, but we did, so it does. What's at stake has clearly been set. We know what Jimmie wants and how badly he wants it because Tarantino has him tell us flat out, hitting it right on the nose in the old "I want" speech.

Like most screenwriters, you may feel reluctant to do this. You've probably heard many times—rightly so—that good screenwriting dialogue is not "on the nose"—but sometimes "on the nose" is where you need to be. My students are always amazed how frequently "I want" speeches appear in good films and how well they work. It may not work for your screenplay, but the option is there if you want to use it.

You might prefer writing a scene that *shows* what Character A wants, like the scene in *Slow Dancin'* that shows how badly Earl wants Maybelline (he's stolen a Polaroid picture of her and placed it on his bathroom mirror; funnier still, he keeps naming her Employee of the Week so he can have a photo to steal):

INT. BATHROOM — SAME

Earl stands in front of the mirror in his brown slacks and a tank top T-shirt, his middle-age pudge hanging slightly over his belt. He pulls the wrapper off a new girdle.

> EARL
> (unsure)
> Maybelline, my heart is a song.

He sucks in his gut, and tightens a girdle around his waist, with all his might, fastening it down. He looks at the picture, and finishes the line, but has trouble due to the tightness of the girdle.

> EARL
> (groaning)
> And you are its melody.

He leans toward the mirror, knocking a can of Ajax off the sink. He starts to pick it up, but the girdle keeps him from bending. He gives up, takes the Polaroid off the mirror and puts it in his pocket.

When we see a character want something this badly, we want him to get it, and that connects us to him and his story.

DEVELOPING STORY AND STRUCTURE

As far as story's concerned, what a character wants is a screenwriter's jackpot. It's the driving force that creates your story, energy system, emotional flow, and pattern of change. Look at *Pulp Fiction*:

Marsellus Wallace wants his briefcase. Vincent and Jules want to get it back for him. Bullets barely miss them. Suddenly, Jules wants to retire.

Marsellus wants Vincent to take Mia out on a date. Vincent doesn't want to, given what happened to Tony Rocky Horror, but he wants to do his duty to Marsellus.

Marsellus wants Butch to throw the fight. Butch wants to double-cross him, and he does, but he loses his precious gold watch in the process. He wants it back. Marsellus wants revenge. They collide—literally— on the street. Butch wants to get away. Marsellus wants to kill him. They stumble into a pawn shop, into the owner's wants. They want to get out. Butch does; Marsellus doesn't. Butch wants to save him.

And so the stories spin out. Want after want. Agenda after agenda. *Crossed* agendas. Wanting breeding new wanting.

Develop your story by brainstorming and playing the consequences of your character's want. What does she *do* to get it from Character B? What strategies does she try? What does Character B do to stop her? What does Character A do when her strategies fail? Or do they? Does she get what she wants? Or not? And what difference does it make to her in the end?

Play the possibilities. Every screenplay has its own rich variations. A character might not get what he wants but he gets what he needs. Look at *Good Will Hunting* and *As Good As It Gets*. Or *African Queen* or *Casablanca* or so many great films, for that matter. Short, ones, too. In *tongue* Joe wants to remain isolated, but life throws him Anna, a young woman with a will of her own, and she wants what Joe does not want to give—connection. A kiss.

"The protagonist has a need or goal, *an object of desire*, and knows it," Robert McKee writes in *Story*. "However, the most memorable, fascinating characters tend to have not only a conscious but an unconscious desire. . . . What he believes he wants is the antithesis of what he actually but unwittingly wants."

Which brings us back to character because at the highest level, story *is* character, to paraphrase F. Scott Fitzgerald.

Once you've developed your story, clearly define its surface action/pattern of change/throughline/spine:

Character A is trying to get (object of desire).

Nail it in one simple dynamic sentence and write it down on a three-by-five card. Then define your story's deep action/character arc, how Character A's inner landscape is changed by the external events:

Character A is (describe the internal change).

Describe the internal change with an -ing verb. This keeps it dynamic. Is your character coming to realize something important? Learning something? Reappraising? Overcoming her fears? Nail the pattern of internal change and write it on a three-by-five card, too.

Then brainstorm and decide what moments of change you will need to show to make the surface and deep action *happen*. These are the pearls in the oysters—the scenes—that you'll write (remember, more than one pearl may occur in one scene). Write each scene on a three-by-five card, arranging them until you find the order you want. Dump any scene that doesn't serve your surface or deep action or illuminate it in some way, like the dreams illuminating Joe's fear in *tongue*. Make sure you establish Character A's want nice and early, so your story/energy system/pattern of change *begins* on page one (as you've seen in *Pulp Fiction*, it can begin on *line one*). And make sure it *ends*. Does Character A fail or succeed? Make sure the precise moment when the outcome is known—your screenplay's climax—happens *on screen*. And make sure we understand the significance of this success or failure to Character A.

When you've done all this—and it is a great deal—outline your screenplay in a Scene-by-Scene. Read the outline over and over, letting the short film play in your head, checking your character's emotional flow.

"A strong emotional line is what drives a film or play and engages an audience," Jan Sardi says in the introduction to his screenplay for *Shine*.

We're never more emotional than when we want something badly and our wanting meets obstacles.

DRAFTING THE SCREENPLAY

Put your surface and deep action three-by-five cards where you can see them so you don't lose sight of your screenplay's spine and your character's arc as you start to write. If your story starts to drift as you draft, or you otherwise get lost in the funhouse, consult these cards to keep your story on track.

Craft your scenes with great care. They're patterns of change in themselves, with a beginning, middle, and end, though you may not want to show all of that. A character's arrival or departure, for example, might not be interesting or contribute to your dramatic purpose. If not, use the magic of the story leap and hit the scene later or get out earlier.

But sometimes you do need to show the beginning, middle, and end, as Robert Benton does in the restaurant boxing match scene in *Kramer vs. Kramer* when Ted and Joanna Kramer meet for the first time since Joanna walked out eighteen months ago. It's a reconnection/disconnection scene between these two characters, so Ted's arrival and departure at Joanna's table are both important.

Cue up this scene on video (it's close to the midpoint) and screen it. It's one of the best examples of a well-written scene, exquisitely crafted with *dialogue beats* (not to be confused with *action beats*—events that move the story forward).

"A beat of dialogue is similar to a paragraph of prose or a verse of poetry," Sam Smiley says.

In the previous chapter I mentioned that the word "beat" in a character's speech indicates a snap pause or a change in subject. You can think of a dialogue beat as a paragraph or short unit of speech about one particular subject.

When you screen the scene in *Kramer vs. Kramer*, outline the beats. Give them brief titles based on each beat's subject. The first beat, for example, might be titled "Hi/hi/chitchat." What are the other beats in the scene?

Why and how do the subjects change or flow to the next beat?

Notice that each *beat* has a beginning, middle, and end. To me, this is one of the most marvelous things about a well-crafted screenplay: The smallest building block—the dialogue beat—is a microcosm for the scene and for the whole screenplay. Each is an energy system that begins, develops, and ends. Somewhere in each beat there's some tiny impulse or change that throws the scene into the next beat (notice the frequent use of questions to trigger new beats). And so the scene and screenplay move forward.

Notice, too, that the beats begin to break down as the scene becomes more emotional. Again, it's Eisenstein's montage applied to dialogue—

accelerating the pace of the cuts (in this case, cut lines) to reflect the scene's rising emotion.

I like to think of beats as Legos because they're the smallest building block of drama (I'm not counting words) and they can be moved around, rearranged in a scene or screenplay for the greatest dramatic effect (Sundance tells Butch he can't swim just before the jump off the cliff into the river). And for the most compelling and credible emotional flow.

Take a close look at this excerpt from Robert Benton's screenplay after Ted discovers that Joanna's been watching Billy from the coffee shop across the street from his school:

> TED
> You sat in that coffee shop across from school—

> JOANNA
> (completing his sentence)
> Watching my son... Ted, I've been living in New York for the past two months.

> TED
> (amazed)
> You've been living here, in the city?

> JOANNA
> (a deep breath)
> Ted... The reason I wanted to see you... I want Billy back.

> TED
> You want *what?!*

> JOANNA
> (firm)
> I want my son. I'm through sitting in coffee shops looking at him from across the street. I want my son.

> TED
> Are you out of your mind?! You're the one that walked out on him, remember?

> JOANNA
> (trying to explain)
> Ted listen to me... You and I, we had a really crappy marriage—

JOANNA (CONT'D)
(hastily)
Look, don't get defensive, okay? It was probably
as much my fault as it was yours . . . Anyway
when I left I was really screwed up—

TED
Joanna, I don't give a—

JOANNA
(she *will* be heard)
Ted, all my life I'd either been somebody's
daughter or somebody's wife, or somebody else's
mother. Then, all of a sudden, I was a thirty-year-
old, highly neurotic woman who had just walked
out on her husband and child. I went to California
because that was about as far away as I could
get. Only . . . I guess it wasn't far enough. So I
started going to a shrink.
(leaning forward, very sincere)
Ted, I've had time to think. I've been through
some changes. I've learned a lot about myself.

Now compare the order of beats to the beats that you outlined when you screened the scene. The lines changed a little, of course—they always do—but sometime, during pre-production or production, the order of the beats was *reversed*. Why? Because emotionally, it just didn't work.

When Joanna tells Ted she wants Billy back, she's dropping a bomb. There's no way in *hell* Ted's going to sit there and listen to her long explanation about going to California and finding herself (a line I never thought anyone could make work, but Meryl Streep does). By reversing the beats—the long explanation *then* the bomb about Billy—the emotional flow is believable. Things are relatively calm when Joanna tells Ted about California—we believe he would listen—but once she says she wants Billy back, he cares about only one thing—keeping her from taking his son. A boxing match.

This switching of beats also makes the scene more dramatic. Now there's a *build* to Joanna's revelation that she wants Billy back (in the screenplay it feels unprepared for, unmotivated, out of the blue). Talk about a moment of change. I mean *kablooey!* The scene explodes, words flying like shrapnel—overlapping, interrupting—the beats breaking down as all hell breaks loose and Ted tells Joanna to go fuck herself. But notice, on screen, he doesn't tell her with words. Benton made a wonderful choice to show it, not tell it, as Ted smashes his glass of white wine—which was a sign of connection—against the brick wall. As Lani Sciandra learned in *Cool Breeze*, the nonverbal reaction is often much stronger.

And so, as you're designing your scenes, noodle your beats. Outline them in the order you think they will happen. But remember they're Legos—moveable pieces—and feel free to move them around until the scene works. Outlining the beats before you draft a scene helps you design scenes that don't spin their wheels—characters talking about the same subject over and over. You may decide to let the wheels spin for dramatic effect. Fine. Just make sure you're not having more fun than your audience. And keep in mind that most scenes work best when the beats change and the story moves forward.

REWRITING THE SCREENPLAY

Beats are also a wonderful tool for revision. A scene you wrote isn't working. Outline the beats. You might well discover what's wrong. You might have a beat that doesn't work in the scene, but it's important to the overall story. Try moving it to another scene in your screenplay. I just critiqued a student screenplay where two young women, total strangers, meet on a train. Right off the bat, one starts telling the other her problems. It felt too early for the character. I suggested moving the beat a bit later, and it worked much better. Of course, if the screenwriter had wanted to create a character who goes around accosting strangers with her personal problems, the beat would have been fine where it was.

This is why feedback from others is so very important. They can tell you if your character's emotional flow rings true in your scenes and story. Find out, too, from others if Character A's want is clear. Do they understand why she wants it? Does Character B provide obstacles to this want? Do you play the consequences of Character A discovering these obstacles and/or deciding to do something different? How could Character A's strategies for getting what she wants be improved? Is the outcome of your boxing match clear? Do we grasp its significance? Does the character's inner change get across?

Be open and listen to the answers they give you. Take notes. And as Joanna says to Ted, "Don't get defensive."

Once you've harvested their responses, set your screenplay aside—if you can—before you rewrite. This allows everyone else's opinions to settle until you know in your gut what you need to do. Your considered opinion is usually best.

NOTES

1. Humphry House, *Aristotle's Poetics*, Madeline House, London, 1956, p. 74. (I'm indebted to Janet Burroway for giving me a copy of House's wonderful book).
2. Quentin Tarantino, *Pulp Fiction*, screenplay manuscript, last draft, May 1993, pp. 1–6.
3. Jeffrey Sweet, "An Object Lesson for Playwrights," *The Writer*, December 1989, p. 19.

4. Arthur Miller, *Death of a Salesman*, Viking Press, New York, 1949, p. 132.
5. Ray Bradbury, *Zen in the Art of Writing: Releasing the Creative Genius Within You*, Bantam Books, New York, 1990, p. 36.
6. Tarantino, p. 123.
7. Robert Benton, *Kramer Versus Kramer*, screenplay manuscript, revised third draft, July 14, 1978, pp. 75, 76.

THE IMPROBABLE CONNECTION

There's no question that conflict is important. And we connect because we also strive, hit obstacles, suffer.

"Life is suffering," Buddha said.

"And such small *portions*," Woody Allen says in *Annie Hall*.

But, as I've said, there is more.

Connection is the other half of the story—of our lives and the stories we tell. Good screenwriters understand this intuitively even though, as I've said, connection is essentially overlooked in screenwriting books.

"Nothing moves forward in a story except through conflict," Chris Keane writes in *How to Write a Selling Screenplay*, putting all our screenwriting eggs in one basket.

But, soft! Doesn't *Romeo and Juliet* take a quantum leap forward when Romeo sees Juliet for the first time? He and the story have slowed to a crawl ("What sadness lengthens Romeo's hours?"), but the moment he sees her, the story takes off at emotional warp speed. ("Did my heart love till now? forswear it, sight!/For I ne'er saw true beauty till this night.") Yes, their star-crossed love creates all kinds of conflict that also moves the story along, but so does this initial—and the ongoing, deepening—connection between the two lovers. Again, it's a dance. Conflict and connection. The best stories have both.

Look at the following scene in Ron Nyswaner's screenplay for *Philadelphia* (and then screen the same scene in Jonathan Demme's outstanding film). Andrew Beckett has been fired from his law firm because he has AIDS. No lawyer will take his case, including Joe Miller. Beckett's will is up against an insurmountable obstacle—prejudice—and though this creates conflict, the story is stalled. Beckett is stuck. He decides to handle his case himself and is doing legal research when Joe Miller sees him again:

A CHAIR SQUEAKS and Joe LOOKS UP TO SEE:

Andrew taking a seat across the room (*the blotches have been reduced by chemo, but he's struggling with a cold*). Andrew removes notepads and pens from his briefcase. He takes out a package of tissues, blowing his nose.

> JOE
> (under his breath)
Shit . . .

Joe slides to the far end of his table, stacking seven or eight HUGE REFERENCE BOOKS in front of him.

JOE'S POV, PEERING THROUGH THE REFERENCE BOOKS:

Andrew opens a book, taking notes. Rubs his eyes. Writes something. Sneezes.

A LIBRARIAN delivers a book to Andrew.

> LIBRARIAN
This is the supplement. You're right, there is a section on . . .
> (lowers her voice)
. . . HIV related discrimination.

> ANDREW
Thank you.

Andrew takes the book from her—but she remains.

> LIBRARIAN
We have a private research room available.

> ANDREW
I'm fine, thanks.

Andrew BLOWS HIS NOSE. Now the other PATRONS are watching.

> LIBRARIAN
Wouldn't you be more comfortable in a research room?

> ANDREW
> (pleasantly)
No. But would it make you more comfortable?

                        LIBRARIAN
        Whatever, sir.

The LIBRARIAN turns away, shrugging to a PATRON, indicating she's done all she can do.[1]

In previous scenes, Joe himself has discriminated against Andrew because he's gay and has AIDS. Earlier, when Andrew came to Joe's office and asked if he'd take the case, Joe refused . . . for personal reasons. And he didn't buy that Andrew had a case.

But now, in the library, hiding behind a wall of reference books he's built between himself and Andrew, Joe *witnesses* discrimination in action and its consequence—disconnection—as the librarian tries to segregate Andrew in a research room and other library patrons quickly exit. Witnessing this—and the suffering it causes—stirs a sense of injustice in Joe—and compassion.

"Compassion is the only energy that can help us connect with another person," Thich Nhat Hanh tells us in *The Heart of Buddha's Teachings*.

It is this compassion—mixed with a sense of injustice and, I would wager, a little guilt—that moves Joe to reestablish contact with Andrew:

Joe approaches, nonchalantly, as if he just *happens* to be sauntering by. Suddenly he "notices" Andrew.

                         JOE
        Oh, Beckett. How's it goin'?

                       ANDREW
        Fine.

When you screen Demme's film, you'll notice a subtle but important change: Demme has Joe *interrupt* the "Whatever, sir" boxing match beat between Andrew and the librarian. The librarian—a man in the film—looks at Joe, realizes he's outnumbered, and backs down. "Whatever, sir," he tells Andrew and goes. So does a nearby patron. By having Joe come to Andrew's *defense*, Demme creates a richer, more significant moment of connection between these two men.

Connecting is a process, a pattern of change made up of moments of change—*connection beats*. A series of connection beats create and deepen the connection that is occurring in this scene:

Joe *discovers* Andrew is being mistreated.

He *decides* to come to his rescue.

He *discovers* that no lawyer will represent Andrew, so Andrew is planning to represent himself.

Then, in a lovely, off-the-point beat, Joe *discovers* Andrew's own humanity when he asks about Joe's new baby. Joe, slightly changed, walks away.

Then he *decides* to come back. He asks Andrew how the law firm found out he had AIDS. Andrew tells him. This *discovery* raises other legal questions and more *discoveries* that play out in a subtle boxing match, Andrew trying to return to his work but Joe keeping him from it, interrupting, wanting answers.

Because of these specific connection beats, Joe is slowly drawn into the case, his connection with Andrew deepening with his understanding of the case law on discrimination and its consequences, stated in bald, unsettling terms in the scene when Andrew reads from a relevant legal precedent:

```
                    ANDREW
        "But because the prejudice surrounding AIDS
        exacts a social death which precedes the actual,
        physical one . . . "

    Joe and Andrew glance at each other, clear their
    throats . . .
```

In the film, the camera cranes up (a lovely shot called for by the screenwriter) and we look down on Andrew and Joe as they continue to work on the case together, passing notes and books back and forth, their hands almost touching. They have connected as lawyer and client and, more important, as human beings. In the following scene—in the screenplay and film—Joe delivers a summons to Charles Wheeler, the man who fired Andrew. And the story is moving forward again.

It is *connection* that moves it—an *improbable connection* between two men who have been legal rivals, who find each other repulsive (Andrew thinks Joe is an ambulance chaser; Joe thinks Andrew is an infectious pervert). This improbable connection occurs in only four pages—less than seven minutes on screen—but creates breathtaking change in both characters' lives. And it jumpstarts the stalled story.

There are moments of change in our lives and stories that are simply not comprehended by conflict.

Moments of change that *create ties between us*, as Stephen Jay Gould so beautifully said. As a screenwriter you can't afford to overlook this crucial fact of narrative life. If you want to write screenplays that connect to others, you need to learn to create and craft a connection.

THE FOURTH SCREENPLAY—THE IMPROBABLE CONNECTION

Write a seven-page screenplay about two characters who initially feel no connection whatsoever—a connection between them is highly *improbable*—but by the end of the screenplay they have come to feel an authentic connection. And follow these guidelines:

1. Establish the improbability of your characters ever connecting.

In *Philadelphia*, the improbability of a connection between Andrew and Joe is carefully set up when Joe refuses to represent Andrew. And it's underlined again in a scene between Joe and his wife—just before the law library scene—when Joe admits that he's prejudiced. He doesn't want to work with a homosexual, much less one with AIDS.

                    JOE
         Would you take a client if you were constantly
         thinking: 'I hope this guy doesn't touch me. I
         don't even want him to *breathe* on me?'

This scene clearly establishes the *revulsion* Joe feels toward Andrew Beckett. Yet, in the following law library scene, in four short pages, Nyswaner creates a credible connection between these two men, a short but significant journey for Joe from prejudice to understanding.

2. Create your pattern of change—connecting—with a series of connection beats—discoveries and decisions your characters make that bring them closer together. Connecting is a path; what are the stepping stones— moments of change—in your screenplay?

3. Make sure the connection beats are clearly rendered so we *see* each moment of change *happen* on paper/screen.

4. The process of connecting between your two characters must be believable. You're creating emotional realism, a pattern of human change and emotional flow that we *buy*.

5. If you need a third character to help effect the connection, as Nyswaner does in *Philadelphia*, you may create one, but remember that the focus of this screenplay is the improbable connection between your two *main* characters.

6. This is a screenplay, not a scene, so feel free to open your story up and move it and your characters through various times and locations.

7. Give us a sense of an ending, how the characters are changed by this unexpected connection.

8. Do not go over seven pages.

9. No skits. Connection is one of the deepest, most profound patterns of human change. It's more than *"You* like Chinese food? *I* like Chinese food!" It may start that way, but you need to dig deeper for a pattern of change that makes a difference to your characters. Your screenplay may be a comedy like *tongue* or *Slow Dancin' Down the Aisles of the Quickcheck*, but the connection must be deeply felt by the characters and the audience alike.

10. Avoid sap. Purple (overly emotional) writing. Sentimentality. Sentiment—authentic feeling and emotion—is important, essential, just don't take it so far over the top that we want to reach for our barf bags.

CHOOSING AN IDEA

As *Philadelphia* so clearly shows, connection is much broader than love or romance. Love isn't off-limits; you just have to work harder to make it fresh, as Thomas Jackson does in *Slow Dancin'*. But be aware, as you choose your idea, that there are many other kinds of human connection.

Keep in mind, too, that the subject doesn't have to be grim city. Compassion is broader and deeper than feeling sorry for somebody's plight in the world. The word comes from the Late Latin *compassion*, past participle of *compassus*, "to sympathize with." This sympathy might manifest itself in laughter, hilarity, joy. Whatever the nature of the connection you write, you're looking for an improbable but plausible pattern of change—connecting—that leads to your characters' shared understanding, humanity, communion, the two of them *seeing* each other in an authentic way.

When human connection occurs, your characters feelings drop into a deeper realm. Look at the dialogue from the improbable connection scene in Disney's animated film, *Beauty and the Beast*. Before this scene, Belle ran away, the Beast went to find her and saved her life by fighting off wolves, though he nearly died doing it. As this scene begins, Belle is wringing out a cloth to wash the Beast's wounds:

                    BELLE
     Here now.
                (he starts to lick his wound)
     Don't do that. Just hold still—

She touches his wound, and he roars.

                    BEAST
     That hurts!

                    BELLE
     If you'd hold still, it wouldn't hurt as much.

> BEAST
>
> If you hadn't've run away, this wouldn't have happened.

> BELLE
>
> If you hadn't frightened me, I wouldn't have run away.

The Beast starts to say something, then stops as he thinks about this.

> BEAST
>
> Well, you shouldn't have been in the west wing!

> BELLE
>
> Well, you should learn to control your temper!

He's taken aback, but looks thoughtful.

> BELLE
>
> Now hold still. This might sting a little.
>   (he growls)
> By the way, thank you for saving my life.

He looks at her, moved.

> BEAST
>   (gently)
> You're welcome.

The camera pulls back to reveal a tender tableau—the Beast looking at her as she touches his arm.[2]

The scene ends with a physical and an emotional connection between them.

DEVELOPING CHARACTER

Again, it's tempting to leap for that first thing that swims by: A racist and a black! An angry teen and an elderly person! A prostitute and a rabbi! Okay, a former student, Aloura Charles, wrote an improbable connection that worked beautifully between a rabbi and a prostitute who meet—and connect—on a subway. But first she had to transcend these character *types* to create specific flesh-and-blood characters who were more than cliches. Cliched characters are the kiss of death in a screenplay. We roll our eyes, thinking what Chris Keane has stated so bluntly but wisely, "hackneyed" characters are "cheap, lazy, and plagiaristic." You can develop unique characters by going *against* type and cliche. Try gender bending. You might be surprised what you come up with.

Look at your menu for springboard characters. If nothing strikes you, go people watch at your local mall, supermarket, skating rink, streetcorner, used-car lot, gas station. This is a wonderful way to get ideas for characters and situations for an improbable connection.

Dimensionalize your characters by asking *why* the connection between them is improbable. What values, beliefs, or opinions does each character have that make the connection highly unlikely? Why do they have these beliefs and opinions? They may be based on experience or, like Joe Miller, pure-d prejudice. Explore this backstory in a brief character bio for each character; you'll be amazed what bubbles up as you start to write their backstory down. Then let your characters tell you what they feel and why in their own voice. This monologue and backstory may not get into your screenplay, but it's important to know it.

Then ask yourself what is it about your characters that allows them to overcome these beliefs and opinions? However subtle, the potential for change must be present in your character, or we won't buy the connection. In *Philadelphia*, though the connection between Joe and Andrew is improbable, we believe it in part because we've seen Joe's humanity and capacity for connection in earlier scenes with his wife and baby. So you're developing two different sides of your characters: Who they are when your screenplay begins and who they are when your screenplay ends. But the seeds of change must be there in them from the beginning.

DEVELOPING STORY AND STRUCTURE

A good way to develop your story is to ask yourself what has to happen to bring about this unlikely connection? What discoveries will force your characters to reappraise one another? To see each other in a new light? To realize they're not so damn different? To begin to feel a sense of communion? What decisions do your characters make—and what actions do they take—that deepen the connection between them? As you sift through the possible answers to these questions—again, play the possibilities—you'll find the building blocks—the connection beats—of your story.

Once you know these, put them on cards. Line them up. Rearrange them. The stand-off between Andrew and the librarian is more interesting and intense in the film because Demme rearranged the beats. Joe's decision to come to Andrew's defense occurs in the middle of the boxing match. And Joe becomes a factor in the librarian's decision to back down. This small shift in the order of events makes the emotional flow more powerful and profound, presaging but not predicting the connection that follows.

Once you know your story, create a shapely structure for your screenplay. Define your screenplay's beginning, middle, and end. Does your story have an inciting incident—a moment of change that unleashes your screenplay's energy system and emotional flow? In the law library scene in *Philadelphia*, that incident is Joe's discovery that Andrew is there in the same reading room. He reacts, hiding behind a wall of reference books. But he keeps watching, and what he sees draws him out.

What are your screenplay's *turning points*—the moments of change that turn your story in a new direction? The scene from *Philadelphia* has two major turning points, giving it a shapely three-part structure. After witnessing the discrimination against Andrew and his suffering, Joe decides to come to his defense. The first turning point. This decision throws the scene out of setup into the second part as the story develops. Andrew and Joe are together, but their relationship is still tentative, distanced. They close the distance a little with the discoveries made in the next two beats—Andrew is representing himself; he cares enough about Joe's life to ask about his new baby—but Joe still decides to leave Andrew and his case behind. Then he changes his mind. He decides to come back. The second turning point. This throws the scene into the third section as Joe and Andrew discuss the relevant case law. As they do, their connection deepens with Joe's understanding, a profound change that leads to the scene's climax—Joe's decision to take Andrew's case. It's an offscreen decision, but one that's clearly implied by the end of the scene.

The structure of this pattern of change is carefully crafted. It's shapely, moving the story effortlessly from one moment of change to another until the characters have arrived at an authentic connection. That's what you're working for in your screenplay—a shapely seven-page pattern of change—connecting—that we can see beginning, developing, and coming to an end.

Design your structure. Draw it. And then, as you draft, make your scenes so delicious we don't notice your structure.

DRAFTING THE SCREENPLAY

By now you know your own process so well, I need only add that you'll need to give yourself plenty of time to draft this screenplay. As my students discover every semester, creating connection is much harder than creating conflict. It's more subtle. Internal. You're rendering internal change, yet you have to find ways to show it on paper and screen. This is *always* tricky. Your connection beats need to be clear, but you don't want to bludgeon us with them.

It's usually too on-the-nose to let your characters *say* that they feel more connected (though there are always exceptions); let your characters' feelings flow underneath what is said, i.e., push it into the subtext. Joe and Andrew never talk about connecting, but they're connecting as they talk because of the discoveries and decisions they're making. A crucial distinction.

Ideally, you'll find a way to show the moments of change/connection beats through your character's behavior and action. And you need to describe this moment of change as it happens. My students almost always resist this. "How do I describe a decision? Or realization?" They're afraid if they write "he decides" it will be telling, not showing.

So I ask them, "Can you *see* a person realizing something? Can you photograph that?"

The answer, of course, is yes. So they—and you—have to find fresh ways of describing these internal changes so we can see them. Avoid hackneyed expressions like "her eyes widen" or "he stands there like a deer stunned in headlights." If you need inspiration, as always, read good screenplays. Lots of them. See how other screenwriters render a realization.

In E. Max Frye's screenplay for Demme's film, *Something Wild*, he describes a secondary character's realization this way:

> Donna looks perplexed, then breaks into smiles when she realizes she's been the victim of a joke (or was it?).[3]

In *Life is Beautiful*, when the father, Guido, translates the Nazi's instructions to convince his young son, Joshua, that life in the camp is just a game, screenwriters Vincenzo Cerami and Roberto Benigni spell out Joshua's realization that his father is right:

> Joshua's face has a completely new expression on it. He is absolutely convinced that all this is one big game.[4]

If we can see it, you can say it, just be sure you say it so we can see it.

REWRITING THE SCREENPLAY

You'll want to work closely with others on the rewrite of this screenplay. You *need* others to know if the connection really *happens* on paper. Do we see your characters, through a series of connection beats, gradually feel an authentic connection? Are the connection beats clear? Are any missing? Is your structure sound? Do you have a clear inciting incident, a turning point that throws your screenplay out of setup into development and a second turning point that throws the story toward the climax? Is this connection improbable in the beginning of your screenplay but plausible by the end? Remember, you're honoring your characters' emotional flow, and the best way to know if it works is to see if others believe it.

Listen closely, take notes, then put them away with your screenplay. Let the elves work on the script for a while. Then, when you come back to it a few days later, you'll have a clearer sense of what you need to do.

And do it. Reshape your screenplay if necessary. You may have discovered that you need to rearrange your moments of change. If so, outline your connection beats again and redesign your screenplay's structure. Cut and add what you must to make sure the screenplay is working, but make sure that the final draft remains seven pages.

And don't despair if getting it right takes a number of rewrites. Crafting a credible, compelling connection *is* harder than crafting a good boxing match, but both, as you'll see in the next chapter, are essential to writing good screenplays.

NOTES

1. Ron Nyswaner, *Philadelphia*, screenplay manuscript, revised draft, October 15, 1992, p. 47, 48.
2. Transcribed from the screen, *Beauty and the Beast*, Walt Disney Productions, 1991.
3. E. Max Frye, *Something Wild*, screenplay manuscript, January 26, 1986, p. 46.
4. Vincenzo Cerami and Roberto Benigni, *Life is Beautiful*, screenplay manuscript, 1998, p. 83.

9

THE LONG SHORT
SCREENPLAY

For the past four screenplays, you've focused on essential elements of drama—discovery, decision, conflict, connection—and you've created and crafted these in short screenplays. In the process, ideally, you've learned to write vivid and economical descriptions of setting, character, action, using higher and more significant detail, and you've learned to sharpen your dialogue, letting your characters say far more with less. And along the way, you've probably noticed that these elements of drama—slippery little devils—are tricky to isolate. They tend to hang out together in screenplays—a discovery precipitating a decision, a conflict giving way to connection, and vice versa.

A dance.

So now it's time to clear the creative floor and let these dramatic elements rip in your long short screenplay.

THE FIFTH SCREENPLAY—THE LONG SHORT SCREENPLAY

Write the best ten- to fifteen-page screenplay you can—using the techniques you've learned to tell a good story that makes us connect. A pattern of human change that makes a difference to your main character. And to us.

And follow these guidelines:

1. Choose an idea that has rich resonance for you, that on some (perhaps not obvious) level, is important to you. If you need inspiration, take a look at the five award-winning screenplays in Part III (and their films) or screen your favorite film of all time, if you have one. Why did you connect? What story could you tell that would connect to others?

2. Make your story simple and your character complex.

3. Make sure the story makes a difference to your main character (otherwise you'll face the dread *so what?*)

4. Articulate a clear surface action and a deep action (character arc) for your screenplay. Make sure that they are, in some way, interrelated. How do external events in your story create inner change in your character?

5. Make sure your surface and deep action are made of specific moments of change—discoveries and decisions—that we can *see* happen on paper/screen.

6. Explore, develop, and weave together—in whatever proportions are right for your story—conflict and connection. In *Slow Dancin' Down the Aisles of the Quickcheck* the conflict and connection (wanting Maybelline but not being able to tell her) are one and the same. In *The Making of Killer Kite*—a send-up of the horrors of filmmaking—there's no connection at all. That's one of the points the story is making.

7. Make sure your story checks out with the Screenplay Paradox: Is it unique *and* universal? A story only you can tell us, but one that we want to see?

8. Don't forget, in case you already have (I do all the time) that the last word in screenplay is *play. Enjoy* the freedom of the form: The power of the image (a picture really *does* speak a thousand words, so let your images do most of the talking); the story leap (hit your scenes late, leave them early); emotional flow (done well, it will connect your scenes and your audience to the story you tell). *Use* the freedom of the form to take your character—and your audience—on a magic carpet ride.

9. Stick to the ten- to fifteen-page limit, unless your instructor and budget allow your script to be longer (at Florida State's Film School, our B.F.A. Thesis Scripts are limited to ten pages).

10. Write the film you want to see

11. Unless it's a skit.

CHOOSING AN IDEA

As you know all too well by now, so much depends upon a good idea. And the best ones—comic or dramatic or a mixture of both—as you also know, come from a deep place inside us:

A passion.
An obsession.
An emotion.
A person.
An experience.
An image.
A perception.
A principle.

You've already tapped some of these in your menu and your four previous screenplays, but now dig even deeper. Explore these deeply felt areas of yourself and your life. What are you yearning to say about life? What stories are you dying to tell?

"Creating begins typically with a vague, even a confused excitement, some sort of yearning, hunch, or other preverbal intimation of approaching or potential resolution," Brewster Ghiselin says in *The Creative Process*. "[The poet] Stephen Spender's expression is exact: 'a dim cloud of an idea which I feel must be condensed into a shower of words.'"[1]

And, for the screenwriter, pictures.

Musing about Muses, Rob McCaffrey came up with a funny perception about being alive: If Muses inspires us, is there a comparable spirit that aggravates and undermines us? Rob came up with the Buse, the cosmic creature who makes us spill coffee down our shirtfront, lock our keys in the car, have bad hair days. To share his perception with others, Rob developed a story about a day in the life of a new Buse, a unique story, to say the least, with universal underpinnings because it's a story about finding one's place in the universe, the subject of all great drama, as Arthur Miller once said.

And to write his film *After Life*, writer/director Hirokazu Kore-eda mined his experience and fascination with memory and his unique perception about its role in our lives—and after. "I developed this idea, at a young age, that you forget everything, and then you die." This belief came from his childhood, seeing his grandfather develop dementia and senility. "One day, he no longer recognized our faces. Finally, he could not recognize his own." So Kore-eda began asking himself the question, "What if you got to hold onto one thing?"[2]

"Dance your own dance," Frank McCourt always tells writers, and he followed his own advice when he wrote his luminous memoir, *Angela's Ashes*.

So create your own version of the list above. Add and subtract categories. Then dive deep into each one. Explore your own experiences, fascinations, perceptions. And play (that word again!) creative pinball, bouncing from one item on your list to another. The richest ideas often occur when categories cross-fertilize. It's called *homospatial thinking*, bringing two disparate ideas together, like Gutenberg inventing the printing press when he connected the functions of a signet ring and a wine press.

My short play *Propinquity* sprang from such a cross-fertilization. My father's father used to say that people fell in love for only one reason—propinquity. Proximity of bodies. There was no sweet mystery to it, no affinity of human nature, just proximity. I disagreed *passionately*. I believed—and still believe—that there are deeper forces at work, or we'd fall in love with every *shlub* we squeeze next to on the subway or bus. And so, when Actors Theatre of Louisville commissioned me to write a ten-minute play, this belief bubbled back up. But it was only half an idea. Luckily, though, the same week a friend and teaching assistant in English said she was sick and damn tired of other teaching assistants complaining about teaching freshmen. She *loved* teaching freshmen because they were young, impressionable, open.

These two passions—hers and mine—intersected, and my play *Propinquity* bloomed whole; I wrote the play in an *hour* ("Good writing doesn't always come hard," Sam Smiley assured me). A simple story: A shy, lovestruck freshman, Dale Bender, is trying to tell his T.A. in English, Alexis, that he loves her, while her significant other, Marshall, is trying to leave her. Crossed lines of action. A ten-minute story told in six scenes that I hit late and left early, each with a small but significant moment of change that swept the story on to the next ("A tender and effortless glissando sweeping gracefully from moment to wistful moment," Sylvia Drake wrote—God bless her—in *The Los Angeles Times*).

In one scene, Marshall tells Alexis that the only reason people fall in love is propinquity. Simple proximity. Alexis passionately disagrees. And so does Dale at the end of the play when he delivers his final essay to Alexis:

> DALE
> Here's my essay. Revised. Very asshole, but it
> has a climax, Miss Saunders. You won't believe
> the climax it has.
> > (beat)
> I didn't write about the House of Usher. I wrote
> an essay on propinquity, what you said the other
> day in your office—that it was the cause of love. I
> hate to tell you this, Miss Saunders, because I like
> and respect you, but that's a crock, a real crock.
> Except possibly for meaning number three—I
> looked it up in the Oxford English Dictionary—
> which defines propinquity as an affinity of
> natures and not simple proximity—

She takes his face in her hands and kisses him.[3]

It is their own affinity of natures that brings them together for this brief moment, and both are changed in the process.

I wrote this short comedy to prove that people fall in love for deeper reasons than proximity, and perhaps I succeeded (the *Irish Times* said "*Propinquity* offers great hope and humanity"), but a play or screenplay cannot succeed on message alone.

"If you want to send a message, call Western Union," Samuel Goldwyn once growled, and I agree, but as Anne Lamott wisely reminds us, "A moral position is not a message." You *can* find wonderful ideas for your screenplay by examining your own beliefs, passion, vision, whatever has the deepest meaning for you, then making a story that shows what you want to say.

"A true plot is an assertion of meaning," asserts Arthur Miller. But it's the *plot* that must assert. Preaching is deadly in drama—I *hate* preaching—and, the truth is, it rarely works anyway.

"You can't tell another," Shelby Foote said, "but with hard work and luck, maybe you can show him."

You must *show* others by creating flesh-and-blood characters going through significant change in specific time-and-place scenes. Screenwriting is an incarnational art. Don't ever lose sight of that.

DEVELOPING CHARACTER

So your not-so-easy task is creating flesh-and-blood characters who will come alive on the page and the screen. You've explored and developed the character checklist, 3-D I.D., the "I want" speech, a passionate speech about the character's values, opinions, beliefs, a brief character bio to create their backstory. All these remain useful tools, but I want to offer a deceptively simple list of questions to answer about your main character in your long short screenplay.

Questions 1–4 define character, Questions 5–9 define story, and Question 10 defines your character arc—how your character is changed by the events of the story. So as you develop your character—*to* develop your character— answer these questions:

1. Who is your character? Answer with a beautifully crafted, significantly specific character I.D.
2. What must your character be connected to in her life or she'll wither up and die (besides the obvious food and shelter)?
3. What does your character want in the story (goal)?
4. Why (motivation)? And why now (how is this day different from any other)?
5. What does your character do to get it (action)?
6. What obstacles—internal and external—does your character meet on the way (conflict)?

7. What's at stake—lost—if your character fails?
8. Does your character succeed or fail?
9. What connections, disconnections, reconnections does your character go through in the story?
10. How is your character changed in the course of the story?

Question 2 always throws my students. What do I mean when I ask what their character must be connected to? Do I mean what the character must be connected to in her life or in the screenplay?

I mean both. If you define what your character must be connected to in her life, you'll bring that *into* your screenplay. Color me stubborn, but I keep this question on the list because I think it offers a less obvious and often richer approach to defining who your character is. Consider yourself and your own life. What must you be connected to or you'll wither and die? This reveals a great deal about your deepest self. For me, it's my family, friends, writing, nature, adventure, and chocolate. Okay, maybe I could thrive without chocolate, but not without the other five things.

Knowing what your character *must* be connected to will help you define who he is, where he is, what he does in your screenplay. As we prepared to write our feature, *Winterfort*, Pam Ball and I kicked this question around for our main character, Jack. Two important things surfaced—he must be connected to Claire (the love of his life) and he must be connected to nature; he feels restless, cooped-up, indoors. Jack's non-negotiable need to be connected to Claire gave us the emotional spine of the screenplay, and his need to be connected to nature gave his scenes richness and resonance—and fresher settings. Pam and I shifted scenes once set in kitchens and living rooms (The First Thing That Swam By) to the great lush outdoors of rural north Florida.

The answer to Question 2 may help you find the answer to 3—what does your character want in the screenplay? The answer to 4—why and why now?—further defines your character, her experience, and her situation when your screenplay begins. And Question 5—what does your character do to get what she wants?—brings us to story, though I'm struck again by the interconnectedness of character and action. They're two sides of the same thing—a human being and a human doing.

DEVELOPING STORY AND STRUCTURE

Doing, as you well know by now, is the root meaning of drama. So answering Question 5 is one of the best ways to define and develop your story. One you've defined what your character wants (goal) and why he wants it (motivation) you can define what he does to get it (action).

Though she's talking about features, Linda Seger offers a method for defining and developing story that's terrific for writing short screenplays. Seger breaks down the story of *Witness* this way:

Motivation	Action	Goal
The murder of a police officer forces John Book to	keep Rachel & Samuel in Philadelphia, to show Samuel a line-up, mug shots, to talk to Paul, to hide out at an Amish farm, to phone his partner, to threaten Paul in order to	expose the villains.

Her example from *Back to the Future* is even more useful because it clearly indicates the obstacles Marty meets as he tries to accomplish his goal:

Motivation	Action	Goal
A beefed-up De Lorean forces Marty into the past	He overcomes Mother's advances, seeks out the Professor, fights with Biff, dresses as Darth Vader to motivate George to ask Lorraine out. He cajoles, persuades, manipulates, in order to	survive and get back to the future.

This exercise—a MAG, I like to call it (motivation, action, goal)—is a dynamic way to develop, define, and clarify your story. You might even create a fourth column—"Or Else"—to clarify stake. (Marty would have never existed, you could say for *Back to the Future*).

It's important to note, however, that wonderful stories have been created where the main character is *not* the *intentional* character—the one with the goal in the story. The main character may be the *focal* character—think Othello—but someone else—Iago—is the intentional one, the character who drives the story. The same is true in *tongue*. Joe Wagner is the *focal* character, but Anna is the intentional one. It is her desire to connect with Joe—and to kiss him—that drives the story. And it is Buzz who drives the story in *Cool Breeze and Buzz*, though Paula is focal. Again, play the possibilities as you develop your story.

When you've answered Questions 6–8, move on to Question 9—what connections, disconnections, reconnections does your character go through in the story? This can yield rich story possibilities you may not have considered, as well as providing the greatest emotional power to your story and thus the moments of the greatest audience connection. The peak empathic moments in films, long and short, are often the moments of connection, disconnection, and reconnection. Think of *Forrest Gump*. For all its historical conflict and sweep, our greatest points of emotional connection to the story are his moments of connection, disconnection, and reconnection with Jenny, Bubba, and his mother.

Last, as you develop your story, explore Question 10—how is your character changed in the course of your story? This is the character arc, the deep action, the difference that external events made to your character's inner landscape. The change may be small—a tiny turn of the screw—but your character will never be quite the same.

Two other excellent tools for developing and defining your story are the *premise* and the *synopsis* or *overview*. "Premise" is the word used by Lajos Egri in *The Art of Dramatic Writing* (Woody Allen's favorite book on playwriting) to mean the "theme, thesis, root idea, central idea, goal, aim, driving force, subject, purpose, plan, plot, basic emotion" of a dramatic work. Egri prefers the word premise "because it contains all the elements the other words try to express and because it is less subject to misinterpretation."

"A good premise is a thumbnail synopsis of your play," Egri writes. It implies a character, an action, and an outcome. The premise of *Romeo and Juliet*, he tells us, is *great love defies even death*. The premise of *King Lear* is *blind trust leads to destruction*, and the premise of *Macbeth* is *ruthless ambition leads to its own destruction*.[4]

Egri's speaking of plays, but the same can be said of good screenplays. The premise of *Back to the Future* is *a moment of courage can change the course of a life*, and the premise of *Babe* is *an unprejudiced heart can change the course of life in the valley*. Neither film ever preaches, but the action of each is a wonderful working out of its premise.

A premise is richer and deeper than a *logline*, which summarizes the surface action in one sentence (think *TV Guide*). Premise moves beneath the surface action of a screenplay to its *deep subject*—what it's *really* about. This can help you dig deeper as you develop your story. And, ideally, every scene in your screenplay will, on some level, be about this deep subject.

If a premise is a thumbnail synopsis of your screenplay, the next step is writing the paragraph-long synopsis or *overview*—as Brady and Lee call it in *The Understructure of Writing for Film and Television*. This is extremely useful in developing story. A good synopsis—as Rob McCaffrey's for *The Buse* shows—touches on the tone of the screenplay and gives a brief overview of the characters and the story:

> *The Buse* is a modern day fairy tale in which all of the daily, little aggravations which happen to people are personified in the form of spirits called Buses. The story follows a day in the

life of a New Buse, whose refusal to torment mortals has gotten him in trouble with the other members of his species. New is desperate to find a line of work which will let him help mankind, but how will he manage it without ticking off his higher-ups? Striking a deal with a Muse which might get him out of his predicament, New agrees to try to inspire a mortal man to win back an old love. The only problem: The lady is getting married to another man the same day!

Rob left us hanging as to the ending (New fails as a Muse but succeeds as a Buse and, realizing how helpful his Buse-ive powers can be, he accepts his rightful role in the great scheme of things), but it's helpful to articulate how your screenplay will end. You might also want to begin your synopsis, as Rob does, by introducing what your screenplay's about ("the daily, little aggravations that happen to people") or as Brady and Lee do in their overview of *Kramer vs. Kramer*, "*Kramer vs. Kramer* is a contemporary marital and family drama about the changing roles of men and women in American society."

You may find it useful, after the synopsis, to develop your story in greater detail in a *treatment*—an expanded prose telling of the story. Bob Gray wrote the screenplay for *The Making of Killer Kite* from a one-page story treatment written by Matt Stevens, who directed the film. Or you may want to bypass synopsis and treatment and develop your scenes and story on cards. The important thing is to know your story and the moments of change that move it along from beginning to end. Once you do, you can begin to design your screenplay's structure.

Which brings us to *plot*, too often equated with story. The two, in fact, are not the same, and the distinction is important and useful. *Story is the events or moments of change in the order they happen*—A to Z. *Plot is the order of events as you choose to tell them*, pure and simple, though there's nothing simple about it.

"Plotting is more than the order of the events," Shelby Foote said.

The events you choose to show and the order in which you choose to show them are major artistic decisions. Why? Because the order of events has a profound effect on how compelling, ironic, or moving your screenplay will be. The whole *is* greater than the sum of the parts.

Your material may work best in a three-act structure—an inciting incident, a turning point at the end of Act One and Act Two, and a climax and resolution at the end of Act Three. But as many fine screenplays—long and short—show, there are other wonderful structural options. Look at *Pulp Fiction*. It's far more compelling and ironic told in a nonlinear structure.

So is *The Making of Killer Kite*. Told in a nonlinear, mockumentary structure, the film intercuts scenes from the cult horror flick *Killer Kite* (shot in film) with scenes of the making of the flick (shot in video), media coverage and reviews of the film, and an after-the-fact interview with the director, Colin Kishman. This structure works extremely well for the subject, increasing the irony and often gut-busting humor (I recently reread the script on the porch at our farm and laughed so loud I startled the ducks from the pond). But it can work well for tragedy, too; *The Sweet Hereafter* intercuts an after-the-fact conversation on an airplane with the story's main action.

We are so tied to seamless realism in this culture, we tend to overlook the fluidity and freedom of film. I recommend Ken Dancyger and Jeff Rush's *Alternative Scriptwriting: Writing Beyond the Rules* if you want to explore alternative structures. Or for sheer inspiration, I strongly recommend screening Michael Verhoeven's German film *Nasty Girl*, a compelling narrative told in a bold mix of past and present, color and black and white, fourth-wall realism and direct address.[5] And, closer to home, take a look at Steven Soderbergh's film *Out of Sight*. The screenwriter, Scott Frank, begins the script with an event that actually occurs very late in the story:

FADE IN:

A MIAMI STREET — DAY

The financial district. Lots of people in suits. A shaky, spasmodic ZOOM in finds . . .

JACK FOLEY—forty, big, focused expression—as he rips a tie from around his neck and throws it down in the gutter. He starts across the street, now peeling off his suitcoat and dropping that, too, right there on the asphalt . . . [6]

We have no idea why Foley rips off his necktie and throws it down in the gutter or peels off his suitcoat, dropping that, too (and we don't find out until late in the film), but it's intriguing. We start asking questions. And curiosity is a fabulous hook, a sure-fire way to hold someone's attention. Just ask Pandora.

If you decide to design a nonlinear plot for your story, be sure you don't lose your audience along the way. And there's no shame in choosing a traditional linear three-act structure if that best serves your story and dramatic purpose. As Jerry Stern used to say in his workshops when students complained that they couldn't come up with snazzy, newfangled plots, "When all else fails, chronology works."

Whatever your structure, once it's designed, type up a Scene-By-Scene for your screenplay—the scenes in the order they happen on screen. When you've read it through several times and you're sure your surface and deep action are clear and your character's emotional flow is convincing, it's time to start drafting your scenes.

DRAFTING THE SCREENPLAY

Whether I'm writing a screenplay by myself or with someone else, I find it enormously helpful to noodle the beats in each scene before I draft it—the action beats/moments of change (what has to happen) and the dialogue beats (what has to be said). When you're noodling your dialogue beats, The First Thing That Swims By will often be on the nose. That's okay for now. You're just roughing out the shape of the scene.

Good scenes, like good screenplays, are shapely, like the restaurant scene in *Kramer vs. Kramer* and the library scene in *Philadelphia*. One creates conflict, one creates connection, but both are exquisitely crafted patterns of change. Chart their structure and see for yourself. Then do the same for your scenes.

Once each scene's shape is roughed out, you can focus on the scene's dialogue, searching for the freshest way for your characters to say what needs to be said (it may take a number of drafts before you find it). You're looking for a fresh but in-character way for your characters to say what they're saying. In the screenplay of *Kramer vs. Kramer*, Joanna asks Ted, "How's the job?" and he answers, "Fine."

But on screen, he adds, "Vice president of nothing." It's an embedding that lets us—and Joanna—know that work isn't the most important thing in Ted's life anymore.

With *Winterfort*, once Pam and I had a good Scene-By-Scene, we chose the scenes we wanted to write. I wrote the first draft of a scene where Claire asks her parents for money because she wants to leave her husband, Hutch. Her parents know he's abusive, but he's also the town's football hero, and they just can't let go of that:

> MR. ANDERSON
> Claire, there are four days in my life I'll never forget. One was the day I married your mother. One was the day you were born. One was the day Hutch threw that football thirty-eight yards, and one was the day he married you.

Claire picks up her purse and walks out the door.

But I wasn't satisfied with the scene. I wanted Claire to reply to her father—it's an important moment of disconnection and growth for her in the story—but I couldn't think of what she could say. I didn't want to go on the nose with something obvious like, "Well, I see whose side you're on." So, at a loss for fresh words, I let Claire be at a loss, too, and I let her walk out. But it made the scene a bit flat.

Pam agreed, and she saved it by coming up with a fresh way for Claire to articulate what she is feeling:

> MR. ANDERSON
> Claire, there are four days in my life I'll never forget. One was the day I married your mother. One was the day you were born. One was the day

>   MR. ANDERSON (CONT'D)
>   Hutch threw that football thirty-eight yards, and
>   one was the day he married you.

A slight pause.

>   CLAIRE
>   Well, that's one for me and one for Mama and
>   two for Hutch. I guess he wins.

She picks up her purse and walks out the door.

The subtext of Claire's speech is "I see whose side you're on," but Pam's text is so fresh, deadly, dead on—scorekeeping!—the moment comes alive. So raise the stakes on yourself as you draft and redraft your scenes for your long short screenplay. Make your dialogue work harder for you. Give it greater richness, irony, and levels of meaning. John Hill wrote an excellent article for *Script Magazine*, "Good Dialogue Is To Dye For," comparing great dialogue to dye markers used by the Coast Guard to mark a place on the ocean so divers can find the place where a plane or ship or "whatever is really important" went down:

> It can't be found on the surface; you have to work a little for it. The communication isn't in the 'text,' the words being said, but in the *subtext* ("sub," of course, means below, just under, out of sight but still very accessible—just work a little for it). Really good dialogue "says it without saying it." And when you create that momentary gap in time and space, between hearing the words and realizing the meaning, making the leap to "get it" is something the audience will love you for because it involves them, it brings them into the character's world view and into the story.[7]

In other words, they connect. They enter a screenplay or film, participating, doing some of the work, having some of the fun.

"Let me play, too," Janet Burroway writes in the margin of short stories when her student writers are spelling everything out.

Great dialogue doesn't.

Hill's favorite example—and mine—is Butch Cassidy's line, "I got vision and the rest of the world wears bifocals." I guffawed when I heard it the first time. It still makes me smile. And I still quote it in conversation because it's so damn witty I never forgot it. Imagine writing a line so fresh, so beautifully crafted, that other people remember it. *That's* connection.

You may not have been born with an ear for great dialogue. Few people are. But I'm convinced that you can improve what talent you have by paying attention.

When you're out in the world, *listen* to the way people talk. The other day, on my daily walk through the park in my neighborhood, I noticed a middle-aged city official scooping water out of our creek. "Taking samples?" I asked.

"Yes," he said, nice and cheerful. "Some of our little fishies are dying." *Little fishies*. The combination of babytalk and the news that our creek was polluted was downright chilling (okay, I'd just seen *Civil Action*). And it's dialogue I've filed away to use in a script later on.

When I interviewed TV movie writer/producer Cynthia Cherbak, she told me she did the same thing.

> In the middle of doing a Kirk Douglas movie for HBO, I was robbed in Rural Canyon at gunpoint by carjackers. They told me to get my ring off or they'd cut my fucking finger off, so immediately I lift that out of my true life. I used the exact dialogue the robbers said.

Life's the best teacher, to coin a cliche, but you can also improve your own dialogue by reading plays and screenplays written by great dialoguists—Clifford Odets, Elaine May, Nora Ephron, David Mamet, Quentin Tarantino, Woody Allen, Tom Stoppard. In Stoppard's play *The Real Thing*, the main character, Henry—a writer—grabs a cricket bat to explain to his lover, Annie, why it's so important for writers to agonize until they get the words right:

> Shut up and listen. This thing here, which looks like a wooden club, is actually several pieces of particular wood cunningly put together in a certain way so that the whole thing is sprung, like a dance floor. It's for hitting cricket balls with. If you get it right, the cricket ball will travel two hundred yards in four seconds, and all you've done is give it a knock like knocking the top off a bottle of stout, and it makes a noise like a trout taking a fly ... (He clucks his tongue to make the noise). What we're trying to do is to write cricket bats, so that when we throw up an idea and give it a little knock, it might ... *travel*.[8]

Ultimately, that's what all of us are trying to do—write cricket bats so our ideas and stories will travel.

REWRITING THE SCREENPLAY

For the long/short screenplay, I strongly recommend that you arrange a *table read*—an informal round-table reading—of a draft of your screenplay. Let one person read the action (they can also read those characters who only have a few lines). Let others read the principal characters. *Do not read yourself.* You need to sit back and listen. This is the best way I know of (short of making a film of your screenplay) to find out which scenes are working and which scenes are not. You'll discover if your dialogue is overwritten, underwritten, if it sounds natural (or stylized, if that's what you want), if your structure is sound, if the story is clear, and if the emotional flow really works. Even a cold reading with inexperienced readers can help you prepare for your rewrite. You might also invite a small audience to the reading and ask for their feedback. Don't object to what they are saying. Listen. Take notes. And look for consensus.

Often, in the early drafts of this screenplay, my students get lost in the funhouse. Their story begins to lose focus. And it's hard for them to get fresh perspective, because they've been so focused on putting words on the page. Once they put words on the page, the words stick like flies on flypaper. They begin to feel married to them. It's hard for them to pull back and see the big picture (believe me, I know; this happens to me all the time when I'm writing). So in script conferences, I'll turn the "flypaper" screenplay face down on the table and draw three shapes on the back:

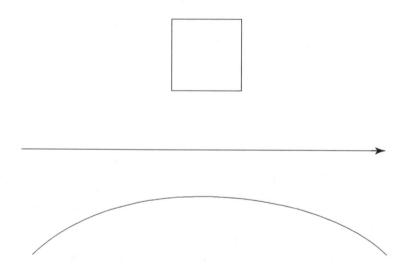

In the square, I ask the student to write what their script is about—in one word. There's almost always a long silence. It's a very hard question. At Bread Loaf, when Terry Tempest Williams asked me the same question about a memoir I was writing, I was staggered. "One *word?*" Then the word hit me—*renewal.* On every level, that's what the story was really about. And knowing this helped me immensely as I began designing and drafting the story.

That's what you're looking for—your *deep subject.* Some writers prefer to use the word *theme.* Whatever term you prefer, the point is to find what your screenplay is really truly deeply about. And in the best screenplays, every scene is, on some perhaps subtle level, about this deep subject.

The horizontal arrow is the screenplay's surface action/spine/through-line. Articulate this, if you haven't already, in one sentence with an -ing verb. How quickly this gets lost as words fly onto the page! Clarifying your surface action before you rewrite is essential.

The arc is, of course, the character arc, your screenplay's deep action. Articulate this for your long short screenplay, if you haven't, in one sentence with an -ing verb. And, again, ideally, there's a close connection between the external events in your surface action and the moments of change that move your character along the arc.

When your screenplay's action—surface and deep—is clear in your mind, you're reading to rewrite. And rewrite. And rewrite. And, in most cases, rewriting doesn't stop there.

"Editing is the final rewrite," said Oliver Stone.

And, as you'll see when you read the following five long short screenplays and screen the five films, rewriting doesn't stop until the film's in the can.

NOTES

1. Brewster Ghiselin, *The Creative Process*, Brewster Ghiselin, New American Library, New York, 1952, p. 14.
2. R. Ruby Rich, "Choose One Memory To Take With You, He Says," *The New York Times*, Sunday, May 16, 1999, pp. 11, 19.
3. Claudia Johnson, *Propinquity/Paternity*, two one-acts, Palmetto Play Service, Pendleton, South Carolina, 1997, p. 23.
4. Lajos Egri, *The Art of Dramatic Writing*, Simon and Schuster, New York, 1960, p. 2.
5. I am grateful to my former colleague, Charlie Boyd, for introducing me to this wonderful film.
6. Scott Frank, *Out of Sight, Scenario: The Magazine of Screenwriting Art*, Summer 1998, Volume 4, No. 2, p. 8.
7. John Hill, "Good Dialogue Is To Dye For," *Script*, Volume 4, Number 3, pp. 19, 20, 60, 61.
8. Tom Stoppard, *The Real Thing*, Faber & Faber, Boston, 1984, p. 51.

PART III

FIVE SCREENPLAYS THAT MAKE IT LOOK EASY

10

SLOW DANCIN' DOWN THE AISLES OF THE QUICKCHECK

INTRODUCTION

At the first crew meeting for *Slow Dancin' Down the Aisles of the Quickcheck*, Thomas Jackson made a brief speech:

> I told everybody the most important thing is I want everybody to have a great experience, have a good time, and learn from the experience. It was important to me that the set was pleasant and everyone felt good about it because there are so many sets you go on that suck. You hate to be there. So it was so important to me that this be a pleasant experience for all involved. Then I said, "But one of our goals is to be the first student film from Florida State to win a student Academy Award." I don't even know if the crew members remember it, but I remember it like it was yesterday because it was such a hard thing for me to say. In the South, you're taught to be self-deprecating, and when you say something like that, even humbly, it sounds like you're being pretentious, even though at the time and even when we won the regional competition I felt *we don't have a chance*. But I've learned in life you have to state things. Just verbalizing it. Putting it out there. There's something about saying it that sort of puts your ass on the line. And you have to live up to it. And if you say it, it puts you in a mindset to make it happen. But I also wanted the crew to know I was taking this seriously. I wanted them to feel they were working on something they could be proud of. And it kind of set the tone.

In May 1999, Thomas was notified that his film was a finalist for the student Academy Award. He would find out in June if he'd won first, second, or third place.

But the journey from idea to the Academy ceremony in June was a long one. In 1998, when Thomas wrote the first draft of *Slow Dancin'*, he did not have a story. *Fifteen rewrites* later, he'd found his story and a whole lot of rich significant stuff in the process:

> What's funny about writing is that I guess in some ways things come out that are somewhat your philosophy but at the same time sometimes they just develop, they just come out of nowhere, you don't know where they come from. They just kind of bubble up. In a way, I mean. I believe it. I mean, the thing is, I've been married twice and divorced twice, but you just have to take those chances, I guess. I'm a hopeless romantic. You have to believe that you can make the connection with the person. You have to look beneath the surface. See who they really are. So I'm in Georgia, and peach season came in the middle of the rewrites, and a peach came to represent this true thing in a person. So, in the screenplay, the produce manager, Jerome, says to Earl:

> JEROME
> You got to look for the peach inside of her, and see her in a way ain't nobody ever seen her. Then talk to her with *your* peach . . . You just look deep into her eyes, past all the flesh, blood and bone, and see that peach inside of her.

Would Earl have the courage to make this authentic connection? That became the central dramatic question of the screenplay and film. As director, Thomas didn't make a great many changes in the screenplay:

> I want to say all the scenes are there. Even in editing, we didn't cut any scenes. There was added dialogue in production, or I would give the actors lines. When you're there, you just have to see what works for you and adjust accordingly. Then there were throwaway lines like when Earl's on the floor, stuff in the background. I'd tell the actors this is what it's about, and they would adlib.

The process of filmmaking, though, like true love, did not always run smooth:

> I watched the dailies the first day and I thought, Oh my God, this is the worst thing. What am I doing? I went home and went paranoid. And I said to my girlfriend, if this film sucks, will you still love me? But you just have to walk on faith.

> No, it's more than just faith. You have to take action. But
> without the faith part, the action doesn't work. Even when
> you think it sucks, you still have to go out there and believe
> it will all come together and it's gonna work. It's all about
> just doing it. And until you have to let go of the film, it's a
> work in progress. That's the greatest thing about film. You
> have chance after chance to make it better.

But the first cut was the one he loved best.

> After that you get lost in detail. The final cut is a million
> times better than the rough cut, but that's the only cut that
> worked for me. I actually saw moments in it, but now . . .
> it's painful. You watch it a million times and it doesn't work
> for you. There are things you just cringe when you watch it.
> That is the saddest part about filmmaking. I don't think I'll
> ever be able to make a film and watch it and say, God, I hit
> the mark. I used to listen to Woody Allen say *Annie Hall*
> doesn't work, and I'd think, God, how could he say that?
> He's just saying that. Now I totally relate.

Many others do not. *Slow Dancin' Down the Aisles of the Quickcheck* won
First Place in the Student Narrative category at the 1998 Ft. Lauderdale Inter-
national Film Festival; the 1999 Cine Eagle Award in Washington, D.C.; Third
Place in the 1999 Student Emmy Awards for Comedy; the 1999 Grand Prize-
Overall and Second Place-Fiction at the Florida Film Festival in West Palm
Beach; First Place at the 1999 Palm Beach International Film Festival Student
Showcase; First Place Featurette Audience Award at the 1999 Filmfest New
Haven, as well as being screened nationally and internationally, including
the Emerging Filmmakers series at the 1999 Cannes Film Festival. And, on
June 14, 1999, in Los Angeles, California, Thomas Jackson received Third
Place in the Student Academy Awards for *Slow Dancin' Down the Aisles of the
Quickcheck*. He's currently developing four feature-length screenplays and
working as Post Production Supervisor at the F.S.U. Film School. He still
lives in Bainbridge, Georgia.

SLOW DANCIN' DOWN THE AISLES OF THE QUICKCHECK

by Thomas Wade Jackson

FADE IN:

EXT. QUICKCHECK — PREDAWN

The parking lot is empty and quiet, except for a green 1979 Toyota pick up, a distant train whistle, and the muffled sound of a guitar coming from inside the store.

INT. QUICKCHECK — SERIES OF SHOTS — PREDAWN

The Quickcheck sleeps as a voice lays lyrics over the music from the guitar.

The meat counter glows under the display lights, stocked with chittlins, bologna, fish roe, pork souse and the feet of both chickens and pigs.

A perfect display of peaches rests happily under a sign that reads, "Nothing's as Sweet as A Georgia Peach."

The magazine rack holds various magazines; a tabloid reads, "Ghost of Hank Williams Haunts Rush Limbaugh." DOLLY TO REVEAL:

The silhouetted back of the man, playing the guitar, sitting on one of the check out counters. CONTINUE TO DOLLY AROUND THE SIDE OF EARL, a plain-looking, 41 year old man. He sings a troubled line and looks over at the Employee of the Month Sign:

EXTREME CLOSE UP of the Polaroid picture of Earl shaking hands with a faded beauty in a cashier's vest.

CLOSE UP of Earl as he finishes his last line and looks from the Employee of the Month sign to a newspaper in front of him.

CLOSE UP of Newspaper. CURTIS, a 38 year old man wearing a Cowboy Hat, and a sparkling red, white and blue suit, grins at Earl from the paper. The headline reads, "Local Country Star Returns Home for Concert."

TITLE

INT. FRONT OF THE STORE — MORNING

The doors of the Quickcheck sit quiet for a second, then
MAYBELLINE, the 38-year-old Head Cashier and woman in the
picture, walks up outside, calling to someone OFFSCREEN.

                    MAYBELLINE
    Come on, Mary Jurgeana, I want you to hear somethin'.

                    MARY (O.S.)
    Hold your horses.

Maybelline comes in the store and makes a bee line to the
radio. She turns it on, and a steel guitar cries out over the
music with a distinctive cheesy Nashville sound. MARY
JURGEANA, a slightly overweight black woman, struggles
through the door.

                    MAYBELLINE
    Hurry up, it's almost over.

                    MARY
              (walking towards Maybelline)
    I ain't got no hurry left in me, girl. Daryl came home
    with some Colt 45 last night, pretendin' he was Billie
    Dee Williams, again.

                    MAYBELLINE
    Let me guess, you had to be the young starlet who
    wanted a part in his next movie.

                    MARY
    No, last night, I had to be a teenage school girl who
    wanted his autograph.

                    MAYBELLINE
              (smiling)
    What did he want to write it with?

A man's twangy voice begins to sing about his Pickup Truck,
over the music.

                    MAYBELLINE
    Remember the guy I was tellin' you about yesterday?
    Curtis?

                    MARY
    You mean the old flame that ran off and became a
    Country Star?

                    MAYBELLINE
Yeah, this is him. Listen.
              (she listens)
He did this on Nashville Now Tuesday.
              (listens some more)
They call him a star on the horizon.

                    MARY
What horizon's that? The hillbilly horizon?

                    MAYBELLINE
They said he had a distinct voice.

                    MARY
Sounds like every other redneck song, to me.

They listen some more.

                    MAYBELLINE
And they said he'd be worth over a million dollars by
the end of the year.

                    MARY
You know, the more I hear it . . .

The deep country voice of a D.J. speaks over the end of the
song. Maybelline and Mary turn their attention away from the
radio, and clock themselves in for the day.

                    D.J. (O.S.)
Whew, that boy can sing it, can't he? That Bainbridge's
own Curtis Anderson, putting the Country back in the
Country.

Maybelline and Mary talk over the D.J.

                    MARY
Girl, I trade my Bille Dee, for an old boyfriend with a
million dollars, any day.

                    MAYBELLINE
I like Daryl.

                    MARY
That's 'cause you ain't ever had to pay Lando
Calrissian's Jerry Curl bill.

                    MAYBELLINE
Who?

Mary pulls a Lando Calrissian action figure out of her purse.

MARY

Billie Dee played him in Star Wars. I keep findin' these
in my pocketbook.

MAYBELLINE
(taking figure)
This don't look nothin' like Daryl.

Mary clocks in and notices the Employee of the Month sign and
that the picture is missing.

MARY
Looks like Earl's runnin' late again.

Maybelline looks at the empty slot and smiles.

INT. BATHROOM — SAME

Earl stands in front of the mirror in his brown slacks and a
tank top T-shirt, his middle-age pudge hanging slightly over his
belt. He pulls the wrapper off a new girdle.

EARL
(unsure)
Maybelline, my heart is a song.

He sucks in his gut and tightens a girdle around his waist with
all his might, fastening it down. He looks at the picture and
finishes the line, but has trouble due to the tightness of the
girdle.

EARL
(groaning)
And you are its melody.

He leans towards the mirror, knocking a can of Ajax off the
sink. He starts to pick it up, but the girdle keeps him from
bending. He gives up, takes the Polaroid off the mirror, and
puts it in his pocket.

INT. STORE FRONT — LATER

Maybelline and Mary sit in the crow's nest, counting the
money for their tills.

MAYBELLINE
She said that Curtis, personally, asked her to call me. I
thought that was kind of surprisin'.

MARY
Why?

                    MAYBELLINE
It's just been a long time.

                        MARY
How long?

                    MAYBELLINE
At least two dress sizes ago.

Behind them Earl walks out from the end of the aisle. He sees
them, then ducks back out of their sight. He pulls the Polaroid
picture out of his breast pocket and looks toward the Employee
of the Month sign.

                        MARY
Well, what was he like?

                    MAYBELLINE
                    (reflecting)
Well, back then he used to play with this band called
East River Junction. He had long hair, and a tattoo on
his arm of a guitar that said, "Honky Tonk Hero."
That's how he saw himself. He always wore a leather
jacket and black boots with silver tips on the toes.

As Maybelline talks, Earl sneaks up to the office, disappearing
behind the wall.

                    MAYBELLINE
And he had this '57 Harley Hydroglide with a 74 cubic
inch overhead valve engine, one just like The King
rode. Curtis sure loved that Harley. You ever do it on a
motorcycle?

Earl, who is about to return the Polaroid picture to the
Employee of the Month sign, misses the slot, and the picture
falls to the floor and under a chewing gum machine. He starts
to reach down for it, but can't bend.

                        MARY
No, but I did it on a lawnmower, once.

Earl struggles for the picture. He squats awkwardly, trying to
reach the picture, but it's just out of his reach.

                    MAYBELLINE
Curtis used to drive that Harley into the bedroom,
wearin' nothin' but a cowboy hat and a smile. And he'd
leave it runnin' while we did it, and when things got
hot, he'd rev it up. I'd feel my whole body vibrate.

                    MARY
I don't think that lawnmower ever ran.

                  MAYBELLINE
Well, let me tell you, there's just somethin' about that
much horse power between your legs.

Earl loses his balance and falls over. As quick as he hits the
ground, he grabs the picture and puts it in his shirt pocket.

Maybelline and Mary hear Earl's fall.

                  MAYBELLINE
Earl, is that you?

Earl lays on the ground, looking up at the ceiling.

                    EARL
Yeah. Ya'll in early this morning.

He tries to sit up, but can't.

                    MARY
It's after eight.

                  MAYBELLINE
Good morning to you, too, Earl.

                    EARL
              (still trying to get up)
Sorry, good mornin'. I guess I'm runnin' a little behind.

Earl bounces up trying to grab the time clock. His fingers
almost touching it.

                MAYBELLINE (O.S.)
Better a little behind than a big behind.

                  MARY (O.S.)
Now, don't go there.

                  MAYBELLINE
        (realizing what they'd been talking about)
How long have you been standin' there, Earl?

There is a crashing sound, and we hear Earl grunt. Maybelline
and Mary react to the sound, and Maybelline leans over the
top of the wall and looks down at Earl, who lays on the floor
with the shell of the time clock in his hands.

                    MAYBELLINE
        Earl? Are you all right?

Mary's head peers over the wall at Earl.

                      EARL
              (pointing to the bottom of time clock)
        Yeah, I'm resetting the clicker.

                      MARY
        Guess what, Earl, Maybelline got invited to that Country
        Star's welcome home party tonight. Did you know that
        they used to be an item? Who knows, you might be
        lookin' for a new employee of the month, tomorrow.

                    MAYBELLINE
        You sure you're all right?

Earl nods, and Maybelline and Mary go back to work.

                    MARY (O.S.)
        So, tell me more about Mr. Harley Davidson.

                    MAYBELLINE
        He also had this thing about showers. For a guy with a
        tattoo he was always clean.

Earl can't stand to hear any more.

                      EARL
        Maybelline.

Maybelline sticks her head back over the wall.

                    MAYBELLINE
        What is it, Earl?

He looks at her like he had at the picture in the bathroom. He
clears his throat and speaks, but the words are difficult.

                      EARL
        Maybelline . . . my . . .

Mary sticks her head back over the wall.

                      MARY
        Oh, yeah, he also gave her backstage passes for the
        concert this weekend. Ain't that something?

Earl gives up and nods.

> EARL
>
> Yeah, that's something.

Mary's head goes back over the wall.

> MAYBELLINE
>
> What was it you wanted, Earl?

> EARL
>
> Just wanted to remind you that we're havin' a two for one special on Check Cream Cola.

> MAYBELLINE
>
> Just like every Friday, right?

Maybelline's head goes back over the wall, and Earl puts the time clock cover over his face.

INT. GROCERY STORE — MEAT DEPARTMENT — LATER

A cleaver slams down, cutting the head off a chicken.

> JOE (O.S.)
>
> Women?

JOE, a 40-something redneck, covered in blood and chunks of meat and bone, turns to face Earl, who stands by the door.

> JOE
>
> There's only two things you got to remember . . . Chittlin's and Mountain Oysters.

GENE, a 30-something redneck, also covered in blood, laughs as he whacks open a Hog's Head.

> GENE
>
> Bullshit! Mountain Oysters my ass.

> JOE
>
> Go ahead and laugh, but there's just somethin' 'bout mixin' intestines and hog balls that makes 'em work like a African-deeshee-act.

> GENE
>
> (laughing)
>
> The only meat I know's gonna make a woman hot is some good ole USDA Tube Steak.

> JOE

Yeah, you must be really firin' up with that Vienna
Sausage you're totin'.

Gene looks at Earl, who looks out the window, down the aisle
to a distant Maybelline.

> GENE

I told you, if you'd bring your ass out to Bookie's once
in a while you could meet some women. Drunk Women.
Women that'd be impressed you was the Manager of
the damn Quick Check. Hell, most of 'em are happy if
you got teeth.

He throws the brainless hog's head in a five gallon bucket and
grabs another head.

> EARL

It's too smoky and there ain't nobody like Maybelline
out there.

Gene with hog's head in hand.

> GENE
> (mock frustration)

Earl, that place is full of Maybellines. You just need to
reconsider your standards. It wouldn't hurt you to
lower 'em a notch or two.

Joe whacks off another chicken head.

> JOE
> (to Gene)

If yours got any lower, people'ld have to start lockin'
their dogs up at night.

Gene splits open another Hog's Head.

> GENE

Earl, you've always been like this. In High School you
carried around that chubby for Lou Ann Cullpepper for
a year, but you never said a Goddamned word to her.
And when you did finally say something to her, she
laughed at you. Why?

Earl turns away from the window and looks at Gene.

> EARL

This is different.

                    GENE
Because you told her some bullshit about your heart
bein' a song.

Earl turns back to the window.

                    GENE
When you gone learn, Earl? Women don't want to hear
poetry, they want you to buy 'em a few drinks, dance a
couple dances with 'em, then take 'em home and pop
your John Henry to 'em a couple times.

                    JOE
Boy, you talk like a man with a paper asshole. When it
comes to women, you don't know a Dick Whistle from a
yo yo.

                    GENE
                  (to Earl)
Ain't you heard? They want it as bad as we do. You
just got to get 'em drunk first.

                    JOE
Look, Earl, I'll see what I can throw together by closin'.
Maybe I can dig up a few Mountain Oysters for you.

Curtis's song starts to play on the radio.

                  D.J. (O.S.)
Here it is again. The new one, our very own Curtis
Anderson.

                    GENE
             (overlapping D.J.)
I just wanta know what the big fuckin' hurry is? You
gone this long without a woman.

Earl stands staring down the aisle at Maybelline.

                    EARL
It just has to be today.

                 GENE (O.S.)
                (to himself)
It just has to be today. The man walks around with a
chubby for months and it has to be today.

INT. REGISTER — SAME

Maybelline is finishing checking out ROY, a heavy-set man
dressed like a cowboy.

                    ROY
     They're having Oyster Night at Bookie's this weekend.
     Pay ten dollars to get in and eat all you want. What
     you think?

Maybelline smiles as she takes his money.

                    MAYBELLINE
     I'll pass this time, Roy.

                    ROY
     Okay, but Country Cruisin's gonna be playin'.

                    MAYBELLINE
     Do you want your green stamps?

                    ROY
     You know, you can have 'em, darlin'.

Maybelline smiles, and Roy winks at her and leaves.

                    MAYBELLINE
     Bye, Roy.

                    ROY
              (calling over his shoulder)
     Bye, darling.

                    MARY
     Look at you, hustlin' customers for their Green Stamps
     just so you can get a set of Elvis Presley china. If you
     get with Mr. Harley Davidson, you won't have to worry
     about stuff like that.

                    MAYBELLINE
     You know, I don't think I'd enjoy doin' it on a Harley,
     now. I don't think I could take the noise.

                    MARY
     So don't do it on a Harley.

                    MAYBELLINE
     The thing is, sometimes I got the feelin' Curtis was
     more into the Harley than he was me.

                    MARY
     And that's bad? Hell, if it wasn't for Billie Dee
     Williams, I don't think Daryl could do it.

                    MAYBELLINE

It's like when Curtis sings a song. It sounds great, but
you don't believe he means it. He's just doin' it to be
cool. You know, like when Elvis sang one, you knew it
was from his heart.

                    MARY

Well, girl, let me tell you, Elvis is Dead.

                    MAYBELLINE

I know. And I'm gettin' too old to keep lookin' for one,
right?

                    MARY

Hell, you've already dated about every man in the
county.
                (pause; small laugh)
Except Earl.

Earl marches up the aisle towards the front of the store ready
to give it another try, but when he hears Mary mention
Maybelline's dating habits, he stops and begins to straighten a
honey display, eavesdropping in on their conversation.

                    MAYBELLINE

Well, most of the men around here ain't good for
nothin' but a havin' a good time. Of course, I ain't ever
been against havin' a good time.

Maybelline smiles.

                    MARY

You know that there ain't no man around here gonna
compare to a rich country star. You just need to get off
your ass and go for it.

                    MAYBELLINE
What do you want me to do? Propose to him?

                    MARY

No, you just need to go back to that party tonight in a
short black dress with a lot of cleavage and spend the
evenin' wavin' it in front of his nose.

Maybelline leans forward, pushes her breasts together to make
cleavage, while considering Mary's suggestion.

                    MAYBELLINE
What'd you think?

Earl, seeing this, turns quickly back to his work, knocking over a bottle of honey. He sits the honey back up right, but it spills onto his hand. He struggles with the sticky bottle.

> MARY
> I think, if you just give Curtis some of that Maybelline charm, he'll be cookin' you breakfast in the mornin', honey.

Earl, flustered, tries to wipe his hands on one of the toilet tissue rolls. It sticks to his hand, and the roll rips open as he struggles to free it. In seconds Earl's hands are covered in tissue as he tries to gather the spilling roll.

> MAYBELLINE (O.S.)
> You think he'd make me a back and grits omelet?

> MARY (O.S.)
> With hash browns and gravy biscuits.

> MAYBELLINE (O.S.)
> Stop it, girl, you're makin' me hungry.

A short elderly black woman pushes her buggy into Earl.

> WOMAN
> (shouting out of deafness)
> Do you know where the napkins are?

He tries to compensate for her shouting by talking real low.

> EARL
> (whispering)
> They're down the aisle.

> WOMAN
> What?

Earl tries to mime that it's down the aisle.

> WOMAN
> You all right?

Earl rushes down the aisle and grabs a package of napkins.

> EARL
> Here.

> WOMAN
> No! Not the table napkins. The Menstruation Napkins! My grandbaby havin' her first visit.

Everyone's attention is now focused on Earl and the Woman.
His face is red. He looks down at his hands and then up to
Mary and Maybelline who are looking around their magazine
racks, laughing. Early takes the woman to find what she
wants.

                              MARY
        He's pitiful.

                           MAYBELLINE
        Yeah, but he's kind of sweet.

Maybelline smiles as she watches Earl walk away, patiently,
with the Woman. Toilet tissue trailing behind them.

                              WOMAN
        Back when I had my first visit, we used rags. We'd just
        have to stop every now and then to wash 'em out.

INT. PRODUCE DEPARTMENT — LATER

Two shapes can be seen through the two small windows on the
stainless steel swingin' doors to the backroom.

                         JEROME (O.S.)
        You see, Earl, the Good Lord ain't made no fruit as
        sweet or as bitter as a woman.

JEROME, the produce manager, a 60 year old black man,
comes through the door, pulling a cart carrying produce, with
Earl in tow. They walk through the dairy section on their way
to the Produce department.

                             JEROME
        And there ain't nothing more addictive. A man will give
        a woman the last penny he's got and smile while he
        does it.

Jerome sits the peach back in the crate and starts pulling the
cart again.

                             JEROME
        You're missin' the point, boy. You got to look for the
        peach inside of her, and see her in a way ain't nobody
        ever seen her. Then talk to her with your peach.

                              EARL
                          (confused)
        I just want to know how to tell her how I feel.

JEROME

That's what I'm tellin' you, boy. You just look deep into
her eyes, past all the flesh, blood and bone, and see
that peach inside of her.

He stops the cart and grabs another peach.

JEROME

And then you speak to her from your peach. Something
like . . .
                    (he looks at the peach as if a lover)
"Baby, your sugar is sweet." But don't say it. Just
think it.

EARL

Jerome, I'm more confused now than when I came over
here.

Jerome puts the peach in Earl's hand.

JEROME

Here, you try it.

EARL

What?

Jerome positions Earl with the peach in front of his face.

JEROME

Now, look into her eyes, boy, and think, "Baby, your
sugar is sweet."

EARL

This is stupid.

JEROME
                    (insisting)
Just do it, boy. Seeee theee Peeaach.

Earl tries the most seductive look he can muster, but he looks
as if he's in pain.

EARL
                    (trying to imitate Jerome)
Baby, your . . .

JEROME

Think it. Don't say it.

Earl struggles with the thought, trying to telepathically seduce
the peach. He strains.

                          JEROME
    Don't hurt yourself, boy.

Jerome laughs, shakes his head, giving up. He takes the peach
out of Earl's hand and replaces it with another one.

                          JEROME
    Here, try this one. I think you scared that one.

Jerome starts pulling the cart again, leaving Earl standing
there with a peach in his hand.

INT. GROCERY STORE — FRONT — LATER

Maybelline sits on her register chewing gum, smokin' a
cigarette, and drinking a Dr. Pepper, while reading a magazine.
Mary sweeps the floor.

                        MAYBELLINE
    There's just this thing missin' from my life. Somethin',
    I don't think no man's gonna satisfy.

                          MARY
    What's that?

Maybelline turns her magazine around to reveal a picture of a
big shiny Peterbilt Truck.

                        MAYBELLINE
    A 359 Peterbilt with a 15 double over, and a Jake
    Brake.

                          MARY
    What?

Mary walks over and grabs the magazine.

                        MAYBELLINE
    When I was nineteen I had this thing for truck drivers.

Mary gives Maybelline a "Are You Kiddin'?" look.

                        MAYBELLINE
    You know, 'cause I ain't ever been nowhere, and they
    had. Anyway, it didn't take long to realize, it was the
    truck and not the man.

                       MARY
           (giving her back the magazine)
You're crazy.

                MAYBELLINE
I'm telllin' you that if it wasn't for my speedin' tickets,
I'd already have my CDL and I'd be haulin' a load of
cows down some lonesome interstate.

                     MARY
Now I know you're crazy.

                MAYBELLINE
           (going back to Magazine)
You've just never driven a Peterbilt.

                     MARY
Thank goodness.

                MAYBELLINE
Curtis never got it, either. He kept tellin' me I'd
outgrow it. The deal was if he made it, and I hadn't
outgrown it, he'd have to buy me a brand new
Peterbilt.

                     MARY
See, now you've got a reason to go to that party
tonight. To get a Peter Truck.

                MAYBELLINE
I guess it wouldn't hurt to go see if he's grown up any.
They say anything is possible.

                     MARY
You just pretend he's got one of them Peter trucks in
his pocket, and you'll be all right.

Maybelline looks back at her magazine and turns the page.

                MAYBELLINE
I don't know. I might could settle for a Freightliner,
long as it had a jake brake.

She shows Mary the picture and smiles.

INT. GROCERY STORE — BACK ROOM — LATER

Earl is sitting alone in his cubby hole, staring intensely at a
peach. Maybelline walks up.

> MAYBELLINE

There you are.

He turns to face Maybelline, hiding the peach behind his back.

> MAYBELLINE

What you got behind your back, Earl?

Earl looks at Maybelline like he practiced on the peach. He strains to send her his thought.

> MAYBELLINE

Damn, Earl, I just asked a question. You don't have to look at me like I pissed in your cornflakes.

He deflates and pulls the peach from behind his back.

> EARL

Sorry.

He sits the peach back on the dog food bag.

> MAYBELLINE

All that fuss over a peach? What's got into you today, Earl?

> EARL

Do you like chittlins?

> MAYBELLINE

What? Look, Earl, I was wonderin' if I could come in late tomorrow. I decided I was gonna go to that party.

Earl tries to hide his disappointment.

> MAYBELLINE

Do you think I can come in after lunch? You never know how late these things run.

> EARL
> (small protest)

Maybelline, you know Saturdays are our big day, and . . .

> MAYBELLINE
> (agitated)

Earl, I can't believe you would be so selfish. It's not like I ever ask for any time off.

                              EARL
                        (reluctantly)
            Well . . . all right.

                           MAYBELLINE
            Thanks, Earl, but it wouldn't hurt you to act like you
            hoped I had a good time tonight.

                              EARL
            Yeah, I hope you have a good time.

                           MAYBELLINE
            Earl, are you sure that you're all right? I think you
            might be comin' down with somethin'. You been actin'
            stranger than usual today.

She smiles.

                           MAYBELLINE
                        (walking off)
            Earl, I thought you were allergic to peaches.

Maybelline leaves. Earl picks up the peach, looks at it, and
tosses it into a box of trash.

INT. GROCERY STORE — SERIES OF SHOTS

This is a montage of people giving Earl advice. A Bugged Eye
PEST CONTROL MAN sprays the produce section as he speaks
to the CAMERA as if to Earl. Distracted, he sprays some of the
produce that is stacked on the floor.

                        PEST CONTROL MAN
            How to get a woman's heart?
                        (slimy smile)
            Try a chainsaw.

A Big Burly HUNTER stands next to the Beer cooler with a
twelve pack of Busch Beer in his hand.

                             HUNTER
            Don't bathe. It's like deer. They got to smell your scent.
            It'll drive 'em crazy.

A middle-age GREASY TRUCK DRIVER stands at the back
entrance of his truck. He tries to tell Earl the answer, but
stutters too bad to get through what he's saying.

DARYL, a 30-something overweight black man, poorly imitating
Billy Dee Williams in both look and voice, stands in the dairy
section holding a grocery basket filled with Colt 45.

                              DARYL
        Earl, Billie Dee don't have to worry about shit like that.

The Truck Driver still stutters.

A Hispanic MIGRANT WORKER stands in the Spanish Food
section of the stroe. He says something in Spanish.

                          MIGRANT WORKER
                            (subtitles)
        You could start by takin' off that fuckin' girdle.

The Truck Driver finally gets it out.

                              DRIVER
        Axle grease.

EXT. LOADING DOCK — SUNSET

Earl sits, despondent, on the loading dock as the sun sets.

EXT. GROCERY STORE — SUNSET

Earl, downtrodden, pushes a cart of groceries out for MR.
SASSER, an old man who talks by pressing one of those
vibrating things against his neck. He has thick glasses and
chews on a cigar.

                            MR. SASSER
                            (subtitles)
        Now, take that Curtis fellow. He's somebody we can be
        proud of. He ain't drivin' up and down these streets
        drinkin' and doin' dope. No, he's up in Nashille makin'
        something of hisself.

Mr. Sasser gives Earl a quarter for unloading his groceries.

                            MR. SASSER
                            (subtitles)
        You know why he made it, don't you?

Earl shrugs.

                            MR. SASSER
        'Cause he knew what he wanted and he went after it.
                          (he climbs in car)
        Most people just spend their lives thinkin' and talkin'
        about shit, but never doin' nothin' about it. Earl, don't
        be a thinker, be a doer. Now, let me hear you say it.
        Come on now.

> EARL
>
> Don't be a thinker be a doer.

Mr. Sasser drives off, smiling.

> MR. SASSER
>
> Now keep that up.

Earl watches, mumbling the line. He smiles as it sinks in.

INT. FRONT OF STORE — SAME

Earl turns the OPEN side to the CLOSED side and stands looking at his reflection in the glass door. He dabs on some cologne and straightens the girdle. Then he turns and walks towards the registers, mumbling Mr. Sasser's line over and over. Mary stands alone, counting her money.

> EARL
>
> Where's Maybelline?

> MARY
>
> She's reshelving the returns. You all right?

Earl takes off in search of Maybelline. Mary sniffs the air and makes a face about Earl's cologne.

> CUT TO:

Maybelline takes an item out of the grocery buggy and puts it back on the shelf.

> CUT TO:

Earl walks quickly down the end of the Aisles looking for Maybelline, mumbling his new mantra. He sees her at the other end of the aisle as she's leaving. Earl rushes quickly down the aisle. He's at the end when Joe comes striding out of the Meat Department.

> JOE
>
> Your troubles are over, my friend.

> EARL
>
> What?

Maybelline pushes the cart out of sight down the dairy aisle, on the other side of the store. Joe pulls Earl towards the Meat Department, while Earl looks back in search of a glimpse of Maybelline.

                              JOE
Wait 'til you see it.

Joe leads Earl, who continues to search through the window
[thinking his mantra] into the meat department. Gene is in the
corner hosing down the bloody floor. Something lies in front of
them on the table under a dirty meat apron.

                              JOE
Are you ready? I call it my Lover's Surprise.

Joe pulls the apron off revealing two mountain oysters placed
below a phallic-shaped pile of chittlins shink-wrapped on a
white Styrofoam tray, shaped like a heart. The chittlins are
supposed to be cupid's arrow.

Earl fakes a smile and then looks back out the window, his
eyes following Maybelline as she comes out the end of an aisle.
He politely listens to Joe, but waits for the opportunity to
leave.

                            JOE
   Now, you want to make sure you mix 'em up in a
   skillet with scrambled eggs and Hogs Brains. Then you
   got all your bases covered. And don't cook 'em over
   five minutes or you'll cook out their potency.

                           EARL
                    (starting to leave)
Thanks, Joe.

Gene steps in front of Earl and snatches the package from
Earl. He looks at it with disgust and then at Joe.

                           GENE
This is just sick.
                    (to Earl)
Who you gone listen to, Earl, a pervert pushin' hog ball
or your cousin who's tryin' to get your ass laid.

                           EARL
Get out of my way, Gene.

                           GENE
Look, Earl, I'll do you a favor. While you close up, I'll
pick us up a fifth of OFC, and then I'll take you out to
Bookie's tonight, and we'll get you a piece of ass. I
guarantee it.

Earl shakes his head and tries to push past Gene.

> GENE
> I guess you think you're too good to go out to Bookie's
> with a lowly meat cutter, huh?

He squirts Earl with the hose.

> EARL
> Now, cut it out.

> GENE
> Just 'cause you Manager of the goddamn Quickcheck,
> you think that you're better than the rest of us.

He sprays Earl again.

> EARL
> Stop it, or I'm gonna have to do something.

> GENE
> Oh, I'm scared.

He sprays again.

Earl looks down, picks up a big tray, and chases Gene, who
continues to spray him, into the freezer. Gene pulls the door
shut, but Earl's momentum can't be stopped, and he slips on
the watery blood and bits of flesh, crashing into the door, then
falling on his ass. We hear the girdle snap on the way down.
He sits wet and panting in front of the freezer door with his
head on his knees.

> GENE (O.S.)
> Let me out of here.

> EARL
> (giving up)
> It's over now.

He pulls the broken girdle out from under his shirt.

> GENE (O.S.)
> Damn it, Earl, it's cold in here, and my pants are wet!

> JOE
> You can't let yourself get so worked up over a woman.

                              EARL
She ain't just a woman. She's why I get up in the
morning. She's the only bright part of this miserable
job, and after tonight, she'll be gone.

Earl sits wet and defeated in watery blood and bits of flesh. He
looks at the unrepairable girdle.

                           GENE (O.S.)
I hope ya'll think this is funny.

                            JOE (O.S.)
Gene, I ain't had this much fun since Betty Sue rented
that Kamasutra Video.

                           GENE (O.S.)
I'm not laughing.

Earl just sits, defeated, holding the limp girdle.

EXT. FRONT OF STORE — CLOSING TIME

Earl, still wet, opens the door to let Jerome out.

                            JEROME
You got her all to yourself. Now's the time.

                             EARL
I think it's a little too late for that now. Goodnight,
Jerome.

Jerome walks back over to Earl and holds out a peach. Earl
doesn't reach for it.

                             EARL
Thanks anyway, but it won't do any good.

                            JEROME
                  (putting the peach in Earl's hand)
Take the peach, boy.

He turns and walks out into the night.

                            JEROME
You can't keep your peach hid forever, Earl.

Earl watches him go, unconvinced.

INT. CROW'S NEST OFFICE — SAME

Earl stands outside the office, by the still-playing radio.
Maybelline sits in the office filling out her paperwork.

                    EARL
    Do you mind if I cut this off?

                    MAYBELLINE
                (not looking)
    Sure whatever.

Earl cuts off the music and climbs into the office, trying to hide
his condition by putting on a coat. He puts the peach on the
counter in front of him and starts making a grocery order.
Maybelline notices the peach and then Earl's condition.

                    MAYBELLINE
    Damn, Earl, what happened to you?

                    EARL
    Gene.

                    MAYBELLINE
    I don't know why you put up with him.

                    EARL
    'Cause he's my cousin.

                    MAYBELLINE
    Still, Earl, you got to start standin' up for yourself.

                    EARL
                (turning back to work)
    Maybe you're right.

                    MAYBELLINE
    You know, a little backbone wouldn't hurt you, none.

They work in silence for a minute.

                    MAYBELLINE
    Earl, I'm sorry if I got a little short with you, earlier.

                    EARL
    It's all right.

                    MAYBELLINE
    You just ain't been yourself today. I think you been
    spendin' too much time in the meat department.

> EARL

I guess my mind's been elsewhere.

> MAYBELLINE

There ain't nothin' wrong with that. My mind spends most of its day in the front seat of a Peterbilt.

> EARL

I think it's good for a person to have dreams, like that. It's somethin' I always like about you. I ain't never had the courage to do much dreamin' myself.

Maybelline stops what she's doing and turns to face Earl.

> MAYBELLINE

You know, you're the only person that's ever called it that.

> EARL

What?

> MAYBELLINE

A dream. Most people think I'm a little crazy 'cause of wantin' to drive a truck.

Earl, nervous by Maybelline's attention, turns back to work.

> EARL

Everybody's got to want something.

> MAYBELLINE

What is it you want, Earl?

He didn't expect this.

> EARL

I can't say.

> MAYBELLINE

Come on, Earl. I know there's got to be something you've always wanted.

Earl pauses, looks at Maybelline, then he turns back towards his work. Trying to think of something to say.

> EARL

Well, nobody knows it, but I'm kind of a closet songwriter.

> MAYBELLINE

I didn't know you were musical, Earl.

> EARL
> > (he goes back to work)
> Yeah.

> MAYBELLINE
> What'd you play?

> EARL
> The guitar.

> MAYBELLINE
> What kind?

> EARL
> I got a couple. I got a Gibson J-45 flattop at home, and
> I keep an old Yamaha FG-460 at the store, for times
> when I'm here alone.

> MAYBELLINE
> You mean you come here on your time off? You need a
> life, honey.

> EARL
> > (explaining)
> I come here because it's quiet, except for the hum a
> sleepin' store makes. I write my best songs here.

> MAYBELLINE
> > (looking around)
> It's kind of sleepin' now, ain't it? Why don't you get
> that guitar and play me one of them songs.

> EARL
> Well, I really need to change the strings.

> MAYBELLINE
> Come on, Earl. I'd really like to hear one of your
> songs.

> EARL
> I couldn't. You're use to hearin' people like Curtis.

> MAYBELLINE
> I'll have you know, I used to be queen of the karioke
> down at the Charter House. And you can't be no worse
> than any of us were.

Earl hesitates and lets out a small sigh.

> EARL
> Well . . . Okay, I guess.

Earl gets up, climbs out of the office, and opens his secret compartment in the hollow under the crow's nest.

> EARL
> Just don't laugh.

> MAYBELLINE
> I might throw tomatoes, but I'd never laugh.

Earl gets the guitar out. He puts his leg on the steps and the guitar on his knee, and makes a few tuning adjustments and starts strumming.

> EARL
> I'm not used to playing with somebody listenin'.

> MAYBELLINE
> Don't be nervous, honey. It's just ole Maybelline. I'm an easy audience.

Earl sees the peach and decides to play a different song.

> EARL
> This one I've been workin' on. It's not quite finished.

> MAYBELLINE
> Okay, Earl, sing the song before we get old.

With his head looking down at the guitar, Earl stands below Maybelline and serenades her with a song that expresses the things he hasn't been able to tell her.* Maybelline sees a side of Earl she never knew existed. As he sings, he finally gets the courage to look up, and Maybelline smiles.

> CUT TO:

LATER

As the song continues to play, Earl and Maybelline dance down the aisles of the Quick Check. We PULL BACK through the register and PAN to the peach.

FADE OUT

* Earl's song:

I've often wondered if this moment came

Would I have the courage to call out your name

And could I look in your eyes without going insane

Darling, I'm calling you now

I've often wondered if I had the chance

Would I find the courage to ask you to dance

And could we waltz into some sweet romance

Darling, I'm asking you now

COOL BREEZE
AND BUZZ

INTRODUCTION

Lani Sciandra wrote *Cool Breeze and Buzz* in my screenwriting class in 1994 and directed it for a B.F.A. Thesis Film in 1995. Recently I asked her how the screenplay changed during production, and she said:

> We really didn't have a solid ending for the story through-
> out production—I had to communicate with and discover it
> through the actors—within the guidelines of the written
> scenes we re-invented as we went along—we all had to
> believe it was happening—I was never really convinced of
> my own dialogue and drew upon the silence more than the
> words for meaning—in fact, it was Sally (Aunt Barbara) who
> came up with the non-dialogue exchange between her and
> Buzz in the last scene that represents the crystalline moment
> of understanding for all of them, and solidifies the ending
> for me.

And the script continued to change in editing:

> There are certainly moments left in the film that don't quite
> land—tiny moments of trying to push meaning—since Jen-
> nifer (the editor) and I were still learning how to juxtapose
> images, the tendency was to relate the elements linearly—
> as we arrived at a fine cut, I became unsettled about what
> we had achieved—it felt stilted and forced, as if the motion
> were dragging itself—I thought it could propel itself more
> by cutting back the bulk—dismantle the safety net and trust
> the danger—we brought in our editing teacher Charlie Boyd
> to help deconstruct the narrative to a more visceral level—

approaching it like a piece of music—despite great opposition, we cut into it with effective results—it turned out to be a monumental lesson in identifying with and nurturing (my) instinct.

In 1995, *Cool Breeze and Buzz* won the Gold Award in the Student Category at Worldfest Charleston and the Gold Award at Worldfest Houston. In 1996 it was the winner of the Independent Film Channel Student Film Showcse, the CINE Eagle Award (Preprofessional/Amateur), the OSU Photography and Cinema Alumni Society Award from the Columbus International Film & Video Festival, and the Student Award at the Florida Film Festival. Also in 1996, *Cool Breeze and Buzz* was named Best Narrative at the Big Muddy Film Festival, Best Narrative Film at the Utah Film and Video Festival, the Trophy Winner for Movies On A Shoestring at the Rochester International Independent Film Festival, and best film in the dramatic category at the Tacoma Tortured Artists Festival. In 1997 it won the Juror's Choice Award at the Victoria Independent Short Film & Video Festival in Canada. In addition, *Cool Breeze and Buzz* has been screened at film festivals worldwide.

Lani is currently living in New York City. When I asked her what she's been doing since *Cool Breeze and Buzz*, she said, "Macrame."

COOL BREEZE AND BUZZ

Lani Sciandra

FADE IN:

BLACK SCREEN

We HEAR four long, deep BREATHS (CREDITS BEGIN)

CUT TO:

EXT. ST. MARK'S RIVER — DAY

CLOSE ON PAULA MCKINNEY

13, up to her shoulders in the water. She takes four more slow BREATHS then quickly ducks under water.

INDIAN SITAR MUSIC FADES IN AS CAMERA HOLDS ON WATER

until Paula emerges from under the surface, out of breath, having uncovered a broken arrowhead.

The year is 1967. Dense woods draped in moss align the river's edge. Nearby is a small delapidated wooden dock garnished with apple snails. A HERON combs the hyacinths on the bank for a meal.

Paula is petite with a gritty edge about her as she sits on the bank, her hair bleached from the sun, cleaning her findings from the river. She's got on a bathing suit, a pair of low-top Chuck's and scrapes on either knee. She holds up a dark specimen.

ANGLE ON SPECIMEN

It is a piece of a large jawbone, blackened from years under water. The teeth still intact.

She then places it in an old cigar box.

ANGLE ON CIGAR BOX

There is a fading b/w photograph of a young couple on the beach amongst various small artifacts.

THE MUSIC FADES (CREDITS END)

We hear LOCUSTS in the canopy of trees above. In the background is a silver Airstream trailer with a large canopy laced with small party lanterns and windchimes.

> AUNT BARBARA (O.S.)
> (from the trailer)
> Pau-la.

Her voice is DEEP AND RASPY. Paula doesn't answer and continues.

> AUNT BARBARA (O.S.)
> (louder)
> Paula!

Paula gathers her things and puts the findings in a bucket and walks to the trailer. She sets the bucket down before entering.

INT. TRAILER — DAY

It is a rather large-sized interior, adorned with a collage of unmatching, outdated furniture and knick-knacks. A large velvet painting of JFK centers over the TV.

Paula enters and the screen door SLAMS behind her. "The Ed Sullivan Show" BLARES from the set as AUNT BARBARA, 46, watches from the couch in a robe and curlers wrapped in a pink scarf. She lights a cigarette. Paula enters the kitchen and fixes a Kool-Aid.

> AUNT BARBARA
> (pointing toward kitchen)
> Paula honey, grab me my purse. I need for ya t' run up to the store fer me.

Paula grabs the purse off the counter and hands it to her.

> PAULA
> What'cha need?

Barb digs through her purse.

> AUNT BARBARA
> I need ya t' git me some Epsom salts.

She looks down to her foot.

                         AUNT BARBARA
     My bunyons r'on fire.

Paula holds herhand out as Barbara counts change from the
bottom of her purse, extinguishing her cigarette in the process.

                         AUNT BARBARA
     An' I got a splittin' headache . . . Please pay attention
     when I call you, girl.
                              (beat)
     Whew! This heat is unbearable.
                              (handing her change)
     Jus' git the smallest one they got.

Paula guzzles down her drink, wipes her mouth with the length
of her arm then sets the glass in the sink. The drink has left
her with a Kool-Aid moustache.

Barbara reaches for her leather cigarette case and discovers it's
empty.

                         AUNT BARBARA
     Ya' got any smokes?

                         PAULA
     No, I've been bummin off'a you, 'member?

Barbara takes a quick check in the purse. No more change.

                         AUNT BARBARA
                              (sighing)
     Well, the salts'll do.

Paula throws on a pullover raincoat and cut-offs over her suit
and exits. Barbara cringes as the screen door SLAMS.

EXT. CANOPY DIRT ROAD — DAY

Paula is walking down the barren dirt road, her coat tied at
the waist. Suddenly, a large red CADILLAC CONVERTIBLE
zooms by from behind, blowing a dense cloud of dust up.

                         PAULA
                              (shouting to car)
     Slow down before you kill somebody!

She begins coughing hysterically, brushing off the dust.

HER POV

of the Cadillac as it drives over a bridge and disappears in the trail of dust.

INT. FLOYD'S KIT N' KABOODLE — DAY

Paula opens the door and the bell RINGS. It's a typical small town general store with short aisles and shelves of medication behind the counter. A large FAN with streamers attached blows in a corner. Paula thumbs through a comic book at the magazine rack.

> FLOYD
> (to someone O.S.)
> Kin I help ya' find sumpthin'?

Paula peers over the comic book down the aisle.

HER POV

She sees a BLACK MAN in a business suit perusing the snack aisle.

She looks back to Floyd, who's becoming increasingly uneasy. Paula quickly shoves the comic book into the front pocket of her coat, unnoticed, then quietly meanders about the store as the Black Man approaches the front counter to pay. Floyd hands him his change.

> BLACK MAN
> No, keep it.

The Black Man leaves, and Floyd shrugs off the courtesy and puts it back in the register. Paula suddenly appears at the register.

> FLOYD
> (startled)
> You nearly scared the wits outta me, little missy.

He leans in, his eyes following the Black Man out the door.

> FLOYD
> You kin never turn yer back on
> 'em. Rob ya blind ev'rtime.
> (turning to her; beat)
> Now, what kin I do fer ya'?

Paula displays a mischievous grin.

                    PAULA
            (looking to shelves behind him)
    Um, yeah. I need a box'a Epsom salts, please.

                    FLOYD
        O-kay.

Just as he turns his back to scan the shelf, she reaches for a
pack of generic cigarettes on the counter.

                    FLOYD
                (slowly)
        Epsom salts . . .
                (grabbing box)
        Here ya'r—

                    PAULA
                (overlapping)
        No! The uh, smaller one.

She quickly shoves the pack in her coat and pulls her hand
back just in time and smiles as if nothing happened.

                    PAULA
                (quickly)
        It's for my aunt.

                    FLOYD
        That'll be sixty-five cents.

She unloads the contents of her pocket onto the counter and
weeds through the change.

ANGLE ON CONTENTS

comprised of a bubble gum comic strip, a polished tiger-eye
stone, a Zippo lighter and strands of twine and lint.

Curiously, Floyd picks up the stone, but Paula quickly rips it
from his hand.

                    PAULA
        I'll take that.
                (admiring it)
        It's my good luck rock. I found it. Cool, huh?

Floyd nods and counts the change.

                    FLOYD
        Fifty-nine, sixty . . . Sixty-five. It's all here.

>   FLOYD (CONT'D)
>   (handing her the bag)
> Thank you.

>   PAULA
>   (taking bag)
> No, thank you.

She smiles and parades toward the door.

>   FLOYD
> A bit hot fer a coat don't 'cha think?

She stops in her tracks then turns.

>   PAULA
>   (beat)
> Nope.

She turns and exits.

EXT. TRAILER — DAY

ANGLE ON PAULA

skipping along the river's edge reading the comic book. She reaches a clearing and the trailer comes into sight.

HER POV

of the trailer. The red Cadillac is parked in front.

She approaches the Caddy and proceeds to investigate.

CLOSE ON

A) her finger running along the side of the car through a thick layer of dust.

B) her hand wiggling the hood ornament.

C) the license plate on the front that reads, "JACKPOT."

Then suddenly, we hear a MALE VOICE.

>   MALE VOICE (O.S.)
> Beauty, ain' she?

HER POV

of a man, BUZZ MCKINNEY, 42, standing in the door at the top of the steps smoking a cigar.

                    BUZZ
              (beat)
Hey, Coolbreeze.

She drops the bag and freezes.

                    PAULA
              (staring up at him)
Hey.

He stands in slacks and a tight short-sleeved v-neck. Upon his belly, a huge brass buckle with a race horse and a large ring on either pinky.

Aunt Barbara appears from behind him.

                    AUNT BARBARA
Paula honey, yer daddy's come to see you.

There's an awkward pause.

                    AUNT BARBARA
Buzz, you gotta be hungry from all that drivin'. What do ya say I fix us a nice lunch. How's that sound?

There is a pause, then Barb enters the trailer.

                    PAULA
              (nodding to the car)
Nice wheels.

He walks down the steps toward the car.

                    BUZZ
              (proudly)
Won her in Atlantic City last Christmas.
              (beat)
Me an' a couple of poker buddies were runnin' the tables that night.

He smiles as he recalls the events. Paula listens.

                    BUZZ
Little did we know, was some House big shot waitin' in the wings all night for his shot. By dawn, he finally
              (reenacting the man's movement)
swaggered down a thick wad of 100's and challenges us a round, double or nothin'. So the boys elected me. An' I ain't never been one to turn down—

Aunt Barbara appears at the screen door.

                    AUNT BARBARA
                    (overlapping)
          Ya'll gonna stand out there all day? Le's eat.

                       PAULA
                     (guessing)
          So, you bought the car with the money?

                       BUZZ
                     (grinning)
          Even better.

He straightens out the hood ornament and takes out a
handkerchief from his back pocket.

                       BUZZ
                 (polishing the ornament)
          Beat him so bad he had to insist on another round.
          She's been mine ever since.

                       PAULA
                    (enchanted)
          Cool.

He looks at her for a moment and smiles.

                       BUZZ
          Come on.

They head for the trailer.

INT. TRAILER — DAY

CLOSE ON PLATE

as Barbara places it on the table, covered with Spam finger
sandwiches and pigs-in-blankets. Toothpicks in their centers.

On the table, a jar of pickles, boiled peanuts and ginger snaps.

                       BUZZ
                    (poking fun)
          Barb, I see you haven't lost your touch.

                    AUNT BARBARA
          Oh, now you jus' back off. If I'da known I'd be
          entertainin'—

> BUZZ
> (overlapping)

You'd still serve up the same slop.

They all dig in at the same time, each one scarfing as much as possible off the plate. Conversation has come to a standstill. We listen to them CHEWING their food.

> AUNT BARBARA

So where'd ya' say you were headed?

> BUZZ

Well, a colleague of mine in Miami gave me a tip that could very well make your little brother a very rich man.

ANGLE ON AUNT BARBARA

rolling her eyes.

ANGLE ON PAULA

listening.

> AUNT BARBARA
> (skeptical)

An' what's this tip?

> BUZZ
> (beat)

Vegas.

> AUNT BARBARA
> (flabbergasted)

Las Vegas? Whatcha wanna move to the middle of the desert for?

> BUZZ
> (wiping his brow)

So what! A little sun never killed no one. Can't be much worse than the swamp you're livin' in.

> PAULA
> (interrupting)

I hear Vegas is wild!

> AUNT BARBARA

But it's the desert, fer Chrissake!

                       BUZZ
What's the difference? You're gonna sweat your balls
off either way.

Barb gives him a look for the comment.

                       BUZZ
           (to Paula)
Sorry, honey.
           (to Barb)
Look, Barb, I got a plan and it's fool-proof. It can't fail.

                   AUNT BARBARA
A plan.

                       BUZZ
What can I say? Business has been good. And right
now, in the trunk of that car, I got enough money for a
down payment on a club of my own.

                   AUNT BARBARA
A what? A club? You know what kinda risk that is?
The things involved in something like that?
           (beat)
And what if it don't work out. Where you gonna go
then?

                       BUZZ
Look, I'm tellin' ya', it's gonna work. It's got to work. I
can feel it, B.

He notices Paula is just playing with her food.

                       BUZZ
Hey, Coolbreeze.

Paula looks.

                       BUZZ
What do you say we go out tonight. The three of us.

                   AUNT BARBARA
Can't. Tonight's single's bingo at St. John's an' I ain't
never missed a night. But you two go, don't worry
about me.
           (looking at watch)
Oh, heavens! It's nearly three-thirty!
           (getting up)
I gotta get ready, do my hair . . .

Barb unties her scarf and scurries to the bathroom.

> **BUZZ**
> (to Paula)
> When's bingo?

> **PAULA**
> Six.

They snicker.

> **BUZZ**
> Wait here, I'll be right back.

He heads out the screen door to his car. Barbara pokes her head out the bathroom door.

> **AUNT BARBARA**
> (indiscreetly)
> Paula, I think the two of you goin' out's a good idea. Give you some time alone to catch up.

She goes back in the bathroom. Buzz returns with a large dress box and hands it to Paula.

> **PAULA**
> For me?

She appears pleasantly surprised. She opens the box and pulls out a frilly pink dress that looks suited for a six-year-old. She holds it up with the tips of her fingers as if afraid to touch it.

> **BUZZ**
> Whatcha think?

> **PAULA**
> (hesitating)
> Wow. It's pink.

> **BUZZ**
> You can wear it tonight!

> **PAULA**
> But . . . I don't wear dresses.

> **BUZZ**
> (enthusiastically)
> It'll look great on you!
> (pause)
> Tell you what. I'll make a deal with you. You wear the dress and we'll do anything you wanna do.

> PAULA
> (surrendering)

Well . . .

> BUZZ

Okay, great!
> (beat)
So, what's to do around here?

Paula looks at the hideous dress then looks to him mischievously.

                                                    CUT TO:

EXT. WOODS — DUSK

Paula is in the dress and her Chuck's seated on a log. Buzz is knelt on the ground trying to light a fire with matches that keep blowing out. The Caddy parked in the background.

> PAULA
> (handing her Zippo)

Try this.

Buzz makes another unsuccessful attempt with the lighter. Paula kneels down and gathers some dry grass then takes the lighter, flips the lid and lights it in one motion. The fire starts.

                                                DISSOLVE TO:

EXT. WOODS — NIGHT

Paula and Buzz are roasting marshmallows over a bright fire. Buzz SMACKS a bug on the back of his neck.

> BUZZ

Ya'ouch!

> PAULA

You get used to it.

There is a pause.

> BUZZ

So, uh . . . your Aunt Barb's been taking good care of ya'?

> PAULA

Oh, yeah. She can have her moments, but I guess I do, too. I take care of her, and she takes care of me and all that junk. Yeah, she's cool.

                    BUZZ
Good, good . . . Glad to hear it.

                    PAULA
So you're really just passin' through then, on your way
to Las Vegas . . . Wow, how cool.

                    BUZZ
Y'well, I'm not just passin' through. I came to see you.
Is that cool?

                    PAULA
Oh, yeah. I just meant most people are just passin'
through anyway.
          (beat)
Woodville ain't nowhere anyone really wants to be,
they just gotta pass through us to get to wherever it is
they're goin'.

                    BUZZ
          (pause)
Y'know, I was a little afraid you weren't gonna
remember me.

                    PAULA
Really? I remember lots of things.

                    BUZZ
          (pleased)
Really? Like what?

                    PAULA
Like . . . I remember you used to have that real long
shaggy beard that used to itch so bad when you picked
me up.

                    BUZZ
          (amused)
Mmhmm.

He SMACKS another bug.

                    BUZZ
Dammit!

                    PAULA
Funny though, I remember you being a lot taller.

He laughs then looks at her profile illuminated by the fire light.

> BUZZ
>
> You know, you look so much like your mother. Do you remember her?

> PAULA
>
> Not really. I guess I was too young or something . . . But I remember everyone being really sad and crying and I didn't really understand all of it. Except when you took my hand and told me not to let go. And I didn't, 'cause I remember I got the worst cramp from squeezing so hard.

> BUZZ
>
> You didn't let go, did you?
> (pause)
> I really loved your mom . . . But when you can finally let go, it's tough turning back.
> (beat)
> I couldn't turn back.

The firewood POPS and the CRICKETS GROW LOUDER. They both stare off into the fire. Paula yawns.

> BUZZ
>
> Whelp. We'd better hit the hay. I'd like to get an early start.

They get up and lay out their sleeping bags.

FADE TO BLACK:

The sound of CRICKETS and FROGS intensifies. We then hear a soft RUSTLING in the woods.

CUT TO:

CLOSE ON BUZZ

as his eyes pop open from the SOUND in the woods.

He springs up in his sleeping bag, waking Paula.

> PAULA
>
> What is it?

> BUZZ
>
> Shh. Listen . . . There's something out there.

He stands and is apparently uneasy.

                              BUZZ
You, you hold tight.
                    (grabbing a stick)
I'll uh, take care of it.

They sit still and listen. Buzz peers into the blackness and
throws the stick. We hear SMALL FOOTSTEPS scurry away.

                              BUZZ
There it is, you hear it!

                              PAULA
Relax, it was just some harmless critter making his
rounds.

                              BUZZ
Oh. Yeah. Well, still, you can never know. Can't be too
careful.

He grabs a bigger stick and lays back down and tries zipping
the sleeping bag as far as it can go. She scoots in closer.

                              PAULA
Don't worry Dad, I'll protect ya'.

She smiles.

                                            FADE TO BLACK:

                                                    CUT TO:

EXT. WOODS — DAY

Paula slowly wakes from her slumber. There is no sign of
Buzz. His sleeping bag is empty. She stands up and scans the
area noticing that their cooler has been tipped over and its
contents are spread everywhere.

                         BUZZ (O.S.)
                    (shouting)
Shit! Ouch! Ooo—

Buzz suddenly appears from behind a tree trying to zip up his
pants.

                              BUZZ
Ants! Ah! Y'ouch!

Paula giggles as Buzz hits the floor swatting his bare feet.

> BUZZ
> What's so funny?! And did you see what your little
> critter friend did! That was my breakfast. Our
> breakfast!

He gets up and marches to the campsite still trying to swat the
ants. Paula is amused by the whole scene.

> BUZZ
> (under his breath)
> Harmless . . . I'll show you harmless . . . Great outdoors
> my . . .

He wraps everything off the ground in one of the sleeping bags
and dumps it into the backseat of the Caddy. Paula, trying not
to laugh, follows his lead and boards the car.

EXT. MOVING CAR — DAY

A funky 60's soul SONG plays as Buzz performs a cigarette
trick for Paula as they drive a long stretch of countryside.

> CUT TO:

EXT. TRAILER — DAY

Paula removes her findings from the bucket on the porch and
lays them out to dry. Buzz exits the trailer in clean clothes
carrying a small suitcase to the car, then joins Paula under the
canopy.

> BUZZ
> (referring to outside decor)
> I like what you did to the place. What'cha got there?

> PAULA
> Just some stuff I found in the river.

He looks at the small collection and picks up the piece of
jawbone.

> PAULA
> Mastadon teeeth.

> BUZZ
> Masta–what?

> PAULA
> Mastadon. Sorta like a wooly mammoth but without the
> wool. They're like ten or twenty thousand years old.

                              BUZZ
Impressive.

He sets the piece down.

                              PAULA
So, you got everything?

                              BUZZ
I'd like to think so.

He sits on the step and watches her sort her findings.

                              BUZZ
                         (beat)
Maybe you can come stay with me.

She looks to him.

                              PAULA
                         (puzzled)
You mean, like visit?

                              BUZZ
No, I mean for real.
                         (beat)
What do ya' say?

                              PAULA
Wow, you mean like all the way to Las Vegas? With
you?

                              BUZZ
All the way. With me.

She is stifled by the offer and doesn't say anything.

                              BUZZ
Well look, I'll have to go out there first to set up camp,
but you think about it and as soon as I get everything
in order, I'll come back for you.

                              PAULA
You know for sure if it'll really work?

                              BUZZ
                         (rubbing her head)
Now that's not for you to worry your pretty little head
over.

He looks to his watch.

> BUZZ
>
> I should really hit the road.

She says nothing. He stands and hugs her.

> BUZZ
>
> You just sit tight and I'll come back.

He boards the Caddy, and she watches him back the car to the road. Suddenly, she dashes out to the road.

> PAULA
>
> Take this.

She hands him the polished rock.

> PAULA
>
> It's for luck.

> BUZZ
> (driving away)
>
> Just hold tight.

She stands in the road and waves.

HER POV

as the car heads down the dirt road.

> CUT TO:

LONG SHOT

from the river of Paula watching the Cadillac drive off. Dust trails the road as the car disappears behind the trees. She goes to the top of the steps and pauses and looks up to the trees overhead and then to the river.

INDIAN SITAR MUSIC FADES IN

She disappears into the trailer.

FADE OUT.

TONGUE

INTRODUCTION

Andy Zare wrote *tongue* in my screenwriting class in 1993 and directed it for a B.F.A. Thesis Film in 1994. When I asked him how the screenplay changed in production, he said:

> I guess as a bunch of film students, we were quite ambitious. But we realized that we couldn't do everything. Scheduling was very difficult because of all the locations. A lot of rewrites involved changing scene locations due to availability and scheduling and sometimes dialogue was transferred from one scene to another. We cut one scene (the pool scene) because we couldn't get enough extras to show up in what turned out to be a very cold morning.

Other crucial factors, such as the actors and even, at times, the set, also affected the script:

> I gave the actors the freedom to improvise. Comedy can't be forced. If something didn't seem right in rehearsal, we'd change it. Sometimes the set would turn out to be a little different than I had initially visualized when writing the script, and that would change things. But I was never concerned with changing or adding lines as long as the story stayed intact.
>   The actor who played Leo, Earl Lamm, was quite charming. He came up with the idea to sing "That Old Joe Wagner" to the tune of "Old Man River."

And, of course, the script continued to change during editing:

The editor, Shawn Matlock, helped with some of the rewrites. He's responsible for a few lines like the "Flytrap" line in the superhero dream.

During the rough cut I stayed away. But I got involved after that. The heart of the story never really changed with editing. Editing was more about how to make the story tighter and easier to follow. In retrospect, there may have been some things we could've tightened, but I think we got it to work pretty well.

In 1994, *tongue* won the Gold Award at Worldfest Charleston and it was a finalist at Worldfest Houston and the U.S.A. Film Festival. In 1995 it won the bronze plaque in the student drama category at the Columbus International Film and Video Festival. And it has been screened at a number of film festivals in the United States and abroad.

After finishing *tongue* and graduating from the Florida State University Film School, Andy moved to Los Angeles where he works at Green Umbrella Productions, a small company that produces science documentaries for PBS's *Nova* and other similar shows. He still writes screenplays, "mainly comedies."

TONGUE

by Andy Zare

FADE IN:

INT. SMALL BATHROOM — NIGHT

The screen is covered by an unidentified pink object.

>   JOE (V.O.)
>   Many people like to say they're different. But I really
>   am.

CAMERA PULLS BACK TO REVEAL THE OBJECT: A HUMAN
TONGUE

Crowded up next to his bathroom mirror is JOE WAGNER,
twenty-something. He is skinny, young, frail, and sporting a
bad haircut. Joe pokes and prods his tongue in intense
examination.

>   JOE (V.O.)
>   My name is Joe Wagner, and I have been cursed.
>   Cursed with a most unusual ability: my tongue. It tells
>   me things I don't want to know. I don't know why or
>   how, but I can't stop it ... or live with it.

EXT. SMALL LAKE — DAY (FLASHBACK)

A YOUNG JOE sits on the edge of the lake. Next to him is a
pretty young girl, SARAH, dressed in traditional female wooing
apparel. The two look into each other's eyes, both nervous yet
willing, and move closer together.

>   JOE (V.O.)
>   I knew something was wrong ever since Sarah. She was
>   my first kiss ...

The two kiss. First a small one, then a bigger.

>   JOE (V.O.)
>   ... and I swore it would be my last.

Just as the kissing is about to lead somewhere, Joe abruptly
breaks contact. Joe's expression turns from curiosity to horror.
Sarah is not sure what is going on.

179

                    JOE (V.O.)
When I kissed Sarah, I kissed every single boy she had
ever kissed before.

                    YOUNG JOE
Sarah? Did you just kiss Adam?

Sarah is not sure what to say. The two stare at each other,
shocked with their discoveries.

EXT. SCHOOL PLAYGROUND — DAY (FLASHBACK)

Young Joe is fighting another boy, ADAM. Adam is about the
same build, but appears to be a bit more agile. A SMALL
CROWD cheers them on. Adam lands a few blows, drawing
blood from Young Joe. Young Joe now whimpers on the
ground. He has been defeated. Adam stands over him.

                    JOE (V.O.)
The trouble with Adam was that he was my best
friend.

                    ADAM
What were you doing kissing her anyway?

A small drop of blood drips from Young Joe's mouth.

                    ADAM
You should keep your tongue out of other people's
business.

                    JOE (V.O.)
I lost Adam's friendship, but I took his advice.

INT. BATHROOM — MORNING

Joe is brushing his teeth. The brushing is vigorous and
forceful. Occasionally the brush will wander onto his tongue,
massaging it.

                    JOE (V.O.)
For years I was afraid to even talk to anyone. I figured
the fewer people I knew, the better.

EXT. JOE'S NEIGHBORHOOD — LATER THAT MORNING

Joe rides an old rusty bike that SQUEAKS when he pedals.

EXT. LEO'S FLORIST — LATER THAT MORNING

Leo's Florist in an old, small shop with no other buildings
nearby. A small parking lot is in front and a small garden is

around the side. Joe rides up to the shop on his bike. He dismounts, leaves the bike up against the wall, and goes into the shop.

> JOE (V.O.)
> So I took the simplest job I could find . . . working with plants.

INT. LEO'S FLORIST — CONTINUOUS

The florist is densely covered with all types of plants. The shop is bright and colorful. A counter is off to the side, and an office is in back. Everything is well organized. The owner, LEO BARYLSKI, a large, cherubic man sporting a Hawaiian shirt, appears from the back of the shop. He greets Joe with a smile.

> LEO
> (singing)
> It's Joe Wagner! It's Joe Wagner, and he's come to work at my flower shop! It's Joe Wagner, gonna work, gonna never stop!

Leo laughs at his own song routine. Joe ignores him and walks into the office in back.

> LEO
> Hey, Joe, aren't you gonna ask me if I have any good news?

> JOE (O.S.)
> No.

INT. LEO'S FLORIST — LATER

Joe is kneeling down taking inventory of the plants. ANNA ZHENIA, a petite girl with a natural smile, a sparkle in her eye, and a bounce in her step, enters the shop. Her energy is contagious. She is beautiful, but not dangerously beautiful. She approaches Joe.

> ANNA
> Excuse me, I'm Anna Zhelia. Are you Leo?

Joe is startled. And when he looks up at Anna he becomes frozen by her simple beauty and composure.

> JOE
> He's in back . . . Can I help?

> ANNA
> I need to speak to him about the job.

                    JOE
              (suddenly puzzled)
        The job?

INT. FLORIST OFFICE — LATER THAT DAY

The office is a small room with two desks on opposite sides.
Various types of plants are scattered all over the room. Leo is
seated at his desk doing some paperwork. Joe stands, fidgeting,
in front of Leo's desk.

                    JOE
        Why didn't you tell me?

                    LEO
        I didn't want you to worry. It's not about you; I just
        need some more help around here.

                    JOE
        What if I don't get along with her?

                    LEO
        Then I'll fire you!

                    JOE
        What?

                    LEO
                  (laughing)
        C'mon, Joe. You get along with everybody.

INT. LEO'S FLORIST — NEXT DAY

Joe and Anna are stocking plants. Joe is stooped down,
working the bottom shelf. Anna is several feet away, working
the top shelf. Joe cannot help taking an occasional glimpse at
Anna. Anna knows why Joe is checking her out. She smiles
back, causing Joe to look away. It is an awkward moment for
Joe.

                    ANNA
        So, Joe, tell me about yourself.

Joe looks up to answer, but he has problems getting any words
to come out of his mouth.

                    JOE
        Ahh . . . Umm . . .

                    ANNA
        What's the matter? Cat got your tongue?

                         JOE
My tongue?

Joe inadvertently drops a few plants on the ground. Anna
moves over to Joe and helps pick up the plants.

                        ANNA
Here, let me help you.

The two begin to clean up the mess. They are very close to
each other now. Anna smiles at Joe. He starts to smile back, a
nervous smile, but turns away to hide it. Joe is blushing.

                         JOE
Thanks.

                        ANNA
Hey, it's okay. I don't bite.

INT. JOE'S BEDROOM — NIGHT

Joe rests asleep in bed.

                      JOE (V.O.)
I have this recurring nightmare that I'm part of this
freak show.

EXT. CITY FAIR — DAY (DREAM SEQUENCE)

We are at a small city fair. There is a great commotion
surrounding a big cage.

The cage is decorated in vivid colors. "THE TONGUE" is written
on it in big letters. Blindfolded and sitting inside the cage is
Joe. There is a small opening in the steel bars of the cage for
his mouth. In front of the cage is Leo, dressed in a bright red
tuxedo. DOZENS OF PEOPLE crowd around.

                         LEO
Step right up! Try to fool the man with the golden
tongue! Feed him anything; he'll identify it for just a
dollar!

An anxious audience watches as Joe is fed a small wad of
gum.

                         JOE
Tasty's Sugarfree Spearmint Gum which has been
chewed on by Roger Tomkins, right after he gobbled
down a plate of barbecue chicken, all dark meat, and
Mrs. Greeley's homemade baked beans.

The crowd, including ROGER TOMKINS, a young man, breaks into APPLAUSE. Leo has a big smile.

Joe is given a small morsel of dog food.

> JOE
> A morsel of Chunky's brand dog food which came from
> the bowl of Mr. Pocklington's Collie, Brutus. And by the
> way, Mr. Pocklington, your dog has been seeing a lot of
> Mrs. Sather's Chihuahua, Minky.

The CROWD LAUGHS. MR. POCKLINGTON, an elderly man, is not amused.

Someone hands Joe a hot dog.

> JOE
> A hot dog with ketchup, mustard, and pickle relish,
> from Walt's Wiener Stand. Pretty fresh; this one was
> alive three days ago.

The CROWD MURMURS. They are somewhat disgusted.

Joe is handed a small cup of ice cream and a spoon. He tastes it.

> JOE
> Ice cream. Tutti Frutti. Belonging to little Dougie
> Gilmour. And I don't know how this happened, but Mrs.
> Gilmour, you dropped your left contact lens in it.

The audience bursts into WILD LAUGHTER. MRS. GILMOUR, a middle-aged woman, looks bewildered.

Suddenly a LARGE AND UNATTRACTIVE WOMAN lunges towards Joe and gives him a big kiss on the mouth. Taken by surprise, Joe fights the kiss, but the woman sticks to him. In panic, Joe flips his blindfold off to see his assailant. Finally, he disengages from her. The LAUGHING OF THE CROWD BECOMES INCREASINGLY LOUDER. Joe SCREAMS!

INT. FLORIST — DAY

Leo licks an "Elvis" stamp as he spies on Joe. Anna wanders through the florist, humming a simple tune and stopping to smell the flowers as she goes. Her movements are graceful and elegant. With sick puppy eyes, Joe spies on her from inside the main shop. His face is full of longing.

> LEO (V.O.)
> Why don't you ask her out?

INT. FLORIST OFFICE — LATER THAT DAY

Joe and Leo are seated at their respective desks wetting
stamps and envelopes. Leo licks with his tongue while Joe uses
a sponge.

                         JOE
        What?

                         LEO
        You like her, don't ya?

                         JOE
        What do you mean?

                         LEO
        You stare at Anna like you're trying to memorize her.

Joe laughs uneasily. Leo stares at him as if he's trying to
probe his mind. A smile creeps onto Leo's face. Joe is aware of
this and is uncomfortable.

                         JOE
        I can't ask her out.

                         LEO
        Why not?

Joe cannot come up with an answer. He freezes for a moment,
hoping that Leo will not follow up.

                         LEO
        Come on, I know she'd say yes.

                         JOE
        I don't know.

                         LEO
        Ask her!
                    (beat)
        Joe, I've known you for a few years. Never have I seen
        you with a girl, you're not . . . you know . . .

                         JOE
        No.

                         LEO
        Okay then, here's a tip from Uncle Leo: Relax, enjoy it,
        and let me know if you score.

Leo laughs again. Joe smiles involuntarily at Leo.

INT. LEO'S FLORIST — DAY

Anna is watering some of the plants. Joe is packing a floral
arrangement, dressing it up to be delivered somewhere. Joe
looks at Anna as if he wants to say something. Anna
approaches Joe.

> ANNA
> Hey Joe, what are you doing tonight?

> JOE
> Excuse me.

> ANNA
> You have any plans for dinner?

> JOE
> (hesitantly)
> No.

> ANNA
> You like Chinese food?

> JOE
> I suppose.

> ANNA
> Great, I'll pick you up at seven, okay?

Joe is caught off guard. He looks like he is not sure about
what has just happened.

EXT. JOE'S NEIGHBORHOOD — THAT AFTERNOON

Joe rides his bike home. He has a smile on his face, and a kick
in his pedaling. The SQUEAKING of his bike is really
prominent.

> JOE (V.O.)
> I started thinking that this would be all right.

EXT. JOE'S APARTMENT — THAT EVENING — 7:00 P.M.

Anna drives up in a yellow Volkswagen bug and TOOTS ON THE
HORN TWICE. Joe trots out to greet her and gets into the car.
The two drive away.

> JOE (V.O.)
> I liked Anna . . . just as long as I didn't have to
> kiss her.

INT. SMALL CHINESE RESTAURANT — LATER THAT EVENING

Anna and Joe are seated across from each other. Both are eating with chopsticks. Joe does not eat any meat. He picks out some of the vegetables and carefully examines them.

> ANNA
> You're mighty particular about what you put in your mouth.

> JOE
> I guess that's just my little quirk.

The two make brief eye contact. Anna gives Joe a warm smile. Joe tries to hide his smile and looks back down at his food.

> ANNA
> So, how long have you been at Leo's?

> JOE
> About four years. What about you?

> ANNA
> Two days.

> JOE
> No, I mean . . . you know.

> ANNA
> Well, actually, I thought it would be interesting to work in a florist shop. I love flowers. I guess you could say I have a little green thumb.
> (laughs)
> And I figured I could also make a little extra money for college. I'm trying to get my degree in theater.
> (beat)
> Actually, what are you doing this weekend?

> JOE
> Why?

> ANNA
> Cause I'm performing.

> JOE
> Performing?

> ANNA
> (smiling)
> Yeah, I'm a clown at the town circus.

                         JOE
          A clown?

                         ANNA
          Yeah.

                         JOE
          Really?

                         ANNA
          Yeah.

Anna nods. Her smile grows into a small laugh.

EXT. JOE'S APARTMENT — LATER THAT EVENING

Anna and Joe walk up to Joe's front door.

                         ANNA
          Well, it was nice.

                         JOE
          Yes, thank you.

Anna stares into Joe's eyes. Joe knows what this means. He
backs off. Anna draws closer, her advance is strong.

                         JOE
          Well, good night.

Joe abruptly turns and heads into his apartment. Anna takes
the cue and disappointedly backs off.

INT. JOE'S BEDROOM — NIGHT

Joe rests asleep in bed.

                         JOE (V.O.)
          I had another weird dream last night.

EXT. PUBLIC SWIMMING POOL — DAY (DREAM SEQUENCE)

DOZENS OF PEOPLE are enjoying the swimming pool. Joe is
sitting in the lifeguard's chair. He does not seem to realize why
he is there. Suddenly, there is a big commotion in the pool. A
girl is drowning. In a moment, we realize it is Anna.

                                        CUT TO:

Anna lies on the pool deck unconscious. Joe kneels down by
her side. He is not sure what to do. A crowd has gathered

around them and everyone is staring at Joe. He slowly makes a move to begin CPR, but stops himself at the last moment. He takes a deep breath and makes another attempt, but is again unsuccessful. The crowd is getting anxious.

Suddenly, Leo emerges from the pool.

> LEO
> What's the matter, Joe? Can't give her CPR?

Anna opens her eyes and lifts up her head.

> ANNA
> Yeah, what are you waiting for?

Joe is still frozen.

INT. LEO'S FLORIST — LATER THAT MORNING

Joe is packing a small floral bouquet. Leo enters the room.

> LEO
> So, did you give Anna the ripe banana?

Leo laughs, but Joe is appalled with him.

> JOE
> Not funny, Leo.

> LEO
> (erupting with laughter)
> You know you love it.

> JOE
> (after a beat)
> What are you doing this weekend?

> LEO
> Me?

> JOE
> Yeah.

> LEO
> I don't know.

INT. CIRCUS — DAY

Anna is dressed as a clown and is doing her routine. Joe and Leo are sitting in the front row amongst a SMALL CROWD.

Anna does a few tricks. Joe and Leo laugh in approval—Leo laughing harder than Joe. Anna comes over to Joe and motions for him to smell the flower on her shirt. Sure enough, when he bends over to smell it, water squirts out and splashes Joe all over his face. Leo laughs even harder and Joe follows.

EXT. MINIATURE GOLF COURSE — DAY

Anna and Joe are sharing the grip on a putter. Joe seems a bit uneasy with the close physical contact. The two putt the ball. It is wildly off target and ends up in a nearby bush. Both laugh. Anna moves to retrieve the ball. Joe hangs on to the putter.

> JOE
> What made you want to become a clown?

> ANNA
> I like making people laugh.

> JOE
> You do a good job.

> ANNA
> Thank you.

Anna puts the ball back down on the course. She moves over to Joe and grabs the putter so that they are both close together again.

> ANNA
> There's something safe about hiding behind a mask—having people laugh at you. It makes me feel good.

The two make eye contact again, and almost kiss. There is a little tension in Joe's face. Joe escapes the kiss by stroking the putter again, shifting Anna's focus to the ball. Both turn to follow it. The ball heads towards the hole and rims out.

> ANNA & JOE
> Ohhhh!

EXT. SMALL LAKE — DAY (DREAM SEQUENCE)

It is the same lake from Joe's past. Joe and Anna sit in the same position that Young Joe and Sarah did earlier. Anna is even dressed like Sarah was.

> JOE (V.O.)
> I had an even weirder dream last night.

The two look into each other's eyes, both nervous yet willing, and move closer together. The kiss. First a small one, then a bigger. Suddenly their lips disengage. Anna backs off. She has an expression of horror.

> ANNA
>
> What's wrong with your tongue?

Joe slowly opens his mouth, revealing a condom placed over his tongue. Utterly shocked and disgusted, Anna screams. Joe has a "why me?" look on his face.

INT. JOE'S BEDROOM — MORNING

Joe awakes, screaming.

INT. LEO'S FLORIST — DAY

Joe waters some small plants while Anna moves a few bags of fertilizer into the main shop. As she walks by Joe, she glances at him. She is looking at his hair. She smiles and catches Joe's attention. Joe continues watering. Anna returns for more bags, pausing before she passes Joe this time.

> ANNA
>
> Joe?

> JOE
>
> Yes?

> ANNA
>
> Who does your hair?

> JOE
>
> Why? Is it funny?

> ANNA
>
> It's just a little long. I can do hair, ya know.

INT. ANNA'S APARTMENT — DAY

Anna's apartment is bright and clean. Joe sits in a chair in the middle of the room with a towel wrapped around his neck. Anna stands behind Joe with a pair of scissors. On the counter is a hand mirror and an electric shaver. Anna moves around Joe, making a few strategic clips. Small clumps of hair rest on the ground. Joe's eyes are shut. He is enjoying the haircut.

> ANNA
>
> You have really thick hair.

                          JOE
          I know. I've always had problems combing it.

                          ANNA
          Oh, you should feel lucky to have hair like this. I'd kill
          to have hair like yours.

Anna stops for a second to examine what she has done. For a
moment she seems unsure of herself. Anna cuts a lock of hair
and winces immediately. Joe cannot see, but Anna's face says
"Oops!"

INT. FLORIST OFFICE — DAY

Joe sits at his desk doing some paperwork. Anna's haircut has
made his hair worse. Leo enters the room and does a double-
take at Joe. Leo walks right up to him and stares at Joe's
haircut, prompting Joe to look up.

                          JOE
          What?

Leo bursts into hysterical laughter. Joe self-consciously runs
his fingers through his hair.

                          JOE
          Anna gave me a haircut.

                          LEO
                    (still laughing hard)
          I'm sorry.

Leo grabs a baseball cap by his desk. He puts it on Joe's head
and leaves the room. Joe takes the hat off and looks at it.

MONTAGE SEQUENCE

HAPPY POP MUSIC PLAYS. Joe and Anna are seen having fun
together. Activities include: shooting pool, foosball, air hockey,
an arcade game, croquet, checkers, connect four (or some
other board game), twister, table tennis and basketball.

EXT. JOE'S APARTMENT — NIGHT

Joe and Anna stand close together.

                          JOE
          I really had fun today.

                          ANNA
          Yeah. Me too.

After a brief staring match, Anna lunges forward to kiss Joe. Joe is taken by surprise but manages to narrowly weasel his way out of the kiss. The two bump each other, triggering nervous laughter from both. Joe quickly slips inside his apartment, leaving Anna alone.

INT. FLORIST OFFICE — DAY

Joe and Leo are sitting at their desks. Leo is reading a gardening magazine. He turns the periodical sideways and gawks at the centerfold.

>   LEO
> Whoa, get a load of this one!
>   (pause)
> You know, if gardening were sex, I'd be a nymphomaniac!

Leo laughs at himself, but Joe ignores him. Leo looks over at Joe with concern.

>   LEO
> Hey, how are things with you and Anna?

>   JOE
> I don't know.

Joe continues working, obviously not interested in talking. Leo seems even more concerned now.

>   LEO
> A little sexual tension, eh?

>   JOE
> I'd rather not talk about it.

>   LEO
> Try it. Women like it.

>   JOE
> Leo, shut up!

EXT. JOE'S APARTMENT — NIGHT

Joe and Anna stand close together after another date. Their lips move closer. Then Joe backs out.

>   ANNA
> Dammit, Joe. What's the matter?

Joe looks away and shakes his head.

> ANNA
>
> You're gay?

> JOE
>
> No . . .

> ANNA
>
> Married?

> JOE
>
> No.

> ANNA
>
> Well then, what is it?

Joe is ashamed. He cannot give bring himself to answer. Anna is very upset, more so than Joe has ever seen her. She struggles to keep her composure.

> ANNA
>
> Is there something wrong with me?

Joe sheepishly shakes his head indicating "no." The two stand in confrontation for a few moments. Both are visibly uncomfortable.

> JOE
>
> I'm sorry. It's just me.

The two are at in impasse.

EXT. APARTMENT — NIGHT (DREAM SEQUENCE)

Wearing "Clark Kent" glasses, Joe knocks on the door. He discovers that it's already open and enters.

> JOE
>
> I had the weirdest dream the other night.

INT. ANNA'S APARTMENT — CONTINUOUS (DREAM SEQUENCE)

The apartment is Anna's. Everything is a mess, furniture tipped over, books scattered on the floor. Someone has deliberately done this.

> JOE
> (looking around)
>
> Anna?

Joe spots a half-eaten sandwich on the table. Cautiously, he approaches it and takes a bite.

                    JOE

Oh my God! Anna's in trouble!

Joe rips open his shirt, revealing a big tongue insignia underneath.

INT. DARK CELLAR — MOMENTS LATER (DREAM SEQUENCE)

We can barely see Anna, who sits in a chair in the center of the room, bound up and gagged. The door opens, letting more light in. We see Joe, dressed in a cheesy superhero outfit, complete with a bright red cape. Anna looks up at Joe.

                    JOE

Anna!

                    LEO (O.S.)
                 (sinister)

Well, if it isn't "The Tongue."

                    JOE

Leo!

                    LEO (O.S.)

Leo?

Leo appears out of the shadows. He is wearing an equally cheesy villain outfit with a big black exclamation point on the front.

                    LEO

Leo's dead my friend. You can call me "Flytrap!"

Leo belts out a boisterous laugh. With his tongue hanging out, Joe darts directly at Leo, jumping on him and wrestling him to the ground. Anna watches intently as the two skirmish.

Leo pulls out a giant "Elvis" stamp and shoves it at Joe. It has the same effect on him that Kryptonite has on Superman. Leo laughs maniacally.

                    JOE

No . . . feel . . . dizzy . . . must . . . save . . . Anna!

INT. JOE'S BEDROOM — MORNING

Suddenly breaking out of his dream, Joe wakes up.

INT. LEO'S FLORIST — DAY

Joe enters the shop and is immediately confronted by an unhappy Leo at the door.

                              LEO
        What the hell happened?

                              JOE
        What?

                              LEO
        Anna quit—said she's had enough of this place. Did
        something happen between you two?

Joe's realizes what this means and his stomach sinks.

EXT. PARK — DAY

Joe sits on a park bench. He has the "why me?" look again.
We HEAR CHILDREN PLAYING in the background. A WOMAN
walks by with a DOG on a leash. The dog's tongue droops
down, almost as if to taunt Joe. In view is a YOUNG COUPLE
kissing on a nearby bench. Joe tries not to look, but cannot
help himself from sneaking a few glances.

INT. ANNA'S APARTMENT — AFTERNOON

The phone rings. Anna picks it up.

                              ANNA
        Hello?

EXT. PHONE BOOTH IN PARK — CONTINUOUS

                              JOE
        Anna?

INT. ANNA'S APARTMENT — CONTINUOUS

                              ANNA
        Joe?

EXT. PARK — LATER THAT NIGHT

Joe sits on the same bench as he did earlier. He waits
nervously. Anna arrives and sits next to him. The two look at
one another for a moment, trying to find a clue as to what
each other is thinking.

                              JOE
        Hi.

                              ANNA
        Hi.

JOE

So, you quit.

ANNA

What did you want to talk to me about?

Joe takes his time to gather up all his thoughts.

JOE

Anna, there's a reason why I can't kiss you . . .
             (beat)
It's my tongue.

ANNA
             (in disbelief)
Your tongue?

JOE
             (rambling)
I have this super sense of taste. It's awful. I'm afraid
to kiss anyone. I'd know their whole past.

ANNA

What are you saying?

JOE

If I kiss you, I'd know too much about you.

ANNA

Well this is a good one. I've been told many things
before. But this one wins on originality.

JOE

You don't believe me?

ANNA

The last one suddenly developed a fear of clowns.

JOE

Spam!

ANNA

What?

JOE

I had it once when I was a kid and I knew exactly
what was in it.

ANNA

What the hell are you talking about?

> JOE

Milk. One sip and I know when it'll expire. I'll know
about the cow it came from. My tongue has these . . .
powers, and it's cursed me my whole life. That's
why I'm afraid to kiss anyone. I know it's weird, but
it's true.

> ANNA

Okay, kiss me and tell me something about myself.

> JOE

I can't.

Anna gets up and starts to leave. Joe gets up a split second
later.

> JOE

Wait.

> ANNA

Joe Wagner, you're a liar and a coward, and I don't
want to see you or your tongue ever again.

Anna leaves. Joe starts to pursue her, then stops. He watches
her until she is out of sight.

INT. JOE'S APARTMENT — LATER THAT EVENING

Joe sits slumped on his couch, depressed and completely void
of energy. An OLD MOVIE is on the TV. It is at the climax of a
love scene. The COUPLE on the screen are on the precipice of a
kiss. Joe squirms a little as the kiss occurs.

INT. ANNA'S APARTMENT — CONTINUOUS

Anna watches the same old movie on TV. But her mind seems
elsewhere. She is upset and confused.

INT. JOE'S APARTMENT — CONTINUOUS

The MUSIC from the old movie gets LOUDER. Joe picks up a
large knife lying on the table next to him. He sticks out his
tongue, lifts up the knife, and closes his eyes. After a long
moment he opens his eyes and lowers the knife.

INT. ANNA'S APARTMENT — CONTINUOUS

Anna is now more involved with the old movie. It seems to
have a soothing effect on her.

INT. JOE'S APARTMENT — CONTINUOUS

Joe grabs his tongue with one hand while holding the knife in the other. He moves the knife around, searching for the perfect point of incision.

INT. ANNA'S APARTMENT — CONTINUOUS

Anna is very calm and pensive. She looks up at the wall to a big picture of a happy clown and studies it for a moment.

INT. JOE'S APARTMENT — CONTINUOUS

Joe closes his eyes again and moves the knife closer to his tongue. He coughs a few times, causing him to lower the knife temporarily. He takes a deep breath. Once more, Joe sticks his tongue out and raises the knife to it.

At that moment, the door swings open. It's Anna. Joe opens his eyes and freezes with the knife next to his protruding tongue. Anna cannot believe what she sees.

                    ANNA
     Joe!

Joe pulls the knife away from his tongue. Ashamed to have been caught, he hastily tosses the knife aside.

                    JOE
     What are you doing here?

                    ANNA
               (shaking)
     I wanted to apologize.
               (beat)
     What are you doing? This is because of me?

                    JOE
     It's not you. It's me.

Joe cannot even bring himself to look at her. Anna's mind is now racing, trying to piece things together. Then something hits her.

                    ANNA
     Close your eyes.

                    JOE
     What?

> ANNA
>
> Do as I say. I'm not going to hurt you.

Joe is confused, but eventually closes his eyes. Anna slowly approaches him.

CLOSE-UP OF JOE

Anna moves into frame and kisses Joe on the mouth. Joe is startled. He opens his eyes and tries to push off Anna. Anna will not be denied and Joe submits after a second. The kiss is gentle and long. When it ends, Anna pulls away slowly, looking into Joe's eyes for his reaction. She smiles a devilish grin and laughs. Joe is in shock.

> ANNA
>
> Now tell me something.

Joe is nearly hyperventilating. He struggles to gain his composure.

> JOE
>
> You had leftover tuna casserole for dinner. Leftover from Tuesday. You washed it down with milk which expires next Monday. After dinner you had a bowl of butter pecan ice cream. Then you brushed your teeth with mint toothpaste. You want lunch?

Anna cannot believe Joe's accuracy. She tries to remain calm.

> ANNA
>
> Who else have I kissed before?

Joe is hesitant to answer. A look of relief suddenly creeps over his face. He looks up at Anna.

> JOE
>
> I don't know.

Joe's eyes are racing. He has been struck by a thousand points of light. His face is alive. Anna is mesmerized by Joe's behavior.

> ANNA
>
> You don't know?

> JOE
>
> I don't know.

Joe begins to laugh, and Anna soon follows. Joe's laughing gradually builds. He becomes delirious, laughing so hard that a tear rolls down his cheek. Not sure as to whether Joe is happy or sad, Anna stops laughing.

                              JOE
        This is beautiful.

                              ANNA
        What?

                              JOE
        I don't know.

                              ANNA
        Don't know?

                              JOE
        No.

                              ANNA
        No?

Joe takes a moment to gather himself. Anna waits patiently.

                              JOE
        I don't know if this will make any sense.
                    (beat)
        My tongue is great with food. I can tell you anything
        about anything. But I guess it doesn't work as well on
        people as I'd imagined.

WIDE SHOT OF THE ROOM

Joe continues talking to Anna MOS. His story seems very strange to Anna, but she seems to accept it.

                              JOE
        I told Anna my story about Sarah and all the trouble
        my tongue had gotten me into. I can only figure that
        Adam was a lucky guess. It turned out that I didn't
        have the "kiss of death" like I thought I did. It felt
        good to have someone to talk to. Anna encouraged me
        to view my tongue as a "gift."

INT. LEO'S FLORIST — DAY

Leo is carrying a huge bag of fertilizer. He whistles as he walks and soon passes by Joe and Anna. They are partially concealed by some plants and are busy kissing.

                    LEO
          He shoots; he scores!

Leo laughs and continues walking. Joe and Anna stop kissing
and laugh as well.

FADE OUT

LENA'S SPAGHETTI

INTRODUCTION

Rachel Witenstein wrote *Lena's Spaghetti* in my screenwriting class in 1994. The B.F.A. Thesis Script Committee (which chooses up to five scripts to produce for thesis films every year) voted unanimously to produce Rachel's screenplay.

I asked Rachel to describe the process of writing the script, and she said:

> The "mail relationship" in *Lena's* is an invention that came about through the process of trying to come up with an idea for your screenwriting class at F.S.U. My first idea had something to do with a plant shop run by an eccentric lady, I think, and I just kept flip-flopping characters and situations until it felt like something I wanted to write. If something wasn't inspiring me, I just changed it. I kept adding in bits that I saw in real life, like the character of the father as a breast surgeon. My father isn't a breast surgeon, but I read an article in the *New York Times* about one, and his flamboyance really tickled me, especially in contrast with a girl who is experiencing a certain amount of anxiety about her own development.

But the journey from script to screen was less joyous, more like Nora Ephron's description of The Process, "a polite expression for the period when the writer, generally, gets screwed."

> I had a horrible experience with the production process. But in the end, I learned a lot, and maybe someone reading this will learn from what's happened to me. The screenplay had been chosen for production unanimously by a committee of

professors and older students at F.S.U. I received a lot of praise for it. But the director added unnecessary scenes and took out a lot of the flavor and humor, even to the point of making references to "going to church" when the family was written as Jewish. Ironically, in the editing process, virtually everything that he added was cut, so I felt somewhat vindicated. But there was something irretrievable that definitely did not make it on to the screen and that still makes me sad, even today.

"If you're very lucky as a writer," Ephron says, "you look at the director's movie and feel that it's your movie, too."

In the end, although she admires the film, Rachel cannot honestly say she feels that *Lena's Spaghetti* is her movie, too:

It did win a lot of awards. The production value was good for a student film. Some of the acting was good. The music was ambitious. The credits were ridiculously long, but they showed that a lot of people worked very hard to make *Lena's Spaghetti*—and worked for free. I feel good that I created a story that moved people to work so hard. It must have touched them on some level. But I never felt comfortable using it as a "calling card" to lead to other work after school because the film doesn't represent my style, my range, or my interests as a writer.

But the version of the screenplay published here is hers. It's the final script from my class and the one selected by the B.F.A. Thesis Committee.

Both the script and the film—though quite different—are wonderful works. The film, directed by Joe Greco, won First Place in the student drama category at the Columbus International Film & Video Festival, First Prize in the comedy category at the 26th Annual Canadian International Film/Video Festival, the OSU Photography & Cinema Alumni Society Award, and the Crystal Reel (First Place) for Best Cinematography and Best Actor at the Florida Motion Picture & Television Association. *Lena's Spaghetti* has also been screened at numerous film festivals at home and abroad, including Telluride.

After graduating from F.S.U., Rachel worked in film production in Los Angeles, then went on to study screenwriting at both USC and UCLA and write the feature *Neither Wolf Nor Dog*, to be directed by John Irvin. Her company, raw©opy, writes for motion picture advertising. She is a two-time recipient of the Academy of Motion Pictures Arts and Sciences grant for screenwriters.

LENA'S SPAGHETTI
by Rachel A. Witenstein

FADE IN:

MAIL. Two hands leaf through a stack of mail. They come across a PICTURE POSTCARD. It fills the SCREEN.

A MAN kisses an almost transparent angel.

The postcard flips over. It is signed in deep red ink:

"With oceans of love, and a kiss on every little ripple, Rosalie."

INT. MAILTRUCK — DAY

Settled back into his seat, postman HERBERT MACK, 33, is absorbed in reading the postcard. He waves it in front of his nose and inhales perfume. He sighs, slips the postcard into a bundle of mail and leans out the window to put it all in a mailbox. From the sack beside him, he grabs a new bundle and leafs through it. He finds another postcard to read.

EXT. MAILTRUCK — DAY

Another mailtruck approaches. The driver, ADELE, inches up beside Herbie for the big scare. She HONKS.

> ADELE
> Caught ya, Herb!

Herb jumps, puts the mail in a mailbox, watches her drive away.

                                                    CUT TO:

EXT. QUAINT SUBURBAN NEIGHBORHOOD — DAY

Herbie's truck passes Southern homes. We hold on HANNAH GOLDIN, 13, who sits on a swing hung from a tree, writing in a notebook. A moving truck pulls out of the driveway. CAROLINE AND STANLEY GOLDIN carry bags to their car. THUNDER grumbles.

                              CAROLINE
              Come on, Hannie! It's time to go!

Hannah scowls and scribbles furiously in the notebook.

                                                    CUT TO:

CREDITS ROLL:

INT. GOLDIN FAMILY CAR — DAY

The Goldin family car starts and pulls out of the driveway.
Rain runs down the back window as Hannah forlornly watches
her house disappear.

                                                 DISSOLVE TO:

EXT. TO INT. MAILTRUCK — DAY

Through windshield wipers we see Herbie trying to stuff
mailboxes without getting wet. He drops a few pieces of mail
into the swirling gutter stream. He splashes out into the rain
and chases the mail down the street.

                                                 DISSOLVE TO:

EXT. HIGHWAY — SUNSET

With the city in the background, the car drives out of town.

                                                 DISSOLVE TO:

INT. THE GOLDIN FAMILY CAR — NIGHT

Sunk real low in the back seat, Hannah stares out the window.
We hear Caroline SINGING soft harmonies with the RADIO.
After giving her mother an annoyed look, Hannah dons
headphones, plays a tape.

                                                 DISSOLVE TO:

EXT. HERBIE'S APARTMENT — DAY

Wearing his postal uniform, Herbie walks to his mailbox. He
opens it, peers inside and closes it, empty-handed.

END CREDITS.

                                                    CUT TO:

INT. HERBIE'S APARTMENT — DAY

Canvasses are stacked against the walls. Some are hung. None of the artwork is figurative. It should reflect a mind in isolation. An empty canvas rests on an easel. A table is cluttered with painter's paraphernalia. The shades are drawn.

COLA PLUM, Herbie's stylish, fragile mother, opens the shades. Disturbed, she flips through the stacks of artwork. Her concern increases as she inspects a dark, shadowy work. She shakes her head slowly. Herbie enters, already unbuttoning his postal shirt.

COLA
(smiling bravely and kissing him)

Darling. How are you?

She licks her thumb to wipe the lipstick off his cheek.

HERBIE

Mom. What a surprise.

COLA

I was just passing by . . . I was looking at your paintings, Herbert.

HERBIE

Oh. Well?

COLA

Very . . . Powerful . . . dark and, well, a little dismal, don't you think, sweetheart?

HERBIE

You see what you want to see, Mom. I didn't ask you to look.

COLA

Let's just stop this right now. I didn't come here to quarrel.
(pulls a number out of her purse)
Herbert, Evelyn's daughter is getting a divorce.

HERBIE

Oh, I'm sorry it didn't work out.

Cola stares at Herbie incredulously.

Herbie exits to the kitchen. Cola follows, calling after him.

                          COLA
      Sorry?

INT. HERBIE'S KITCHEN — SAME

Herbie pulls out a can of spaghetti and opens it with an
electric can opener. He starts eating it right out of the can.

                          COLA
      She's going to be single! Use a plate. Herbie dumps the
      spaghetti on a plate.

                          COLA
      Here's her number. You should—

Herbie exits with the plate. Cola follows.

INT. HERBIE'S APARTMENT — DAY

Herbie sits down at the art table and eats amongst the paints
and brushes. Cola stands across from him.

                          COLA
      Can't you allow me just this small happiness? I'd like
      to see you paint something . . . beautiful for a change!

                          HERBIE
      Mother, I'm sorry. I'm just not interested in that kind
      of thing.

                          COLA
      I see. Should I have gotten her ex-husband's number
      instead?

                          HERBIE
      What?

                          COLA
      I've seen your painting, Herbert. Not even one picture
      of a woman!

Cola exits, leaving Herbie speechless.

                                                    CUT TO:

INT. HERBIE'S APARTMENT — NIGHT

ANGLE ON: Herbie's eyes. We pull out to see him slouched by
his easel, tapping his teeth with a dry paintbrush. The dirty

plate is next to him. He stares at the blank canvas. With one sweep, he knocks it off the easel, revealing the naked window behind it. He sees his neighbors through the window of another apartment. Herbie crosses to the window to get a better look.

EXT. TO INT. DANNY AND JULIE'S APARTMENT — SAME

HERBIE'S POV: DANNY holds the ladder as JULIE climbs it to unscrew a dead lightbulb. From the ground, he hands her a fresh one. The window brightens. He climbs the other side of the ladder to face her. They kiss and descend the ladder, somehow still joined at the lips. The lights go off.

INT. HERBIE'S APARTMENT — SAME

Frustrated, Herbie sighs and pulls down the shades.

                                                    CUT TO:

EXT. APARTMENT COMPLEX IN HERBIE'S ROUTE — DAY

Herbie stands beside his truck, stuffing the grid of mailboxes. A young couple, FORD and MAY, approach him hand-in-hand.

                        AMY
        Got anything for apartment "M"?

Herbie hands them a letter.

                        AMY
        Ford, it's from you?

                        FORD
        Read it, Honey.

Herbie stands next to Amy, waiting for her to move. He tries to tell her, but can't. Oblivious, she leans back against the mailboxes to tear open the envelope.

                        HERBIE
        Uh, excuse me . . .

                        AMY
                  (reading the letter)
        Amy Madison. I love you with everything I have. Will
        you marry me?
                  (looks at Ford)
        Really, Sugar?

> FORD
> Yes, Angel. Will you marry me?

> HERBIE
> (under his breath)
> I can't believe this!

> AMY
> (throws her arms around him)
> Of course I will! Yes! I do I do I do!

Herbie tries to sneak behind the smooching couple. Amy bumps him.

> AMY
> Oh, I'm sorry. I didn't realize . . .

> HERBIE
> It's okay.

Herbie watches as Ford and Amy walk back to their apartment.

                                        CUT TO:

INT. NEWSPAPER BUILDING — DAY

People swarm around the lobby. Herbie stands in a long line of CUSTOMERS under a SIGN which reads: "Classifieds: Employment, Lost & Found, Pets, Automobiles, Garage Sales, Personals, Obituaries." He steps forward, accidentally kicking the back of the shoe of the woman, GINA, in front of him. She gives him a cold look.

> HERBIE
> So sorry.

The clerk, CLARK, is a bodybuilder, a real "stud." He fills out a form as Gina dictates, but he is actually busy checking her out.

> CLARK
> Reward?

> GINA
> Of course.

Adele passes though the office, carrying a package. She is in uniform, but her knee socks are bunched around her ankles. She walks with a spring in her step and has sparkling eyes. She spots Herbie.

                        ADELE
Hiya, Herb!

                        HERBIE
Hi, um . . .

                        ADELE
Adele. Read any good postcards lately? Just kiddin',
everyone does it. Well, I do anyway. Whatcha doin'?

                        CLARK
Can I help you?

                        HERBIE
Oh, I uh, lost my cat.

                        ADELE
Wow, how sad. What's he look like?

                        HERBIE
Well, he's . . . black. And he looks pretty much like
a cat.

                        CLARK
Reward?

                        ADELE
Well, I'll keep my eye out. Bye.

She walks away, balancing the packages precariously on her
head.

                        CLARK
Hey! Reward?

                        HERBIE
No. No reward. No cat.

                        CLARK
What?

                        HERBIE
                   (quietly)
An ad. A personal ad.

Clark snorts a laugh. He pulls out a different form and slaps it
down on the counter with a hand.

                                        CUT TO:

EXT. HARVEST STREET FAIR — DAY

A FERRIS WHEEL. A CAROUSEL. And LOTS OF PEOPLE. Three
school buses line the street. Bouncing above a CROWD of
jostling fairgoers, Hannah Goldin jumps on the trampoline of
the HUMAN FLYTRAP. She is dressed in a velcro suit. Small
earrings frame her clean face. Each of her fingernails is
painted a different color. A DJ broadcasts live over speakers,
piping GRUNGE MUSIC through the sunny fair. Hannah smiles
at ADAM, a fourteen-year-old boy teddy bear of a boy. He
tosses a baseball and watches with JARRETT, DICKIE, and a
group of four BOYS. The radio music tails out.

                    DJ (O.S.)
     We're havin' a blast here at the Harvest Fair! So come
     on down! Bring the kids!

                    DICKIE
               (elbowing Adam)
     That new girl likes you, Adam!

All except Jarrett laugh. Jarrett scowls.

                    DJ (O.S.)
     I think they're ready for a new volunteer at the dunk
     tank! Only two tickets gets you the chance to get this
     lovely Hooter's girl wet!

Adam and the boys dart through the crowd over to the dunk
tank. Hannah turns as she bounces, helplessly watching Adam
walk away.

                    DJ (O.S.)
     We've got lots of rides, lots of games, and of course,
     what fair would be complete without the Human
     Flytrap!

Frustrated, Hannah flings herself at the velcro wall and sticks,
spread eagle. She laughs, then realizes that she is unable
to move and panics. She yanks furiously with her arms
and legs.

                    DJ (O.S.)
     Oh my God! A little boy is stuck to the wall for our
     enjoyment! Everybody look!

The crowd looks and LAUGHS. Hannah closes her eyes and
grits her teeth. Her face burns.

DJ (O.S.)
Oh, sorry, a little girl! I didn't see the earrings. Gotta
come out folks . . .

CUT TO:

INT. SCHOOL BUS — SAME DAY

Hannah sits alone on the empty school bus, scribbling furiously
in a journal.

HANNAH (V.O.)
I hate this school. I hate Adam. I hate our new house. I
hate velcro. I hate my nose—

The greasy BUS DRIVER opens the door. Hannah slams the
notebook shut as kids with carnival prizes pass her seat. Adam
passes without noticing her. Jarrett stops next to Hannah.

JARRETT
(yelling to the back)
Dickie Nelson, get the hell out of my seat!

He notices Hannah and snorts a laugh before pushing to
the back.

EXT. SCHOOL BUS — SAME DAY

Hannah gets off the bus alone, her backpack over her shoulder.
As the bus pulls away, Jarrett and his gang are seen pressed
up spread eagle against the back window, imitating Hannah.
She runs for home.

CUT TO:

EXT. NEIGHBORHOOD STREET — SAME DAY

Hannah runs down the middle of the road. She stops to catch
her breath. A MOVING VAN drives by. She hurls a rock at it as
it passes.

HANNAH (V.O.)
Hello, I'm back. Dad says I hate everything because I'm
thirteen and that I need to put things in perspective.

CUT TO:

EXT. RAILROAD TRACK — SAME DAY

Hannah kicks rocks along the tracks, still toting her backpack.

                                    HANNAH (V.O.)
          So I've decided to start writing to "Lena," since when
          I'm older, I'll be a famous actress with lots of
          perspective, and "Lena" will be my stage name.

                                                        CUT TO:

EXT. HANNAH'S HOUSE — DAY

Hannah trudges through the yard of her new house. She opens
the front door and disappears inside, slamming the door
behind her.

                                    HANNAH
          So, dear Lena, I'm sure you can remember, this has
          been the most humiliating day of my life.

                                                        CUT TO:

INT. HANNAH'S ROOM — NIGHT

Hannah sits on her bed under a SMALL READING LAMP,
writing in her journal. She closes it, CLICKS OFF the lamp and
walks to her desk to put her journal away. Moonlight spills
into her room.

EXT. TO INT. HANNAH'S BEDROOM — SAME

Looking very small and young in her nightgown, Hannah
stares out her window.

                                    HANNAH (V.O.)
          Lena, you are the only friend I have.

                                                        FADE OUT:

FADE IN:

INT. HANNAH'S BEDROOM — NEXT MORNING

Hannah lies on the very edge of her bed, awake. The bed is
covered with mounds of meticulously arranged stuffed animals.
The room is filled with unpacked boxes. Caroline pokes her
head in as she buzzes the house. She wears a smart business
suit with no makeup.

                                    CAROLINE
          Hannah! I'm not going to tell you again.

> HANNAH
> (weakly)
> But Mom, I don't feel good.

Stanley enters the room with a newspaper in one hand, a thermometer in the other. He places his lips on her forehead.

> STANLEY
> You don't feel warm. What hurts?

> HANNAH
> My stomach and my head. And I have the chills.

> STANLEY
> Let's take your temp, Babe.

He sticks the thermometer in her mouth.

> CAROLINE (O.S.)
> She's normal, Doctor Goldin.

> STANLEY
> (calling to Caroline)
> With our genes? I doubt it.
> (Hannah rolls her eyes)
> Keep it under your tongue.

Stanley sits at the front of the bed and opens the newspaper. He offers Hannah a section.

> STANLEY
> Got the old paper form back home. Comics?

She puts them aside. Humming an opera, Stanley reads but feels Hannah looking at him. He looks up and speaks after a pause.

> STANLEY
> I know this move was hard on you, Babe.

Hannah's eyes fill with tears but do not spill over.

> STANLEY
> But there's only room for so many breast surgeons in one town. Do you understand?

Hannah nods. Stanley looks a little relieved. He tries something.

> STANLEY
> But you know what? I'll tell you a secret if you promise not to tell any of my patients. They're all beautiful.

Hannah rolls her eyes. Stanley plays now. He acts out the following shapes of breasts to Hannah while he sings this rhyme.

> STANLEY
> There are tubular boobies and conical domes. Ptotic droopies and little young ones . . .

Hannah laughs. She spits the thermometer out.

> HANNAH
> Dad!

Stanley picks up the thermometer and reads it.

> STANLEY
> Well, Mom's right, kiddo. You're normal. Congratulations.

> HANNAH
> Daddy, I feel sick. Can't you take my word for it?

Hannah gives him puppy dog eyes.

                                                    CUT TO:

INT. HANNAH'S BEDROOM — LATER

Hannah jumps on the bed. She flops onto her stomach, picks up the comics, looks them over with a straight face. She turns the page and sees the personal ads. She brightens as she reads.

THE PERSONAL AD FILLS THE SCREEN:

"Like to write? Single male seeks unique female for pen-pal. Please write: Herbert Mack. 8013-B Duck Lane. Savannah, Georgia, 41256."

MUSIC SWELLS.

                                                    CUT TO:

INT. HERBIE'S APARTMENT — NIGHT

Herbie stares at the blank canvas. The phone RINGS. Suddenly inspired, he feverishly mixes paints. After four RINGS, his ANSWERING MACHINE can be heard.

> HERBIE (V.O.)
> Hello, this is Herbert Mack. I'm not home, Mom. I'm on a date with Cindy Crawford. And no, I haven't gotten a letter yet.

Herbie strokes a deep blue on the canvas. The machine BEEPS.

> COLA (V.O.)
> Herbert, change your message!

He stops and looks at what he has done. Dissatisfied, he opens a tube of black and paints over it.

> COLA (V.O.)
> What if I was a girl calling? It sounds like the only calls you ever get are from your mother. Call me when you get home.

Herbie finishes painting the entire canvas black

> FADE INTO THE BLACK:

IN BLACKNESS:

The sound of RAIN ON ALUMINUM is heard.

INT. HERBIE'S MAILBOX — DAY

Herbie opens the SQUEAKY mailbox door, throwing light into the deep cavern. It is empty. Herbie's disappointed, wet face fills the hole. He slams the mailbox shut.

EXT. MAIL TRUCK OUTSIDE HERBIE'S APARTMENT — DAY

Settled back into her seat, Adele is absorbed in a postcard. She wears her postal uniform but looks more polished than usual. The sound of a DOOR closing startles her. She sees Herbie exiting his apartment. She smoothes her eyebrows. Herbie jogs to the mail truck.

> HERBIE
> Anything for 8013-B?
> (recognizes Adele)
> Oh, hello. When did you get this route?

                          ADELE
                  (hands him his mail)
A while ago. I hope you found your cat, 'cause I saw a
black one. On the road.

                          HERBIE
Uh . . . Oh! No. Nope.
                  (holds up the postcard)
Did you, uh . . .

                          ADELE
Yeah. She sounds nice.

                                              CUT TO:

INT. HERBIE'S APARTMENT — DAY

Herbie runs into his apartment, reading the postcard. After a
moment he picks up the phone and dials.

                       COLA (V.O.)
Hello?

                          HERBIE
Mom! I got a letter!

                       COLA (V.O.)
Finally. From a woman?

                          HERBIE
Yes from a woman!

                       COLA (V.O.)
Well, read it to me.

                          HERBIE
Okay. "Dear Herbie. Hi. I am writing because I usually
write myself, but I thought it would be a nice change to
actually get a response.
                  (he chuckles)
I'm an actress. I'm from the West and I miss my home
in the mountains. My favorite food is spaghetti. I have
two Siberian Huskies with ice blue eyes, named Lapis
and Lazuli. What about you? Lena."

                       COLA (V.O.)
That's it? What does she look like? Did she send a
photo?

He waves the postcard in front of his nose and inhales, grinning.

                              HERBIE
     She's beautiful, Mom.

MUSIC BEGINS: It is a simple, yet lyrical piece.

                                             CUT TO:

EXT. HANNAH'S HOUSE — DAY

Hannah sits on the front steps, writing in her journal. A mail truck pulls up to the house. She runs to it. The POSTMAN hands her a bundle of mail. She pulls out a letter on the way back to the house and slips it in her journal.

INT. HANNAH'S HOUSE — SAME

Hannah enters the house. It is a mess with boxes and furniture in the wrong places. There is a grand piano in the foyer. She puts the mail on top and squeezes past it.

                         CAROLINE (O.S.)
                    (calling from the kitchen)
          Time for lunch, Hannie!

                              HANNAH
     Not hungry.

Caroline appears behind the kitchen counter with a phone propped up to her ear by her shoulder. She places a bowl on the counter.

                              CAROLINE
          I made Spaghetti O's.

Hannah takes the bowl without her mother noticing.

INT. HANNAH'S BEDROOM — SAME DAY

Hannah closes her bedroom door, flops down on her bed and tears open the letter. She eats as she reads it, delighted.

                              HANNAH
          Dear Lena. I can't believe how lucky I am. Your letter
          was wonderful. You are a charming and witty woman.
          Life in the theatre sounds so exciting. It's funny, the
          only thing I cook is spaghetti . . . and not very well.
          Could you send me your recipe? Herbie.

Wide-eyed, Hannah drops her spoon into the almost empty bowl of Spaghetti O's.

                                                    CUT TO:

INT. HERBIE'S KITCHEN — NIGHT

The flame of a gas burner IGNITES. Onions are simmering, tomatoes are basting, water is boiling. The counter is a mess with spices and dirty cutlery. Holding a postcard, Herbie carefully measures ingredients into a steaming pot of sauce. He opens a can of pineapple chunks, checks the postcard again and doubtfully stirs them in the pot. He tastes a spoonful and smiles.

ANGLE ON: The back of the postcard fills the screen. It reads: LENA'S SPAGHETTI, and is followed by a recipe.

                                                    DISSOLVE TO:

INT. SCHOOL BUS — DAY

ANGLE ON: A small painting of a mountain range.

Hannah sits alone among the CHAOS of the school bus, leaning her head against the window, staring dreamily at the painting. Jarrett passes by her seat and gives her a dirty look. She takes out a postcard and begins to write.

                    HANNAH (V.O.)
          Dear Herbie. Thank you for the mountains. When I look
          at them, I breath in golden air and exhale silver.

                                                    DISSOLVE TO:

INT. MAIL TRUCK — DAY

A PILE OF MAIL is stuffed into a mailbox. Herbie stuffs mailboxes without reading any postcards.

                    HANNAH (V.O.)
          I can see through the ceiling to the stars.

EXT. MAIL TRUCK IN A SUBURBAN NEIGHBORHOOD — DAY

Herbie drives down the beautifully foliated road.

                                                    DISSOLVE TO:

INT. HANNAH'S HOUSE — DAY

Hannah helps her father hang a swing in a tree in the front yard.

                    HERBIE (V.O.)
     Dear Lena, Even though it's only once a week, it's so
     good to talk to someone who understands me, who
     thinks the same way I do.

                                        DISSOLVE TO:

INT. HERBIE'S APARTMENT — NIGHT

Herbie sits at his easel, rereading a postcard. He sets it on top of a stack of postcards and letters, and begins to paint.

                    HERBIE (V.O.)
     I wish I could see your play. I'm sure you'll make a
     great Juliet. I'll be thinking of you. Break a leg, Lena.

MUSIC ENDS.

                                        CUT TO:

INT. SCHOOL BUS — DAY

SOUNDS OF CHAOS. Hannah sits in her usual seat, alone, reading a letter. Across the back seat, Jarrett, Adam, Dickie and a few other BOYS play a bouncy game of poker, using a backpack as a table. Several CLASSMATES watch, hanging over the back seat.

                    JARRETT
               (chewing on an unlit cigar)
     Adam, you in? Don't be a wuss.

The bus hits a bump, the cards go flying.

                    ADAM
     I'm not playing unless we get a flatter table. This
     sucks.

Jarrett takes the cigar out of his mouth and stands.

                    JARRETT
     How about your girlfriend?
               (bellows to Hannah)
     Hey!

Jarrett wads up a piece of paper and tosses it. It lands on Herbie's letter. Hannah quickly folds it into the envelope.

                    JARRETT
    Hey! New Girl!

Hannah is caught by the address on the envelope. It reads: "Miss Lena Gold."

She takes a deep breath, then stands to face Jarrett.

                    HANNAH
    My name is not "New Girl." It's—

                    JARRETT
    —New Boy? That's right! Adam says we need
    something flat to play on, New Boy. Any Ideas?

Jarrett's BOYS laugh, give him five, and do the "spread eagle."

                    BUS DRIVER
    No standing on the bus!

                    HANNAH
              (walking towards him)
    Yes, Jarrett, I do have an idea. Your flat Neanderthal
    head!

The entire bus reacts in amazement.

                    JARRETT
              (steps into the aisle)
    Eat me!

                    HANNAH
    Barely a mouthful!

                    STUDENTS
    Oooooooooo!

ANGLE ON MIRROR: The bus driver's eyes dart to the back of the bus.

                    BUS DRIVER
    Sit down, both of you!

They stand eye-to-eye.

                    BUS DRIVER
    Jarrett Buxell! Sit down or I'll write you up.

Defeated, Jarrett sits. His BOYS react, disappointed.

> BUS DRIVER
>
> You too, Girl!

> HANNAH
> (to the driver)
>
> Hannah!

> BUS DRIVER
>
> Sit down or walk!

She doesn't move. The entire bus is quiet. Everyone looks at Hannah with wonder.

> BUS DRIVER
>
> Now!

Hannah sets her jaw.

CUT TO:

EXT. BUS — DAY

The bus WHEEZES as the door opens. Hannah trudges down the stairs and starts walking with her head down.

As the bus drives off, we see the faces of her classmates, including a girl, JJ, staring at her out the window.

CUT TO:

EXT. HERBIE'S APARTMENT — DAY

As Adele drives up, she see Herbie leaning up against his mailbox. With paint smudged on his face, he whistles merrily as he waits for the delivery. She checks her hair, leans out the window, hands him his junk mail.

> ADELE
>
> Hiya Herb.

> HERBIE
> (flipping through the mail)
>
> Hey . . . Isn't it Wednesday?

> ADELE
>
> Can't fool you! Yep, it's Lena Day. And it's a goodie, too.

She holds out the postcard, looking at him oddly. He grabs it but she doesn't let go. She rubs the side of her nose. He doesn't get it. She wipes the paint off of his face.

DISSOLVE TO:

INT. CAROLINE'S BATHROOM — DAY

Hannah sits on the counter and opens a fashion magazine as if it were a Bible. She holds it up to the mirror and mimics the model's expression. She opens a drawer full of Caroline's makeup.

HERBIE (V.O.)
. . . My mother doesn't believe that you're real. She thinks I'm writing letters to myself. Will you send a picture to prove . . .

ANGLE ON: HANNAH'S FEATURES

She applies loads of lipstick, eye shadow, blush, etc. . .

HANNAH (V.O.)
. . . will not send a photo, because I believe that pen-pals should remain a bit mysterious. But I will describe myself to you. I have long black hair . . .

Hannah spies a box of tissues.

ANGLE ON: BOX OF KLEENEX AS HANNAH PULLS OUT TISSUES.

CUT TO:

EXT./INT. CAROLINE'S BATHROOM — LATER

Caroline approaches the bathroom and opens the door, revealing Hannah. She spins around, stuffed to a size "double D." Caroline jumps back, startled.

CAROLINE
Hannah! You scared the crap out of me! Look at you.
(looks her over and smiles)
You want me to teach you how to put it on right?

Hannah nods. Caroline sets down her purse and things and reaches for a washcloth and soap. She wipes the makeup off Hannah's face.

CUT TO:

INT. HANNAH'S BEDROOM — NIGHT

Stanley and Caroline bend over Hannah's bed to kiss her
goodnight. Her room, unpacked now, looks like a little girl's
room.

> STANLEY
> (picks up a stuffed dog)
> Don't let ol' Lapis push you out of bed tonight.

He kisses her forehead.

> HANNAH
> He's Lazuli.

> CAROLINE
> Goodnight, Dolly. I had fun today. Did you?

Hannah shrugs, then grins. Caroline kisses her cheek.

> CAROLINE
> Sweet dreams.

Their arms around each other, Caroline and Stanley turn off
the light and exit. Moonlight shines on her bed.

> HERBIE (V.O.)
> Dear Lena. Last night I dreamt that we met. I had
> cooked for you a nest of spaghetti the size of a
> bathtub. You insisted on throwing it to the ceiling to
> see if it was done. It never stuck . . .

                                                    CUT TO:

INT. HERBIE'S APARTMENT — NIGHT

Herbie sits at his easel reading a postcard.

> HANNAH (V.O.)
> Dear Herbie. Sometime tonight have you looked up at
> this beautiful full moon? If you have, then we've seen
> each other, because I've been watching it too . . .

He sets the postcard next to the canvas and continues
painting.

                                                    CUT TO:

EXT. RAILROAD TRACKS — SUNSET

Hannah lies back on the hill, wearing a flowing skirt and a bit
of makeup. Her hair is longer. She tears open a letter and
begins reading. As she does, her face becomes worried.
A TRAIN IS OFF IN THE DISTANCE.

> HERBIE (V.O.)
> Lena, have you ever noticed the way stars seem to
> fade if you look straight at them? Well, I need to look
> straight at you, Lena.
> > (she sits straight up)
> All I know is that you are an actress, you have a
> beautiful mind, beautiful handwriting, your perfume
> smells like baby powder and . . . I think I'm in love
> with you.

Hannah stops reading. THE SOUND OF THE TRAIN
APPROACHING. She runs down the hill. The train rushes past
as Hannah runs off.

EXT. STREET — SUNSET

Hannah runs up the street and driveway to her house.

> HERBIE (V.O.)
> What was your childhood like? Do you like red or white
> wine? Angel's hair or fettuccini? How old are you?
> When can I meet you?

Hannah runs into her house and SLAMS the door behind her.

> DISSOLVE TO:

EXT. HANNAH'S HOUSE — NIGHT

> CUT TO:

INT. HANNAH'S BEDROOM — NIGHT

Hannah sits on her bed, rereading the letter. There is a KNOCK
at her door. She hides it under her animals. Stanley enter
wearily and kisses her goodnight.

> STANLEY
> Sweet dreams, babe. I'm going to bed.

> HANNAH
> Okay.
> > (Stanley walks to the door)
> Dad? Um . . . Nothing.

                              STANLEY
'Night, kiddo.
                    (sighs)
I guess I shouldn't call you that anymore. You're really
growing up fast.

                              HANNAH
I am?

                              STANLEY
Yeah. And you were such a cute kid. Whatever
happened?
                    (he chuckles)
Don't let ol' Lazuli push you out of bed tonight.

He exits. Hannah moves to her desk and spreads out the
collection of Herbie's letters. She puts her head in her hands,
then looks at herself in the mirror and steels herself for the
task ahead . . . She picks up a postcard and her purple pen and
writes.

                              HANNAH
Dear Herbie.

                                                    CUT TO:

EXT. SCHOOL BUS — MORNING

ANGLE ON: Hannah's face in the harsh morning light as she
runs for the bus. We hear the RUMBLE of the school bus's
engine. She pauses at the corner to drop the postcard into a
mailbox, then disappears into the school bus. The doors close
in our face.

                                                    CUT TO:

INT. Herbie's APARTMENT — SUNSET

The finished "Lena painting" fills the screen. It is a nude,
reclining female. Her head is tipped back in profile, her hair
cascades abundantly over her body. It tangles with and
becomes a forkful of spaghetti which she holds over her open
mouth as if it were grapes. It looks vaguely like Adele.
Propped up against it is the new postcard from "Lena." The
phone is RINGING. We HEAR Herbie pick it up.

                              HERBIE (O.S.)
                    (softly)
Hello.

                                   COLA (O.S.)
                          (heard faintly on the other end)
                   Herbert, Evelyn and her daughter are meeting us for
                   lunch on Sunday. Don't say no . . . do it for me . . . as a
                   favor . . .

Herbie stands in front of the painting, the phone to his ear. He
reaches for the postcard. Cola's voice FADES as we HEAR . . .

                                 HANNAH (V.O.)
                   Dear Herbie. Guess what! I got a job with a touring
                   company. I won't have an address for a while, it could
                   be years if the show goes well. But you have been a
                   magnificent friend, Herbie, and artist. I'll never ever
                   forget you. Your pen pal, Lena.

                                   HERBIE
                   All right, Mom. I'll meet her. I've got to go. Bye.

Herbie hangs up.

                                                                  CUT TO:

INT. SCHOOL BUS — MORNING

WE MOVE with Hannah down the aisle as she heads for her
usual seat. She stops dead in her tracks. Her seat is not
empty.

JJ, a girl with glasses and a soccer ball, stares out the
window. Hannah looks around. There are no empty seats.

                                   HANNAH
                                 (cautiously)
                   You saving this seat?

                                     JJ
                   No.

                                                                  CUT TO:

EXT. HERBIE'S APARTMENT — DAY

Herbie walks across the parking lot with groceries under his
arm. He sees Adele's truck turning into the parking lot. He
ducks behind some bushes, unsure of what to do.

Adele gets out of the truck to stuff mailboxes. She has a new
hat. It is fairly outrageous, but she wears it with style. She
looks radiant.

Herbie finally stands up from the bushes.

> HERBIE

Hi.

Adele jumps slightly. They are face-to-face, closer than they
have ever been.

> ADELE

Hi, Herb.

There is an awkward moment.

> ADELE

I'm sorry about Lena. She might write soon.

> HERBIE

She might.

> ADELE

Well, see ya.

> HERBIE

I like your hat, by the way. It's a great color.

> ADELE
> (touches the hat)

Oh, do you? Wow. Thanks. It's my birthday.

> HERBIE

It's your birthday?

> ADELE

Yeah.

> HERBIE

How old are you?

> ADELE

Um . . . twenty-nine. Hah! No, actually, I'm thirty-three.

> HERBIE

No kidding. Me too. Hey, um . . . would you want to grab
something to eat? Just as friends, I mean. Or dinner?
Do you like Italian?

> ADELE

Oh wow. Yeah, I do. I'll pick you up at seven?

                         HERBIE
     I'll cook.

                                        DISSOLVE TO:

EXT. BUS STOP — DAY

Hannah runs off the bus, followed by JJ. JJ gives the soccer
ball a swift kick. The girls chase it down the sun-dappled road
together.

                                        FADE TO BLACK:

THE END.

THE MAKING OF
KILLER KITE

INTRODUCTION

The Making of Killer Kite, written and shot in 1991 as an M.F.A. Thesis Film, is a reincarnation of a spoof that Matt Stevens wrote, directed, and shot on Super 8 mm in high school:

> Like every other young male filmmaker—I'm talking about when I was in high school—I made the obligatory inanimate-object-attacking-people film. *Killer Kite 2*, a supposed trailer for a sequel that, of course, didn't exist. I decided to do the attacking kite in the context of a spoof since I was relentlessly bombarded by ads for *Jaws 2* during my latch-key kid phase of watching hours and hours of television after school. So it was a spoof of the trailer for *Jaws 2*. Maybe it was my war on over-hyped cheesy horror films!

Years later, as a graduate student at the F.S.U. Film School, Matt turned *Killer Kite* into a one-page story treatment for a mockumentary about the making of a low-budget horror film, *Killer Kite*:

> The plan was to follow an inept crew during the difficult production of a beleaguered project. In an ironic twist, the film (within my film) would turn out to be so bad that it would be good—becoming an instant cult classic, a la *Rocky Horror Picture Show*. *The Making of Killer Kite* would include interviews with cast and crew (who would take themselves *way* too seriously), as well as clips from the supposed film. I think I was partly making fun of filmmakers who took themselves too seriously—and filmmakers who hadn't evolved beyond that phase of producing films about

inanimate objects attacking people. Of course, I was also making fun of the filmmaking process itself, which is so inherently on the edge of farce anyway! And, hey, I was just trying to make people laugh.

After the faculty selected Matt's story for an M.F.A. Thesis Film, they selected Bob Gray to write the screenplay:

I was given the assignment of writing the screenplay and, it became apparent that, in order to tell the story of the making of the fictitious film, *Killer Kite,* I would first have to write, at least, a detailed treatment of the "film" itself. I decided to use the classic structure and characters from any of a dozen horror films from the 50's and 60's (ie., the Mad Scientist and Young Assistant who unwittingly unleash the terror, the Niece of the Mad Scientist who becomes the love interest and partner of the Young Assistant in destroying the beast, and, of course, the final scene that leaves open the possibility of a sequel). Once the story of *Killer Kite* was set in my mind, it became possible to write about the making of the "film."

Matt credits Bob with most of the ideas about the plot of the film-within-the-film, but also with most of the verbal wit in the script ("What is she trying to achieve?" "An orgasm."/"Get the ugly kid out of here or I'll cut your stinking heart out . . . P.R., that's all I do."). Matt stuck to shtick:

I remember that I had always proposed a number of gags, including: A conflict between the filmmakers—one who wanted raw sex and violence on the screen, and another who thought he was making an artistic masterpiece; terrible actors auditioning for the film; on-set disasters that would lead to continuity errors which would be revealed in the clips; a dolly that wouldn't work or had to be returned, so that the crew had to resort to ridiculous things like using a kid's red wagon to get that money shot; a stunt kite that wouldn't work, so the actress would have to wrestle with the kite to make it look like a fight; a ridiculously overdone scene where a girl with a lollipop would be chased by a kite, and it would cut to a stand-in finishing the scene for her because of shooting difficulties. And I believe that I had large brushstroke ideas for certain set-pieces—the creation of the Kite; a chase scene involving a child actress who is tortured by the crew and a stage mother; a sex/nude scene that turns disastrous; a final climactic battle with the Kite; and rabid fans of the film outside a showing.

As for the mockumentary part of the screenplay, Bob took a different approach:

> I decided to pattern *The Making of Killer Kite* after *Spinal Tap*, which is to say I would try to make the "documentary" as real and believable as possible to help sell the wacky, over-the-top subject it purported to document. I consider it the greatest compliment when someone finds the "documentary" so convincing that they want to know where they can rent a copy of the "film" *Killer Kite*.

A feeling I had myself when I saw the mockumentary the first time. But pulling the two stories together on paper and screen was tricky, Bob said:

> The greatest challenge lay in telling both stories simultaneously. I tried to weave the stories, dropping hints and skipping around, referring back in a scene to something that was set up several scenes earlier. I think it works and, in the end, the viewer has a good grasp of both stories.

Getting there, though, wasn't easy:

> Creating the script and the eventual film became an exercise in schizophrenia. All of the "documentary" portions would be shot on video and should have the sound, look and feel of hand-held, impromptu footage, while all of the "film" portions would be shot on film and have the sound, look and feel of a scripted and rehearsed—albeit schlocky—motion picture. Hence the VIDEO or FILM at the head of each scene in the script. This schizophrenia carried through the production for me as well since I was also the Director of Photography/Camera Operator. I would spend a morning shooting run-and-gun video and the afternoon shooting traditional, motion-picture-style tripod/dolly cinematography.

In production, a number of changes occurred. As director, Matt threw in some "visual things" during production just as Bob did as D.P. on the project.

And the actors, Matt said, made valuable changes in the screenplay and film:

> I depended a lot on the contributions from the actors— improvisations, etc.—while rehearsing and shooting. Especially since much of it was supposed to have a documentary feel, I wanted to give them that freedom to play. And there

are several funny ad-libbed moments that made it into the film.

Matt also did some restructuring during post. He and Bob both said they were happy with the final product. As Bob summed it up:

> In the end, I think *The Making of Killer Kite* is a good script that became a very good film through the efforts of the multi-talented Matt Stevens and the incredible cast who were, to a person, able to take the "documentary" and make it seem off-the-cuff and personal and then turn around and play the intentionally-bad "film" script right to the top without going over. The film was as much fun to make as it is to watch, and the many accolades it's received have been very gratifying indeed.

In 1991, *The Making of Killer Kite* won First Prize for Comedy from the Academy of Television Arts & Sciences College Television Awards—a.k.a. the student Emmies. It won First Place in narrative from the Ft. Lauderdale International Film Festival, and Best Student Entry from the Canadian International Film Festival in Ontario. It was a Top Five Finalist in the Lucille Ball Festival of New Comedy in 1992, and it has been screened in various venues across the United States, including the Director's Guild of America.

Since *The Making of Killer Kite*, Bob Gray has been "working steadily but wearing a lot of different hats to work steadily," he told me. He recently finished shooting an independent feature, *Samantha*, and is currently writing a Movie-of-the-Week, *Invisible Angels*, based on the book *Born to be Hurt* by Ida Muorie. He's also developing and producing a cable series about boating, *Sail Away*, with former CNN anchor Patrick Emory. Bob lives in Sarasota, Florida, with his wife and two children.

Since *Kite*, Matt Stevens has taught screenwriting and directing at the F.S.U. Film School, produced and directed a second-unit segment for the feature *Curdled*, executive-produced by Quentin Tarantino, and was a finalist for the Sundance Screenwriters Lab. Matt now lives in Los Angeles where he has sold two feature-length screenplays and continues to write and produce.

THE MAKING OF KILLER KITE

Story by Matt Stevens

Screenplay by Robert S. Gray

FADE IN:

EXT. HARLAN LaRUE'S MANSION — NIGHT (FILM)

The ancient stone building sits dark and lifeless. A single light shines from a room near the roof. Lightning flashes as THUNDER ROARS.

CUT TO:

INT. LaRUE'S MANSION — NIGHT (FILM)

The laboratory is cluttered with giant batteries, transformers and dials.

PROFESSOR HARLAN LaRUE, an elderly, disheveled man in a white lab coat, hurriedly makes a last minute inspection of a melange of coiled wires, flashing lights and bubbling beakers.

His assistant, JONATHAN SCOTT, a young, handsome all-American lad, stands looking out the window.

Lightning flashes.

> JONATHAN
> (checking his watch)
> It's moving in this direction, Professor LaRue. In five minutes, we'll be in the center of the storm.

> PROFESSOR
> All right Jonathan. No time to waste. Ten years of research and it all comes down to this moment. Prepare the kite.

Jonathan throws a large switch and a glass case begins to pulse with green light, growing brighter until a black, bat-shaped kite becomes visible inside. The two stand staring into the case, their faces an eerie green.

> PROFESSOR
> Think of it my boy. In the future when they power an entire city with the power from one storm, men will

                    PROFESSOR (CONT'D)
    speak of this night. The night Harlan LaRue changed
    the course of history.

Jonathan opens the glass case and connects two wires to
either "wing" of the bat kite. He carefully removes the kite
from the case.

                    JONATHAN
    The kite is ready, Professor.

                    PROFESSOR
    Onward, into the future.

The two go up the stairs to the roof.

                                          CUT TO:

EXT. ROOF — NIGHT (FILM)

The Professor and Jonathan, with kite in hand, come out onto
the roof. They set the kite to sail almost effortlessly. The
Professor grabs the kite string and holds on tightly, wind
gusting, lightning flashing and THUNDER CRACKING.

                    PROFESSOR
                  (yelling)
    Check the connections.

Jonathan runs back down into the laboratory as the Professor
looks mechanically into the sky.

Suddenly, a bolt of lightning hits the kite and the Professor.

Jonathan returns to the roof.

                    JONATHAN
    It worked. The batteries are charged. Professor?

He sees the Professor's empty shoes sitting on the roof,
smoking.

                    JONATHAN
    Professor LaRue?

He looks up to see the kite as it flies off. Now, there is the hint
of an evil smile on its face.

                                          CUT TO:

EXT. LABORATORY ROOF — NIGHT (VIDEO)

From a different angle, we see Jonathan standing on the roof,
watching the kite.

>   LIZ (O.S.)
> Cut.

The VIDEO CAMERA zooms out until we see a film camera on a
dolly sitting only a few feet in front of Jonathan. Behind the
camera is COLIN KISHMAN.

As the shot continues to widen, we see the roof is actually a
set on a soundstage. CREW MEMBERS wander about.

>   COLIN
> Perfect everybody. Really. Good job. Let's just do it one
> more time.

GROANS are heard from the Crew.

>   CUT TO:

INT. COLIN'S OFFICE — DAY (VIDEO)

Colin Kishman is in his late 20's and very hip; in a black
shirt, buttoned to the throat, wire rim glasses and hair that is
lacquered straight back.

Awards, film posters and books decorate his tastefully-
conservative office. He sips a mineral water as he sits back
casually in his over-stuffed chair.

>   COLIN
> "Kite" had been a dream of mine since I was in film
> school in Iowa but it was too far ahead of its time for
> school and none of the studios were interested so we
> did it as an independent.

>   JUMP CUT:

>   COLIN
> It's set in the horror film genre but it's actually neo-
> expressionistic vision of the classic struggle between
> man and his inner demons.

>   CUT TO:

INT. BARREN ROOM — DAY (VIDEO)

CARL KISHMAN, mid-thirties and looking older, is dressed in a plain blue work shirt as he sits at a metal table. Behind him is a cold concrete wall.

He smokes constantly as he runs his fingers through his hair. There is a nervous tic in the corner of his eye.

> CARL
> Well, yeah, that's the great thing, you know, it's got something for everybody. I mean, it scares your pants off to begin with plus, it's got a little . . .

He uses his hands to indicate breasts.

> CARL
> You know? I mean, you've got to show a little skin if you're going to sell the thing.

                                                    CUT TO:

INT. COLIN'S OFFICE — DAY (VIDEO)

> COLIN
> I just didn't want to do that same old, tired, bedroom love scene that's been done to death. Setting it in the laboratory, I thought, was not only thematically correct but very sensual.

                                                    CUT TO:

INT. CARL'S ROOM — DAY (VIDEO)

> CARL
> And, where the guy ends up buffing the broad right on the giant battery . . . I mean, is that great, or what?

                                                    CUT TO:

INT. COLIN'S OFFICE — DAY (VIDEO)

> COLIN
> Casting? Don't remind me. No, honestly, ours was tough but worth it. We ended up getting the best talent in Hollywood.

                                                    CUT TO:

EXT. KISHMAN PRODUCTION TRAILER — DAY (VIDEO)

An old trailer sits on a vacant lot. Concrete blocks serve as stairs. Next to the door is a sign that reads, "Kishman Brothers Productions—Hollywood, Florida."

There are about a DOZEN ACTORS lined up in front.

LIZ BOWDEN exits the trailer and addresses the actors.

> LIZ
> All right, who hasn't filled out a form?

A few actors raise their hands. She goes to the FIRST ACTOR and offers them a form.

> LIZ
> (coldly)
> Any union affiliations?

> FIRST ACTOR
> No, ma'am.

> LIZ
> Good.

A COWBOY exits the trailer, slamming the door.

> COWBOY
> Don't waste your time, boys. These idiots don't know talent when they see it.

> LIZ
> Well, I do. And, believe me, I didn't.

> CUT TO:

EXT. TRAILER — DAY (VIDEO)

An OLDER ACTOR is practicing his lines in a baroque and theatrical voice.

> OLDER ACTOR
> The night Harlan LaRue changed the course of history.
> (beat)
> The night Harlan LaRue changed the course of history.

> CUT TO:

EXT. TRAILER — DAY (VIDEO)

A definite CHARACTER ACTOR.

                              CHARACTER ACTOR
        I'm going to read for the lead. I've paid my dues doing
        characters and I think I'm at that leading-man stage in
        my career, now.

                                                            CUT TO:

EXT. TRAILER — DAY (VIDEO)

A precocious YOUNG GIRL stands reading her lines while her
doting STAGE MOTHER kneels beside her, brushing her hair.

                              YOUNG GIRL
        Mother, do you mind? I'm trying to learn this.

                              STAGE MOTHER
        Sorry, honey. Go ahead.

The Young girl goes back to the script, pauses and then lets
out a blood-curdling SCREAM.

                                                            CUT TO:

INT. KISHMAN PRODUCTION TRAILER — DAY (VIDEO)

The two Kishman brothers sit at a table stacked with resumes
and photos. Carl is now wearing a shirt and tie that is
loosened at the neck. He does not run his fingers through his
hair or have a nervous tic.

Colin has much longer hair than before and wears a T-shirt
that says, "Film Iowa". Film and Iowa share the letter "I".

The two appear very fatigued.

                              COLIN
                          (unenthusiastically)
        Very good. Really.

He looks to Carl for confirmation but gets only a glaze of
disinterest.

                              COLIN
        Really, very nice.

We see that it is the Character Actor.

                              COLIN
        It's not exactly what we had in mind for the lead but,
        if we decide to go that way, we'll be in touch.

We jump through a series of lines being read by different actors. Each one is worse than the last:

FIRST ACTOR
It's moving in this direction Professor LaRue.

SECOND ACTOR
I can't stop seeing that poor child's face and that . . . thing.

OLDER ACTOR
The night Harlan LaRue changed the course of history.

THIRD ACTOR
Tammy, it's too dangerous. We should . . . wait, can I start over?

FOURTH ACTOR
We should leave it to the authorities. That fiend has already killed five red-haired children.

FIFTH ACTOR
(snickering)
Make love to me, Jonathan.

SIXTH ACTOR
(seductively)
Make love to me, Jonathan.

SEVENTH ACTOR
(sternly)
Make love to me, Jonathan.

The Brothers are rocked awake by the Young Girl's SCREAM.

YOUNG GIRL
Shall we proceed with the audition, gentlemen?

CUT TO:

INT. LABORATORY — DAY (VIDEO)

ASHLEY DAVENPORT is sitting on the laboratory set for her interview.

ASHLEY
Tammy is the pivotal character here. It's really her story and I want to give her a very positive, can-do, sort of 90's-woman quality.

JUMP TO:

> ASHLEY
> (proudly)
> Yes, I was the, "Love-My-Floor-Wax" lady. It ran for six
> months in the Jacksonville area.

JUMP TO:

> ASHLEY
> I'd rather continue doing dinner theatre here than
> move to California. It's just that whole L.A., show-biz,
> starlet thing is definitely not me.

CUT TO:

BILL PRINZ is sitting on the same set.

> BILL
> This is Jonathan's story. He is the central character
> around which all the supporting characters revolve. I
> mean, he helps build the beast, he destroys the beast
> and he gets the girl. Gets her right here, in fact. That
> should prove interesting.

JUMP TO:

> BILL
> My looks are holding me back as an actor, I think. I
> mean, all I'm offered are the leading-man roles and,
> just once, I'd kill for one of those juicy, character
> parts. Oh, well.

CUT TO:

INT. COLIN'S OFFICE — DAY (VIDEO)

Colin holds up a large poster for "Killer Kite". Near the bottom
of the poster, we see a child sitting on the sand, a small shovel
in hand and a pail at her feet. Near the top of the poster is a
large, menacing bat-shaped kite.

> COLIN
> This was the original poster idea but I felt it was too
> derivative of Jaws, so . . .

He holds a up a second poster. Instead of the child at the
bottom, we now see a couple, running in terror from the kite.

> COLIN
> We came up with this which I thought was better but
> still didn't grab me so . . .

He holds up the final poster. It is a close shot of Ashley and Jonathan, partially undressed and in passionate embrace. On the wall, in the background, is a small shadow of a kite.

>   COLIN
> I designed this one myself. I just felt the story was not about some kite, really. It's about people.

                                                        CUT TO:

INT. BARREN ROOM — DAY (VIDEO)

CARL is once again in the stark concrete room where we first saw him.

>   CARL
>   My advice to young filmmakers?
>   (beat)
>   Hire Lizzy Bowden as your A.D.

                                                        CUT TO:

EXT. IRICK PARK — DAY (VIDEO)

Film equipment and CREW are everywhere.

Colin sits behind the camera atop the dolly crane while Carl paces nervously, checking his watch.

Liz holds a red wig and addresses the Young Girl in a whisper as her Mother looks on from the background.

>   LIZ
> Yes, your mother did a wonderful job but the kite only attacks red-headed children. So, you can either put on the wig or I'll shave your head with a rusty razor. Got it?

                                                        CUT TO:

EXT. IRICK PARK — SHORTLY LATER (VIDEO)

The child is now wearing the red wig. Just behind her the kite is being suspended in the air by ASPEN GREENWALD, the stunt coordinator.

>   LIZ
> Ready on set?

Aspen looks high in the tree to his assistant SHORTY LOGAN, who holds the other kite line.

                    ASPEN
    Ready, Shorty?

                    SHORTY
    Ready.

                    LIZ
    Okay, quiet everybody. This is a take. Roll sound.

                    SOUND MAN
    Speed.

                    LIZ
    Roll camera.

                    COLIN
    Speed.

                    LIZ
              (slating)
    Killer Kite. Scene 43, take 1.

                    COLIN
    And . . . action.

The Girl runs from the kite which is closing in on her. She looks back, SCREAMS and falls.

                    LIZ
    Cut. Good for everybody?

                    SOUND MAN
    Sound good.

                    COLIN
    Sorry, I lost her when she fell. Let's just do one more.

                                        CUT TO:

EXT. IRICK PARK — LATER (VIDEO)

Liz, agitated, holds the slate in front of the camera.

                    LIZ
    Scene 43, take 15.

She marks and drops the slate to reveal the Young Girl spattered with dirt and wig askew.

                    COLIN
    Action.

The Young Girl starts running and turn to scream. This time, it
is a raspy and pale imitation of its former self.

                    LIZ
    Cut.

                                        CUT TO:

EXT. IRICK PARK — LATER (VIDEO)

Carl paces as he talks to Colin.

                    CARL
        You just don't get it, do you? We've got the dolly for
        two more hours. That's it. Then, no more dolly.

                    COLIN
    We only need it for three more shots.

                    CARL
    You've already spent four hours on this one.

                    COLIN
    We're fine.

Carl's cell phone RINGS. He turns it on and puts it to his ear.

                    CARL
        Your brains are in your ass.
                (becoming nervous)
        Oh, no. Not you, Mr. Van Arsdale. Ha, ha. No, it was
        just . . . one of the actors.
                (to no one in particular)
        You'll never work in this town again.

                                        CUT TO:

EXT. IRICK PARK — LATER (VIDEO)

The Stage Mother sits comfortably as the Young Girl limps
over, tired, defeated and on the verge of tears.

                    YOUNG GIRL
                (hoarsely)
    I can't do't again.

The Mother sprays antiseptic in the Young Girl's throat.

>   STAGE MOTHER
>   Like hell. You'll do it all day if they tell you to.
>   (softly)
>   Okay, honey?

The Young Girl turns and lets out a piercing SCREAM, right into the microphone.

The Sound Man rips off his headphones and begins chasing the Young Girl, murder in his eyes.

Liz jumps up and brings him down with a flying tackle. She looks up with a face full of dirt.

>   LIZ
>   Okay people, that's lunch.

>   CUT TO:

EXT. IRICK PARK — LATER (VIDEO)

Everyone is again in position to re-take scene 43.

>   LIZ
>   Scene 43, take 22.

>   COLIN
>   Action.

The Young Girl takes off running and screaming. She falls, looks up and, instead of screaming, begins choking.

>   LIZ
>   Cut. What the hell's the matter now? Aspen?

>   ASPEN
>   The line's wrapped around her throat. Give me some
>   slack.

>   CARL
>   Careful. Easy, you're tearing the kite.

The Stage Mother runs over to assist the Young Girl.

>   STAGE MOTHER
>   My baby.
>   (to Carl)
>   You'll be hearing from my lawyer.

Liz yanks the line and, unnoticed by anyone, Shorty is pulled from the tree, landing with a THUD.

The Young Girl and Stage Mother head for their car.

> LIZ
>
> Where are you going?

> STAGE MOTHER
>
> I'm taking my daughter to the hospital, if that's all right with you, bitch.

Liz yanks the wig off the Young Girl's head.

> LIZ
>
> Christ, never work with kids.
>
> (to Colin)
>
> Okay, we've wasted five hours, we still don't have this shot and we've lost our actress. So, who are we supposed to get to finish this scene?

Colin turns slowly to look at Liz, the only woman on the set. The implication of his look sinks in.

> LIZ
>
> Oh, no. No, no. No way.

> CUT TO:

EXT. IRICK PARK — LATER (VIDEO)

Liz is now in the red wig as an ASSISTANT is strapping her breasts with an Ace bandage.

> COLIN
>
> Believe me, it will cut. No one will ever notice.

He gives her a quick kiss on the cheek and leaves.

> LIZ
>
> (to the assistant)
>
> I can't believe this. I've worked with Bob Altman, Mike Nichols . . .

The Assistant is unimpressed.

> LIZ
>
> Anson Williams.

The Assistant looks up, awestruck.

ASSISTANT

Really?

CUT TO:

INT. BARREN ROOM — DAY (VIDEO)

Carl continues his interview.

CARL

Of course, the ironic thing is that the special effects are
what made the film, in some ways, but also what . . .
broke it, actually, with the lawsuit and all but, God,
don't remind me of that.

He takes a long drag off his cigarette and blows smoke into the
air, staring blankly as his eye twitches quickly.

EXT. LABORATORY ROOF — DAY (VIDEO)

Aspen stands next to Shorty, who's dressed in a full-body, bat-
kite costume. A patch covers one eye; a scar on the cheek
below.

ASPEN
(to camera)

This next stunt is really revolutionary. It's never been
tried before. This kite costume, that my test pilot
Shorty here is wearing, is like a small hang glider so,
when he jumps off here, they'll be able to get these
great shots of the kite circling and circling. Really
menacing looking stuff, man. But the really wild thing
is, there's a camera stuck inside Shorty's costume here
so, at the same time, he'll be getting these great aerial
shots. I told him, "Hey, make 'em pay you D.P. rates".

He slaps Shorty on the back, playfully.

Shorty looks over the rail, panic stricken. It is a long way
down.

ASPEN
(to camera)

No, we haven't had time to test it yet but, if anybody
can do it, Shorty can.
(to Shorty)
Right, buddy?
(to camera)
There's nothin' he won't do.

CUT TO:

INT. COLIN'S OFFICE — DAY (VIDEO)

Colin's interview continues.

>   COLIN
> Probably the most rewarding thing about "Kite" was
> the relationships that developed on the set, especially
> between the actors and myself. There was a real
> simpatico there.

CUT TO:

INT. LABORATORY — DAY (VIDEO)

The set is lit, the equipment in place and the actors in
costume.

Colin, fatigued and nervous, addresses Bill and Ashley.

>   COLIN
>   (to Ashley)
> No, I don't think they would go to his room. This is
> something they do in the heat of passion. Okay? This
> isn't a romantic weekend in the Keys. This is raw
> animal lust. Get it . . . got it . . . good.

>   ASHLEY
> But, I don't understand Tammy's motivation here. It
> seems so submissive. What is she trying to achieve
> with this?

Carl, with a three-day growth of beard and clothes straight
from the floor, passes through.

>   CARL
> An orgasm.

LAUGHTER is heard around the set.

>   COLIN
> All right, people. Let's have quiet. This is a very
> difficult scene for everybody so, let's just cooperate.
>   (to Ashley)
> Tammy realizes she is becoming the same isolated,
> lonely, embittered person that her uncle Harlan had
> become and the only way she can avoid that is to dare
> to love another and her disrobing is merely symbolic of
> her losing the veils of secrecy that have enshrouded
> her soul.

Ashley is moved by his words.

                              COLIN
          Okay, let's try one.

                                              JUMP TO:

                              ASHLEY
          Jonathan, we may not live to see another day and I
          don't want to die a woman who never knew love. Make
          love to me, Jonathan.

          They embrace and kiss passionately. Ashley begins snickering.

                              LIZ
          Cut.

                                              JUMP TO:

                              ASHLEY
          Make love to me, Jonathan.

          They kiss, her face to the camera side of his.

                              BILL
          Sorry, but shouldn't my face be on the other side?

                              LIZ
          Cut.

                              COLIN
          No, Bill, we'll want to see Tammy's face here.

                                              JUMP TO:

                              ASHLEY
          Make love to me, Jonathan.

          They embrace and kiss. She rips the buttons from his shirt. He
          unbuttons her blouse and, as he finishes, she self-consciously
          begins to re-button it.

                              LIZ
          Cut. Damn it, what are you doing?

                              ASHLEY
          Sorry, I'm . . . I just . . . Can we do it again? Sorry.

                              LIZ
          Okay, let's get Jonathan another shirt.

                                              JUMP TO:

They are set to retake the scene. Bill's shirt is a different color, now.

> ASHLEY
> Make love to me, Jonathan.

Again, they embrace, kiss and begin to disrobe each other. This time, as he finishes un-buttoning her shirt, she manages to turn her back to the camera. He wrestles to turn her back around, kissing all the while.

> LIZ
> Cut. Where does it say, "Tammy and Jonathan wrestle"?

> ASHLEY
> I'm sorry. This isn't easy, you know?

> LIZ
> I don't care. Act if you must.

> ASHLEY
> Fine. You think it's so easy, then you get naked in front of them.

She points to the crew, who look around embarrassed and guilty.

Ashley leaves the set in tears.

> CUT TO:

INT. SOUNDSTAGE — SHORTLY LATER

Carl and Liz are off to one side of the set, talking quietly.

> CARL
> We've got to have this scene. I mean, we've got to have it. No "R" rating, no sale. It's that simple. We've got to have it.

Colin joins them.

> COLIN
> It's no use. She says it's purely exploitive and she won't do gratuitous nudity.

> CARL
> We'll pay her.

                         COLIN
     I offered. She said, "I'm an actress, not a stripper".

                         CARL
     That's it. We're screwed.

                         LIZ
     That's your answer.

The brothers only look confused.

                         LIZ
     Pay someone to body double the rest of the scene.

Colin and Carl come alive at the simplistic genius of her
suggestion. Together, they turn to look at Liz.

                         LIZ
     Oh, no. Absolutely not. N O, no. Forget it. Hire a body
     double.

                                                      CUT TO:

INT. COLIN'S OFFICE — DAY (VIDEO)

Colin's interview continues.

                         COLIN
     The love scene, as it stands now, is different than we
     had originally planned but, I think it works very nicely.
     I still get a lot of comments on it.

                                                      CUT TO:

INT. LABORATORY — DAY (FILM)

Tammy and Jonathan enter.

                         TAMMY
     Oh, Jonathan, I can't stop seeing that poor child's face
     and that . . . that thing.

                         JONATHAN
     Shh. Try not to think about it.

                         TAMMY
     Jonathan, we may not live to see another day and I
     don't want to die a woman who never knew love. Make
     love to me, Jonathan.

When we cut back to Jonathan he is wearing the different colored shirt.

The scene plays through until her shirt is unbuttoned and her back is to the camera and then there is an awkward cut-away to a flashing light.

The scene plays through to the end in close up, a body-double now standing in for Tammy. He removes her shirt and the body-double has tassels glued to her nipples.

The two crawl upon the giant battery to consummate the relationship and the camera dollies to a bubbling beaker.

CUT TO:

INT. BARREN ROOM — DAY (VIDEO)

Carl's interview continues.

> CARL
> I've gotta be honest with you, I don't remember the last five or six days of the production. I've heard some pretty weird stuff, though. As long as they can't prove it, 'eh?

CUT TO:

INT./EXT. TAMMY'S CAR — DAY (FILM)

Tammy sits in the driver's seat with Jonathan next to her. In the middle of the back seat is a mannequin wearing a red wig.

> TAMMY
> Okay, we know all the children were attacked in Irick Park, right?

> JONATHAN
> Right.

> TAMMY
> And, they all had red hair, right?

> JONATHAN
> Right.

> TAMMY
> And, since the curfew prohibits children from being outside alone, little Rusty here will be the perfect decoy.

> JONATHAN
> Let's hope the kite has the Professor's same bad
> eyesight.

CUT TO:

EXT. IRICK PARK — DAY (VIDEO)

Tammy and Jonathan enter the park carrying little Rusty and
two machetes. CHILDREN and PARENTS scatter at the sight.

The camera dollies beside them, only now, instead of a dolly
and track, Colin and the camera ride atop a children's red
wagon.

Tammy and Jonathan prop Rusty in the middle of the
playground.

> TAMMY
> Okay, you take cover in those bushes and I'll wait in
> the car.

In the background, a CHILD continues to play on the
playground, her MOM beside her.

> LIZ
> Cut.
> (to Mom)
> You're supposed to be gone by now. You see these two
> people with machetes and you grab your child and
> leave. Got it?

Carl comes over.

> CARL
> (to Mom)
> That's it. You're off the film. Goodbye. Leave.

> MOM
> We were never in your stupid film, remember? You told
> us you'd already cast everyone.

> LIZ
> Well, you'll have to leave. We can't get this shot with
> you in the way here.

> MOM
> You Hollywood people are all the same.

> LIZ
> Lady, please, just leave before we call the cops.

Carl takes the machete from Jonathan's hands.

                    MOM
Why don't you go make your smutty movie somewhere
else.

                    CARL
Look, bitch, this smutty movie has already put me fifty-
thousand in debt. I've mortgaged my house, my boat
and my Beemer. I haven't slept or bathed in three
days. My wife has moved out and I think my dog may
have starved to death. Trust me, I'm losing my sense
of humor. So, you can either take that ugly child and
get out of here or I swear I'll cut your stinkin' heart
out.

The Mom grabs the child and runs off.

                    CARL
P.R., that's all I do.

                                        CUT TO:

INT. T.V. STUDIO — DAY (VIDEO)

                    FILM REVIEWER
It was twenty-five months ago tonight that I had the
unimaginable burden of watching "Killer Kite" for the
first time and, as I said at the time, "the film is not
worthy of a serious review." So, of course, every child
between nine and twenty has been to see it at least six
times. It's now made the greatest profit of any
independent film in history and, tonight, it begins a
record 105th consecutive week at Los Angeles' famous
Polk Theatre. Yes, I've been to see "Killer Kite" again
and, no, I haven't changed my review. What everyone
takes to be that camp, Kishman style of comedy is
nothing more than inept filmmaking. The fact that
these guys got a three-picture deal with Paramount is
an inauspicious statement on the health of the
American film system. Just take a look at this awful
segment from an even worse film.

                                        CUT TO:

EXT. IRICK PARK — DAY (FILM)

We see the segment where the kite is chasing the Young Girl.
She falls and looks back at the kite.

                                                              CUT TO:

KITE'S POV

Of the Young Girl lying on the ground, screaming.

RETURN TO SCENE

Only, now, it is Liz in a red wig, wrestling with the kite. She
screams and acts as badly as anyone has ever screamed and
acted.

                                                              CUT TO:

INT. COLIN'S OFFICE — DAY (VIDEO)

                         COLIN
        Of course the critics didn't like it. None of them
        understood it. Not one realized that the kite is an
        analogy for prejudice. It only attacks red-haired
        children. Get it?
                      (disgusted)
        Critics.

                                                              CUT TO:

INT./EXT. TAMMY'S CAR, IRICK PARK — DAY (FILM)

Tammy sits behind the wheel, looking up at the sky. Slowly,
the kite rises beside the car until it is looking through the
window.

                         TAMMY
                      (startled)
        Uncle Harlan, no. It's me, Tammy.

The kite backs away.

Tammy grabs a machete and lunges at the kite, missing. The
kite takes off.

Tammy jumps out of the car and calls Jonathan.

                         TAMMY
        Jonathan, be careful. He knows we mean to destroy
        him.

ANGLE ON JONATHAN

As the kite swoops down and attacks him. He falls to the
ground, bleeding.

The kite then attacks the mannequin. A loud CRUNCH is heard and the kite falls to the ground, injured.

Tammy and Jonathan quickly descend on the kite and stab it with their machetes. Trickles of blood come from the kite's wounds.

                    TAMMY
                  (sobbing)
        Oh, no. Uncle Harlan, no.

Jonathan helps her up.

                    JONATHAN
        Come on. It's over. The Professor is in a better place,
        now.

They walk off, arm-in-arm, toward the car.

                                            CUT TO:

EXT. POLK THEATRE — NIGHT (VIDEO)

A long line of YOUNG PEOPLE extends from the front door. OTHERS wait behind barricades. Many are in costume, wearing kite suits and waving kite puppets.

TWO BOYS are dressed as the Professor, ANOTHER as Jonathan and ONE as Ashley.

Shrieks are heard as a stretch limo pulls up. Ashley gets out.

                    ADOLESCENT BOY
        I love you, Tammy.

Ashley enters, the epitome of the Hollywood starlet. She is dressed in a low-cut gown and poses for the myriad flashbulbs.

Bill Prinz gets out next, looking tan and manicured. There are more SHRIEKS from the crowd.

                    TEENAGE GIRL 1
        Make love to me, Jonathan.

                    TEENAGE GIRL 2
        Make love to me, Jonathan.

Another limo pulls up and Colin gets out, dressed in a tuxedo and escorting Liz who looks elegant in an evening gown. She swats away a child who asks for an autograph and hurriedly pulls Colin inside the theatre.

A black motorcycle pulls up on the sidewalk and PEOPLE scatter. The rider gets off and we see it is Aspen.

Next, the Young Girl arrives in a wheelchair and wearing a neck brace. She is being pushed by her Mother. They are swarmed by a pack of pre-pubescent girls and the last we see of them is the wheelchair tipping over.

                                                    CUT TO:

INT. POLK THEATRE — NIGHT (VIDEO)

We see several of the AUDIENCE MEMBERS, the light from the screen shimmering on their faces. They deliver the final lines of the film with the actors on the screen.

                    FEMALE CROWD
        Oh, no. Uncle Harlan. No.

                    MALE CROWD
        Come on. It's over. The Professor is in a much better
        place, now.

                                                    CUT TO:

EXT. IRICK PARK — DAY (FILM)

After Tammy and Jonathan walk off, the camera remains on the kite. A breeze lifts it and turns it over, revealing a dozen baby killer kites below.

The Crowd OOOH'S and AAAH'S.

                                            FADE TO BLACK:

FADE IN:

GRAPHIC:

"This Film Is Dedicated To Shorty Logan. 'There's nothing he wouldn't do'."

                                                    CUT TO:

INT. COLIN'S OFFICE — DAY (VIDEO)

                    COLIN
        I am very busy, right now. We begin principle
        photography on "Prom Bomb" next week and I'm just
        finishing the script for "The Town That Couldn't Spell,"

COLIN (CONT'D)
which we hope to have in production by the time Carl
gets out . . .

if we can straighten out this I.R.S. thing.

CUT TO:

INT. BARREN ROOM — DAY (VIDEO)

Carl finishes the last of a cigarette butt and looks nervously
over his shoulder. He checks his watch.

CARL
Do I have any advice for young filmmakers?

On the SOUND of a jail cell opening, the camera pans over to
reveal the jail bars beside Carl as the GUARD enters.

CARL
Yeah, take care of the legal work first. Trust me.

The Guard leads Carl out of the cell.

FADE TO BLACK:

ROLL CREDITS.

---15---

CONCLUSION

What's left to say? Only this: Having stressed the importance of craft in screenwriting, I have to be honest: Craft can only take you so far.

"The rest," as William Gibson so wisely said, "is art and up to God."

"Young screenwriters forget they're writers," Mark Spragg told me. "They believe too much in craft—form—and not enough in the art of the piece. It is organic."

Messy. Mysterious. Ultimately, creating a screenplay and film that connect is a mysterious process. And the act of connecting with others, Peter Weir suggests, may be more unconscious than conscious:

> You have to remember that the audience is sitting in their seats dreaming and if you can connect with their unconscious, you really have a powerful connection between viewer and screen. You want them to let the stuff come up from their unconscious, provoked by your energies with just enough logic to feel like you know what you're doing and the picture is under control. That's the challenge, to have enough logic without inhibiting the unconscious.[1]

Enough logic, yes, but not *rules*, as Academy Award winner, Nicholas Kazan, says in *American Screenwriters*:

> In essence, there are *no rules* with film. It's like a dream: it can take many different forms. The important thing is that what happens should be continually surprising and in retrospect seem inevitable. If you have that it doesn't matter what your structure is.[2]

Learn the craft, then give yourself permission to go beyond it.

260

"Research, think," as Mark Spragg says, "then turn the dogs loose and see where they go."

So the last thing I'd like to say is what I've been saying all along: *Play*. Or, as Seamus Heaney says in "Station Island":

> *You are fasted now, light-headed, dangerous.*
> *Take off from here. And don't be so earnest,*
> *so ready for the sackcloth and the ashes.*
> *Let go, let fly, forget.*
> *You've listened long enough. Now strike your note.*[3]

NOTES

1. Linda Seger and Edward Jay Whetmore, *From Script to Screen: The Collaborative Art of Filmmaking*, Henry Holt, New York, 1994, p. 145.
2. Karl Schanzer and Thomas Lee Wright, *American Screenwriters: The Insider's Look at the Art, the Craft, and the Business of Writing Movies*, Avon Books, New York, 1993, p. 248.
3. Seamus Heaney, *Selected Poems 1966–1987*, Farrar, Straus & Giroux, New York, 1990, pp. 211–212.

AVAILABLE SCREENWRITING SOFTWARE

Software	E-Mail	Phone
Final Draft	info@finaldraft.com	1-800-231-4055
Scriptor	www.screenplay.com	1-800-84STORY
ScriptThing	sales@scriptthing.com	1-800-450-9450
ScriptWorks	video@videouniversity.com	1-800-464-7511
Scriptware	http://scriptware.com	1-800-788-7090
SideBySide	sidebyside@simon1.com	1-888-234-6789

FILMS REFERENCED

Title	Availability
Romeo and Juliet (1968)	amazon.com ASIN# 6304145217
Death of a Salesman (1985)	amazon.com ASIN# 630478578X
The Fugitive	amazon.com ASIN# 6304406088
Red (Trois Coleurs: Rouge)	amazon.com ASIN# 6303486762
Apollo 13	amazon.com ASIN# 0783216890
Pulp Fiction	amazon.com ASIN# 630395345X
Metropolis	amazon.com ASIN# 6304019513
M	amazon.com ASIN# B00000610N
The Big Heat	amazon.com ASIN# 6302797675
The Full Monty	amazon.com ASIN# 6305064679
Star Wars	amazon.com ASIN# 6304539258
Babe	amazon.com ASIN# 0783229011
Marty	amazon.com ASIN# 630290210X
The Hospital	amazon.com ASIN# 6302241111
City Lights	amazon.com ASIN# 6302561833
Dr. Strangelove	amazon.com ASIN# 6302799066
As Good As It Gets	amazon.com ASIN# 0767811712
Courage Under Fire	amazon.com ASIN# 6304973160
Nick of Time	amazon.com ASIN# 6304008716
Ulee's Gold	amazon.com ASIN# 079289992X
Butch Cassidy and the Sundance Kid	Movies Unlimited #041022 1-800-4-MOVIES
The Princess Bride	amazon.com ASIN# 6304718551
Everything That Rises	Unavailable
Poison Ivy	amazon.com ASIN# 6303914926
Shine	amazon.com ASIN# 078061755X
Marnie	amazon.com ASIN# 6300183947
When Harry Met Sally	amazon.com ASIN# 0792837207
Bull Durham	Unavailable
Grosse Point Blanke	amazon.com ASIN# 6304578458
Shawshank Redemption	amazon.com ASIN# 0780623134

Rain Man	amazon.com ASIN# 6304428952
Annie Hall	amazon.com ASIN# 6301963911
Hannah and Her Sisters	amazon.com ASIN# 6303232663
Philadelphia	amazon.com ASIN# 0767809270
sex, lies and videotape	amazon.com ASIN# 0800100964
Say Anything	amazon.com ASIN# 6301412761

APPENDIX C
FURTHER READING

You have a great many books on writing in general and screenwriting in particular to choose from, but if I could only take a dozen to a desert island for the rest of my writing life, I would choose these for instruction and inspiration:

Burroway, Janet. *Writing Fiction: A Guide to Narrative Craft*, 5th ed. New York: HarperCollins, 1999.

Dancyger, Ken and Jeff Rush. *Alternative Scriptwriting: Writing Beyond the Rules*. Boston: Focal Press, 1995.

Egri, Lajos. *The Art of Dramatic Writing*. New York: Simon and Schuster, 1960.

Gibson, William. *Shakespeare's Game*. New York: Atheneum, 1978.

Goldman, William. *Adventures In the Screen Trade: A Personal View of Hollywood and Scriptwriting*. New York: Warner Books, 1983.

Lamott, Anne. *Bird By Bird: Some Instructions On Writing and Life*. New York: Pantheon, 1994.

McKee, Robert. *Story: Substance, Structure, Style, and the Principles of Screenwriting*. New York: HarperCollins, 1997.

Rodale, J.I. *The Synonym Finder*. New York: Warner Books, 1978.

Seger, Linda. *Making a Good Script Great*, 2nd ed. Hollywood: Samuel French, 1994.

Smiley, Sam. *Playwriting: The Structure of Action*. Englewood Cliffs, New Jersey: Prentice-Hall, 1971.

Stern, Jerome. *Making Shapely Fiction*. New York: Norton, 1991.

Strunk, William C. and E. B. White. *The Elements of Style*, 3rd ed. New York: Macmillan, 1979.

REFERENCES

Aristotle. *The Poetics*. Translated by Gerald F. Else. Ann Arbor: University of Michigan Press, 1978.

Atchity, Kenneth. *A Writer's Time*. New York: Norton, 1995.

Baker, George Pierce. *Dramatic Technique*. Boston: Houghton Mifflin, 1919.

Benton, Robert. *Kramer versus Kramer*. Screenplay manuscript, revised 3rd draft, July 14, 1978.

Bettelheim, Bruno. *Surviving*. New York: Knopf, 1979.

Bradbury, Ray. *Zen in the Art of Writing: Releasing the Creative Genius Within You*. New York: Bantam Books, 1992.

Burroway, Janet. *Writing Fiction: A Guide to Narrative Craft*, 4th ed. New York: Harper-Collins, 1996.

Cameron, Julia. *The Artist's Way: A Spiritual Path to Creativity*. New York: G.P. Putnam's Sons, 1992.

Capra, Fritjof. *The Tao of Physics*, 3rd ed. Boston: Shambhala, 1991.

Cooper, Dona. *Writing Great Screenplays for Film and TV*, New York: Prentice Hall, 1994.

Cowgill, Linda. *Writing Short Films: Structure and Content for Screenwriters*. Los Angeles: Lone Eagle Press, 1997.

Csikszentmihalyi, Mihaly. *Creativity: Flow and the Psychology of Discovery and Invention*. New York: HarperPerennial, 1996.

Dancyger, Ken and Jeff Rush. *Alternative Scriptwriting: Writing Beyond the Rules*. Boston: Focal Press, 1995.

Egri, Lajos. *The Art of Dramatic Writing*. New York: Simon & Schuster, 1960.

Ephron, Nora. *When Harry Met Sally*. New York: Knopf, 1992.

Field, Syd. *Screenplay: The Foundations of Screenwriting*. New York: Dell, 1982.

Friedan, Betty. *The Fountain of Age*. New York: Simon & Schuster, 1993.

Froug, William. *Screenwriting Tricks of the Trade*. Los Angeles: Silman-James Press, 1992.

Gibson, William. *Shakespeare's Game*. New York: Atheneum, 1978.

Gilligan, Carol. *In a Different Voice*. Cambridge: Harvard University Press, 1982.

Goldman, William. *Adventures in the Screen Trade: A Personal View of Hollywood and Screenwriting*. New York: Warner Books, 1983.

Goldman, William. *Butch Cassidy and the Sundance Kid*. New York: Bantam Books, 1969.

Gould, Stephen Jay. "Counters and Cable Cars." *The Best American Essays 1991*. New York: Ticknor & Fields, 1991, pp. 78–86.

House, Humphrey. *Aristotle's Poetics*. London: Madeline House, 1956.

Hyde, Lewis. *The Gift: Imagination and the Erotic Life of Property*. New York: Vintage Books, 1979.

Keane, Chris. *How to Write a Selling Screenplay*. New York: Broadway Books, 1998.

Lamott, Anne. *Bird By Bird: Some Instructions on Writing and Life*. New York: Pantheon Books, 1994.

Lerner, Harriet. *The Dance of Anger: A Woman's Guide to Changing the Patterns of Intimate Relationships*. New York: HarperCollins, 1989.

Lindgren, Ernest. *The Art of the Film*. New York: Collier Books, 1970.

Lucas, George, Gloria Katz, and Willard Huyck. *American Grafitti*. New York: Grove Press, 1973.

McKee, Robert. *Story: Substance, Structure, Style, and the Principles of Screenwriting*. New York: HarperCollins, 1997.

Miller, Jean Baker. *Toward a New Psychology of Women*, 2nd ed. Boston: Beacon Press, 1986.

Olds, Linda. *Metaphors of Interrelatedness: Toward a Systems Theory of Psychology*. Albany: State University of New York Press, 1992.

Raphaelson, Samson. *The Human Nature of Playwriting*. New York: Macmillan, 1949.

Rich, R. Ruby. "Choose One Memory to Take With You, He Asks." *The New York Times*, Sunday, May 16, 1999, p. Henry Holt, 1994.

Schanzer, Karl and Thomas Lee Wright. *American Screenwriters: The Insider's Look at the Art, the Craft, and the Business of Writing Movies.* New York: Avon Books, 1993.

Seger, Linda. *Making a Good Script Great.* Hollywood, Samuel French, 1994.

Seger, Linda and Edward Jay Whetmore. *From Script to Screen: The Collaborative Art of Filmmaking.* New York: Henry Holt, 1994.

Shelton, Robert. *Bull Durham,* Screenplay manuscript, May 1, 1987.

Sherman, Eric. *Directing the Film: Film Directors on Their Art.* Los Angeles: Acrobat Books, 1996.

Smiley, Sam. *Playwriting: The Structure of Action.* Englewood Cliffs, New Jersey: Prentice-Hall, 1971.

Stern, Jerome. *Making Shapely Fiction.* New York: Norton, 1991.

Sweet, Jeffrey. "An Object Lesson for Playwrights." *The Writer,* December 1989, pp. 18–20.

Tarantino, Quentin. *Pulp Fiction,* screenplay manuscript.

INDEX